Civil Service Reform
in the States

SUNY series in Public Administration
Peter W. Colby, Editor

Civil Service Reform in the States

Personnel Policy and Politics at the Subnational Level

Edited by

J. Edward Kellough and Lloyd G. Nigro

State University of New York Press

Published by
State University of New York Press, Albany

For information, address State University of New York Press,
194 Washington Avenue, Suite 305, Albany, NY 12210-2384

Production by Diane Ganeles
Marketing by Susan M. Petrie

Library of Congress Cataloging-in-Publication Data

Civil service reform in the states : personnel policy and politics at the subnational
level / edited by J. Edward Kellough and Lloyd G. Nigro.
      p. cm. — (SUNY series in public administration)
   Includes bibliographical references and index.
   ISBN-13: 978-0-7914-6627-8 (hardcover : alk. paper)
   ISBN-10: 0-7914-6627-2 (hardcover : alk. paper)
   1. Civil service reform—United States—States. I. Kellough, J. Edward. II. Nigro,
Lloyd G. III. Series.
   JK2465.C58 2005
   352.6'2367213'0973—dc22
                                                                    2005002757

10 9 8 7 6 5 4 3 2 1

Contents

Personnel Policy and Public Management: The Critical Link

J. Edward Kellough
Lloyd G. Nigro

Government jurisdictions in the United States have frequently reformed their administrative systems as they have struggled with changing political and economic circumstances. These administrative reforms are typically designed to reflect popular new models or emerging paradigms for public management. They are driven by complex and not necessarily congruent combinations of values and purposes ranging from the purely partisan to the largely technical. During the twentieth century, for example, there were at least twelve highly visible efforts to reform federal administrative arrangements—about one every eight years.[1] There were also innumerable similar reforms enacted by state and local governments. With each reform, changes, both large and small, in the administrative machinery of government are implemented, and the effects of those changes often last long after the reform itself has become a distant memory. It is interesting to observe that, more often than not, public personnel or civil service systems are at the top of the reform agenda.

The fact that personnel policy is the frequent target of reform bears witness to the central importance of personnel management to technically and politically effective government operations. It is through the personnel function that public agencies recruit, select, develop, pay, and hopefully retain highly qualified employees. These civil servants, in turn, directly influence the content and execution of public policies. They are the individuals responsible for translating objectives contained in legislative enactments or executive orders into the daily operations of government programs. Since the 1960s, as important new issues have arisen to demand the attention of public personnel managers and the constituencies they serve, the scope and impact of the public personnel function have grown and become even more socially and politically critical. Equal employment opportunity, pay equity concerns, labor relations, and constitutional protections are but a few of the issues now central to the field.[2] As a result, public personnel policy and management are increasingly dynamic and complex, and it is always the case that the technical, ethical, and political aspects of the civil service attract attention.

Since the rise of merit systems in the United States, civil service processes have been designed in large part to insulate public servants from politics and partisanship. The goal has been a neutral and technically competent career service. At the same time, however, there is a need for democratic oversight of the public bureaucracy by elected officials, and management must have the flexibility necessary to achieve public policy objectives in a timely and efficient manner. The challenge has always been to find a way to temper the control and flexibility that are required with appropriate levels of protection for public employees.

In this context, and in a system where public expectations are high, effective public management can be quite difficult. Indeed, the thrust of most civil service reform efforts in recent years has been to find ways to cope with the perceived need for flexibility in public management while maintaining adequate levels of centralized oversight to ensure employees are protected from abuse. Recent reforms have pushed steadily toward making the administrative agencies of government more responsive to political (especially executive) direction and toward overcoming what is seen as an overly restrictive structure of merit system rules and procedures that arguably has the effect of severely limiting management capacity and organizational performance.

Obviously, proposals for reform focusing on these specific issues are not new. They have antecedents that date to the Brownlow Committee recommendations of the late 1930s, and similar ideas are reflected in the U.S. Civil Service Reform Act of 1978. Consistent with concepts associated with the "new public management," current reform initiatives stress reinvention, re-engineering, decentralization, deregulation, employee empowerment, results-oriented management, and executive control. Recent initiatives reflect the notion that human resources functions in government should be strategically integrated with the planning and management control tasks in agencies and, most importantly, should emphasize support as opposed to regulatory activity. Reinventing themes relevant to the civil service were reflected in the Clinton Administration's National Performance Review and in the report of the National Commission on State and Local Public Service of 1993. In this volume, the reader will encounter two types of civil service reform. One of these focuses, in the Brownlow tradition, on making structural and technical improvements in the personnel function. As such, it is in the long-standing tradition of government modernization, and therefore does not represent an anti-government point of view. It seeks to improve the performance of government. The second type of reform, consistent with the new public management perspective, often seeks to dismantle existing civil service systems and to replace them with models closely resembling those found in the private sector.

This book will examine the kinds of public personnel reforms noted above and the extent to which they are being implemented in state government. An assessment of reform at the state level is particularly important given the significance of states in the delivery of public programs and the historic role the states have played as incubators of administrative change. The purpose here is to provide readers with a contemporary analysis and assessment of civil service reforms undertaken by state governments during the last decade of the twentieth century and the first years of the twenty-first. Some states have implemented dramatic reforms during that time, while in others, reforms have been resisted, often successfully. The chapters presented here were prepared for this volume by nationally recognized experts on civil service and civil service reform in the United States, and we believe they will be of wide interest to public policy makers, practitioners, students, and academicians. In general terms, we sought a regional distribution of states and variation in history and politics that should be associated with attitudes toward reform. With these goals in mind, we selected states that had engaged in reform and others where reform efforts had been less successful. Our selections were also controlled by the availability of highly qualified authors who could speak knowledgeably about to the intricacies of civil service reform in each state.

We expect this book will be useful as a text for advanced undergraduate and graduate courses on public administration and public personnel administration or human resources management. It is divided into two major sections. Part One, which is comprised of the first five chapters, examines the context of personnel reform in the states. Donald E. Klingner of the University of Colorado at Denver provides a useful general background on personnel policy and civil service reform in chapter 1. He identifies alternative approaches to structuring personnel systems driven by differing value orientations. In chapter 2, Hal G. Rainey of the University of Georgia reviews federal trends in the quest for flexibility in public personnel systems and other currently popular reform ideas and their implications for state government. Rainey considers what it will take to achieve effective change in public organizations and the preconditions necessary for successful reform. Sally Coleman Selden of Lynchburg College presents an empirical analysis of recent civil service reforms in the states and their causes and potential consequences using data generated in part by the Government Performance Project conducted at Syracuse University. Chapter 4, by Richard C. Kearney of East Carolina University, reviews the role of public employee unions in civil service reform, notes the impact of unions, and explains how that impact differs by time, state, and legal environment. Finally, in chapter 5, Stefanie A. Lindquest of Vanderbilt University and Stephen E. Condrey of the University of Georgia, discuss the legal framework within which public personnel systems operate and the implications of some civil service reforms for constitutional due process.

Part Two of the book examines the experiences of selected states with civil service reform. In chapter 6, for example, we review the dramatic reforms that occurred in the state of Georgia in the mid-1990s. The Georgia reforms were comprehensive, and in many ways went beyond what has occurred in other states. The state removed merit system protections from all employees hired after July 1, 1996, and placed authority for most personnel management decisions in line agencies and departments, leaving the state's central personnel agency to serve primarily as a consultant to those organizations rather than a regulator of the system. This chapter reports the findings of a statewide survey of supervisory and nonsupervisory employees working within the Georgia system. The findings indicate that supervisory and nonsupervisory employees alike are quite pessimistic about the effects of the reforms on the personnel management process in the state.

In chapter 7, James S. Bowman of Florida State University, Jonathan P. West of the University of Miami, and Sally C. Gertz of Florida State University examine civil service reform in Florida, which became, in the year 2000, the second state to enact comprehensive reform removing merit system protections from public employees. Bowman, West, and Gertz trace the historical antecedents of the reform effort in Florida and explore the provisions of the law, its major implications, and its impacts.

Steven W. Hays of the University of South Carolina and Chris Byrd and Samuel L. Wilkins of the South Carolina Budget and Control Board review reform efforts that have taken place in the state of South Carolina in chapter 8. They note that thanks to a variety of political and administrative catalysts over the past decade, South Carolina's government has become a leader in managerial reform, and that by far the most celebrated facet of that reform movement was a complete redesign and reorientation of the state's centralized human resource management function. Borrowing heavily from the contemporary wisdom of reinvention, the personnel system was decentralized and line managers were empowered to make almost all of the staffing and human resource decisions that once required outside review and approval. The authors chronicle the many structural and procedural changes implemented in South Carolina and provide an assessment of their effects.

The nature of the public personnel management system in Texas is next explored by Jerrell D. Coggburn of the University of Texas at San Antonio. Coggburn reviews Texas' unique approach to public sector human resources noting that it is the only state with no centralized personnel office to direct or even work in a consultative role with line agencies. Instead, the state has had for a very long time an almost fully decentralized personnel function in which agencies and departments assume primary responsibility. The implications of this decentralized approach and its impact on the effectiveness of human resources management in Texas are reviewed.

In chapter 10, N. Joseph Cayer of Arizona State University and Charles H. Kime of Arizona State University—East analyze personnel system changes in the state of Arizona. The review of human resources policies and practices in that state reflects consideration for more than twenty years of specific suggestions for change. In 1980 the state made major changes in its personnel system to reflect some of the changes made at the national level through the Civil Service Reform Act (CSRA) of 1978. While much of the spirit of the CSRA reform influenced the Arizona effort, the state was not ready to adopt the panoply of reforms represented by CSRA. The 1980 reform in the state was an effort to modernize state personnel and place personnel activities on a professional level. Over the past two decades, the state has made piecemeal changes. Unfortunately, numerous political upheavals in the state have stunted efforts at real change, but nonetheless, efforts now are under way focusing on such issues as classification and compensation reform, broadbanding, performance evaluation systems, and modernizing benefits plans for employees.

Chapter 11, by Katherine C. Naff of San Francisco State University, contains a discussion of efforts to reform the civil service system in California and how its experience stands in marked contrast to states such as Florida, Georgia, and South Carolina. Despite California's reputation as a "trendsetter"; that is, the place where the tax revolt, environmental movement, and immigration debate began, the state's civil service system has changed little since the introduction of the merit system in the early 1900s. One important reason has to do with the state's political environment. In contrast to many other states, California has strong unions representing its civil servants and the relationship between those unions and Governors Wilson and Davis had a significant effect on prospects for serious reform. The chapter concludes with a rather pessimistic assessment of the likelihood that major civil service reform in California will occur over the coming decade.

In chapter 12, by Peter D. Fox, former Secretary of the Wisconsin Department of Employment Relations and Robert J. Lavigna, Senior Manager for Client Services of CPS Human Resource Services, discuss significant reforms of the Wisconsin state civil service system. Fox and Lavigna review the state's progress in reforming the hiring process, position classification, and labor relations systems. The focus of the effort was on bringing significantly increased flexibility and efficiency to personnel program management. According to the authors, these reforms have yielded more timely hiring, better qualified job candidates, new ways to reward and retain talent, and more cooperative relationships with labor unions. Above all, Fox and Lavigna assert that these improvements have been achieved without sacrificing the principles for which progressive civil service systems are known—merit, fairness, and openness.

In chapter 13, Norma Riccucci of Rutgers University, Newark, examines recent efforts by the state of New York to reform its civil service system. Riccucci finds that the system is administered through a fragmented structure, and efforts to reform this structure have been frustrated by a lack of legislative support. However, incremental reforms have been achieved by an effectively led centralized civil service department. Riccucci observes that while some may argue that many of the reforms are rudimentary, they have "pulled New York State's civil service up to par with other state's civil service systems."

In chapter 14, we provide a summary of some of the lessons we believe may be learned from the reform experiences in various states. Prospects for the future, including issues that are certain to become central in future reform debates, are set forth for the reader's consideration.

Before closing this introduction, we think it is important to emphasize a central premise upon which this book is based: government and its employees matter. As noted earlier, the tasks accomplished by government workers include everything from the maintenance of public facilities to the interpretation, formation, and implementation of public policy. They perform the critical work of government and bring public programs to life. In a very real sense, then, they are the government, or at least, they are the people in government with whom citizens are most likely to have regular contact. As a result, and because government service matters, civil service reform matters. Nothing less than the effectiveness of government and popular perceptions of its legitimacy are at stake. The chapters that follow do much to underscore this important reality.

Notes

1. Among the major reform efforts of the twentieth century at the federal level, one may count Commissions or Committees including the Commission on Department Methods of 1905 (i.e., the Keep Commission), the Commission on Economy and Efficiency of 1910 (i.e., the Taft Commission), the Joint Committee on Reorganization of 1920, the President's Committee on Administrative Management of 1937 (i.e., the Brownlow Committee), the First Hoover Commission of 1947, the Second Hoover Commission of 1953, the Task Force on Government Organization under President Johnson, the Advisory Council on Executive Organization from 1969 (i.e., the Ash Council), the President's Reorganization Project under President Carter, the President's Private-Sector Survey on Cost Control established in 1981 (i.e., the Grace Commission), the National Commission on the Public Service established in 1987 (i.e., the Volcker Commission), and the National Performance Review under President Clinton. See Ingraham (1992) for a discussion of each of these efforts excluding the National Performance Review under President Clinton.

2. Hays and Kearney (1990) discuss the emergence of these important issues in greater detail in the preface to the second edition of their edited text on public personnel administration.

References

Ingraham, Patricia W. (1992). "Commission, Cycles, and Change: The Role of Blue-Ribbon Commissions in Executive Branch Change," in Patricia W. Ingraham and Donald F. Kettl, eds. *Agenda for Excellence: Public Service in America*. Chatham House, NJ: Chatham House Publishers.

Hays, Steven W., and Richard C. Kearney, eds. (1990). *Public Personnel Administration: Problems and Prospects*, 2nd. ed. Englewood Cliffs, NJ: Prentice-Hall.

PART ONE

Civil Service Reform in the States
Process and Context

CHAPTER 1

Societal Values and Civil Service Systems in the United States

Donald E. Klingner

Over the past two centuries, the evolution of public personnel management in the United States (in national, state, and local governments) has been driven by the emergence of alternative competing values (Klingner and Nalbandian 2003). As each emergent value has gained political strength, its increased importance has been reflected in the forming of corresponding public personnel systems and their related techniques. Traditionally, conflict in the United States has centered around four fundamental values: political responsiveness, organizational efficiency and effectiveness, individual rights, and social equity.

Political responsiveness is the belief that government answers to the will of the people expressed through elected officials, and the public workforce must, in turn, be made to answer to those in elective office. In a system grounded on this value, the political and personal faithfulness of public employees may best be ensured through an appointment process that considers political loyalty, along with education and experience, as indicators of merit. Often, in order to promote responsive government, elected officials are authorized to fill certain jobs through political appointments.

Organizational efficiency and effectiveness reflect the desire on the part of elected officials and the public to maximize productivity. This suggests that employment decisions about whom to hire, reassign, or promote should be based on applicants' and employees' competencies, rather than on their political loyalty.

The concept of individual rights suggests that citizens must be protected from unfair actions of government officials. In the context of civil service systems, public employees' rights to job security and due process are maintained through merit system rules and regulations that protect them from inappropriate partisan political pressure. In parallel fashion, public employees who are union members

11

will have recourse to work rules contained in collective bargaining agreements that protect them from arbitrary management decisions.

Social equity as a personnel value places emphasis on fairness to groups such as women, racial minorities, the disabled, and veterans, which may otherwise be disadvantaged by a market economy that accepts the legitimacy of discrimination in hiring and in pay. As is the case with individual rights as a principal value, social equity is concerned with fairness. But unlike individual rights, which are based on personal attributes like education, experience, or seniority, social equity is concerned with employment preferences based on membership in a protected class or group.

Within the past quarter century, these four traditional values have been supplemented by increasingly powerful emergent "anti-government" values. Early evidence of the rise of these values is found in the 1976 presidential campaign, won by Jimmy Carter, who ran against the national government as a Washington "outsider." Following the election, Carter proposed the 1978 Civil Service Reform Act on grounds that included poor performance in the public service and difficulty in controlling and directing bureaucrats. Beginning in 1980, the Reagan administration, though starting from fundamentally different values and policy objectives, continued to cast government as part of the problem, and to campaign against the infrastructure of public agencies and public administrators.

The ascendant anti-government assumptions behind this shift were paralleled by a related general transition from political to economic perspectives on public policy. That transition emphasized the role of market forces on individuals and the economy, rather than program implementation by government agencies and employees, as the most efficacious tools of public policy (Beckett 2000). Economic perspectives and the value of administrative efficiency clearly placed intense political pressure on the public sector to "do more with less." The pressure *to do more* caused government to attempt to become more accountable through such techniques as program budgeting, management by objectives, program evaluation, and management information systems. The pressure to do more *with less* money caused governments to lower expenditures through tax and expenditure ceilings, deficit reduction, deferred expenditures, accelerated tax collection, service fees, user charges, and a range of legislative and judicial efforts to shift program responsibilities and costs away from each affected government. Since from 50 to 75 percent of public expenditures go toward employee salaries and benefits, efforts to increase accountability and reduce costs have necessarily focused to a large extent on the field of public personnel management.

These underlying contemporary political and economic forces shaped three specific emerging anti-government values with implications for personnel policy: individual accountability, limited and decentralized government, and community responsibility for social services. First, proponents of individual accountability expect that people will make individual choices consistent with their own goals, and accept responsibility for the consequences of these choices, rather than passing responsibility for their actions onto the rest of society. Second, proponents of limited and decentralized government believe, fundamentally, that government is to be feared for its power to arbitrarily or capriciously deprive individuals of their rights. Advocates of this view also believe that it is easier to connect public policy, service delivery, and revenue generation in a smaller rather than larger unit of government. Decision makers are known, revenues are predictable, and services are directly visible in such circumstances, and for some, the reduction in size and scope of government is justified by the perceived ineffectiveness of government; by the high value accorded to individual freedom, responsibility and accountability; and by a reluctance to devote a greater share of personal income to taxes. Third, proponents of community responsibility for social services believe that local government agencies need to be supplemented by not-for-profit, nongovernmental organizations responsible for social services, recreation, and community development activities. For public personnel management, the most significant consequence of this value has been the creation of thousands of nonprofit organizations that routinely provide services funded by taxes, user fees, and charitable contributions.

These forces—mistrust of government and increased reliance on market mechanisms—have significantly affected public management at state and local government levels as well as the federal level. In 1993 the National Commission on the State and Local Public Service, generally referred to as the Winter Commission after its chair William Winter, issued a report that was generally critical of traditional public personnel management practices. An essential tenet of that report was that while civil service systems had traditionally been designed to promote efficiency and employee rights by protecting the public service against political interference and patronage-based turnover, these systems had gradually evolved to a point where "red tape" had overly restricted management flexibility, and due process had unreasonably protected incompetent or insubordinate employees. Its fifth recommendation called for an "end to civil service paralysis" through the adoption of practices designed to make personnel management more responsive to executive leadership, more supportive of innovation and risk-taking, and more rewarding of performance (National Commission on the State and Local Public Service 1993, Thompson 1994).

Personnel Systems

These critiques of traditional public personnel management values were not articulated directly, but rather through efforts to change personnel systems—the laws, policies, rules, regulations and practices through which personnel functions are fulfilled (Freyss 1995). There are four basic public personnel systems corresponding to the traditional values underlying public personnel management: political patronage, civil service, collective bargaining, and affirmative action.

Political patronage means legislative or executive approval of individual hiring decisions, particularly for policy-making positions, based on the applicant's political or personal loyalty to the appointing official. To ensure their loyalty, political appointees may be fired at any time; they serve at the discretion of those who appoint them.

Civil service is the predominant traditional system, and the only complete system (because it includes all functions and can incorporate all four traditional competing values). It is also the dominant organizational culture underlying the practice of public management. Civil service system proponents favor a professional public service as the best way to achieve the values of efficiency and individual rights and a bureaucracy responsive to political direction. They think that staffing public agencies rationally (based on jobs needed to carry out specific programs and the competencies needed to accomplish these goals), and treating employees fairly are the best ways to maintain an efficient and professional public service. This means giving employees good pensions and health benefits; giving them equal pay for work of comparable worth; hiring and promoting them on the basis of competencies; treating them impartially once on the job; and protecting them from partisan political influences. Overall, elected officials, who often appoint agency heads responsible for managing the bureaucracy, control policy objectives of civil service systems. The legislature maintains control over resources by limiting the total number of employees an agency can hire, staffing levels in particular agencies or programs, and the personnel budget. These tools help ensure political responsiveness. Civil service systems are supported by citizens and groups who want to keep "politics" out of public personnel decisions and to manage public agencies rationally and efficiently. At least initially, these groups proposed to accomplish this by creating personnel procedures that protected employees from political "interference" and allocating jobs based on competencies. But because advocates of privatization and "cutting the fat out of big government" also believe in running government rationally and efficiently ("like a business") there are some conflicts among proponents of this objective.

Collective bargaining systems exist within civil service systems. Even though collective bargaining is commonly associated with negotiation over wages and benefits, the primary motive is to ensure equitable treatment by management. It reflects the value of individual rights (of union members), achieved by basing personnel decisions like promotion on seniority. Contracts may also provide additional protection for individual employees against disciplinary action or discharge. Because some overlap exists in the grievance procedures available under civil service and collective bargaining systems, employees are usually required to select one procedure but not both. In all cases, contracts negotiated between an agency's managers and leaders of the union representing its employees are subject to legislative approval.

Affirmative action systems also usually exist within civil service systems. For the affirmative action system to operate, the government must have acknowledged an imbalance in the percentage of minorities or women in its workforce and those qualified minorities or women in a relevant labor force. Alternatively, members of a group protected against discrimination may have sued the employer, resulting in a judicial ruling or consent decree requiring the agency to give special consideration to members of the "protected class" in various personnel decisions, especially hiring and promotion. Affirmative action is supported by members of underrepresented classes (such as females, ethnic and racial minorities, and disabled job applicants and employees), and by advocates who contend that the effectiveness of a democracy depends upon the existence of a representative bureaucracy.

As would be expected, the rise of anti-government values has led to the emergence of alternative or reformed personnel practices, and as those reforms have spread, they have had a fundamental impact on the way public services are delivered. Two trends are apparent with regard to these reforms. One stresses a reduced role for government and reductions in the number of public employees brought about by using alternative organizations or mechanisms for providing public services (International City Management Association

1989). The second involves increasing the flexibility of employment relationships for those public employees that remain.

The alternative mechanisms comprising the first trend include various forms of privatization and contracting including purchase-of-service agreements, franchise agreements, subsidy arrangements, vouchers, volunteerism, and regulatory and tax incentives. Many of these arrangements have become relatively common place (Mahtesian 1994). They may enable state and local governments to offer services within a given geographic area, utilizing certain economies of scale, and as a result, governments may be able to reduce capital costs and personnel expenditures. In addition, the use of outside consultants and businesses (hired under fee-for-service arrangements on an "as needed" basis) can increase available expertise *and* managerial flexibility by reducing the range of qualified technical and professional employees that a government agency must otherwise employ.

Increasingly, public employers also seek to enhance flexibility by meeting minimal staffing requirements through career (civil service) employment and by hiring other employees "at will" into temporary or part-time positions (United States Merit Systems Protection Board 1994). For examples, see chapters 6 and 7 of this volume. These contingent workers usually receive lower salaries and benefits than their career counterparts and are unprotected by due process entitlements or collective bargaining agreements. Where commitment *and* high skills are required on a temporary basis, employers may seek to save money or maintain flexibility by using contract or leased employees in positions exempt from civil service protection. While contracts may be routinely renewed with the approval of the employee and the employer, employees may also be discharged at will in the event of a personality conflict, a change in managerial objectives, or a budget shortfall. Managerial and technical employees hired into these types of contracts usually receive higher salaries and benefits than can be offered to even highly qualified traditional civil service employees, and they enhance managerial flexibility to trim personnel costs quickly should this be necessary, without having to resort to the bureaucratic chaos precipitated by the exercise of "bumping rights" in a layoff situation.

Evolution: Conflict and Compromise
Among Values and Systems

Conflict among public personnel values and systems is limited and regulated by the dynamic realities of the competition itself.

Because the number of public jobs (and the money to pay public employees) is finite, jobs allocated through one system cannot be allocated through others. Advocates of each value and its associated system strive to minimize the influence of others. But because each value, carried to its extreme, creates distortions that limit the effectiveness of personnel management, attempts by each system or value to dominate lead inevitably to stabilizing reactions and value compromises.

Responsiveness carried to extremes results in the hiring of employees solely on the basis of patronage, without regard for other qualifications; or in the awarding of contracts based solely on political considerations (corruption). Efficiency, carried to extremes, results in over-rationalized personnel procedures—for example, going to decimal points on test scores to make selection or promotion decisions, or making the selection process rigid in the belief that systematic procedures will produce the "best" candidate. Individual rights, carried to extremes, results in overemphasis on seniority, or on due process and rigid disciplinary procedures. Social equity, carried to extremes, results in personnel decisions being made solely on the basis of group membership, disregarding individual merit or the need for efficient and responsive government.

With respect to emergent anti-government "systems," the weaknesses of market models—primarily their inability to address issues such as distributive equity or indivisible public goods—act to limit reliance on service contracting, privatization, user fees, and other "anti-government" personnel systems. Increased use of flexible employment mechanisms might lead to a government functioning primarily as a contract compliance office—the "hollow state" (Milward 1996) or the "subscriber state" (Roberts 2002). Or it might lead to unacceptable declines in political neutrality (Brewer and Maranto 2000), employee rights (Hsu 2000), social equity, or organizational effectiveness (program continuity, expertise, and organizational memory) (Milward 1996). Increased outsourcing makes contract compliance the primary control mechanism over the quality of service rather than traditional supervisory practices. This creates a real possibility of fraud and abuse (Moe 1987).

Continual budget cuts and pressure to do more with less result in agencies that are budget driven rather than mission driven. And budget-driven agencies that address public problems with solutions designed to meet short-term legislative objectives are not likely to be effective. Long-range planning, or indeed any planning beyond the current budget cycle, is likely to become less important. Agencies will not be able to do effective capital budgeting or to adequately maintain capital assets (human or infrastructure).

Public personnel management in the United States is complex because there are multiple levels of government and thousands of governments, each with its own personnel system or systems. But there is general agreement that its development has proceeded according to a pattern (Heclo 1977; Sayre 1948; Fischer 1945). First, public jobs were allocated primarily among elite leaders—the small group of upper-class property owners who had led the fight for independence and established a national government. Next, the emergence of political parties created a patronage system that rewarded party members and campaign workers with jobs once their candidate was elected. The spoils system expanded as the functions of government and the number of government employees grew after the Civil War. Political "machines" developed in big cities, supported by newly arrived immigrants. With electoral victory of candidates who had been nominated in conventions of loyalist delegates came the opportunity and obligation to dispense patronage or public jobs to those who had worked hardest for the party. Party loyalty would be verified, a political clearance might be issued and in return the new jobholder would pay (often monthly) a "voluntary" assessment to the party. This went to pay the party officials who had provided the job and to finance future election campaigns.

The period between 1883 and 1937 is important in the development of public personnel administration based on merit principles. These principles of merit and political neutrality reflect the civil service ideal—the belief that a competent, committed workforce of career civil servants is essential to the professional conduct of the public's business. A civil service system grows out of the following principles (Civil Service Reform Act 1978):

1. Recruitment should be from qualified individuals from all segments of society, and selection and advancement should be determined solely on the basis of relative ability, knowledge and skills, after fair and open competition that assures that all receive equal opportunity.
2. All employees and applicants should receive fair and equitable treatment in all aspects of personnel management without regard to political affiliation, race, color, religion, national origin, sex, marital status, age or handicapping condition, and with proper regard for their privacy and constitutional rights.
3. Equal pay should be provided for work of equal value with appropriate consideration of both national and local rates

paid by employers in the private sector, and appropriate incentives should be provided for excellence in performance.

4 All employees should maintain high standards of integrity, conduct, and concern for the public interest.

5. The workforce should be used efficiently and effectively.

6. Employees should be retained on the basis of performance, inadequate performance should be corrected; and employees should be separated who cannot or will not improve their performance to meet required standards.

7. Employees should be provided education and training where such education and training would result in better organizational and individual performance.

8. Employees should be protected against arbitrary action, personal favoritism, or coercion for partisan political purposes prohibited from using their official authority or influence for the purpose of interfering with or affecting the result on an election or a nomination for election.

9. Employees should be protected against reprisal for the lawful disclosure of information which the employees reasonably believe evidences: a violation of any law, rule, or regulation; or mismanagement, a gross waste of funds, an abuse of authority, or a substantial and specific danger to public health or safety.

While the Pendleton Act of 1883 espoused efficiency as well as the elimination of politics from personnel decisions, efficient methods of recruiting, selecting, and paying employees were not then available. In the twentieth century, "scientific management" began to provide the tools to do so. As a result of the U.S. Army's experience selecting officer candidates during World War I, psychologists developed aptitude, ability, and performance tests that were carried over into private industry during the 1920s.

The relationship between patronage and civil service centers around the enduring question of how governments can bring expertise to bear on public policy development and implementation while retaining the supremacy of political values. This combination of efficiency and effectiveness required that most positions be covered by the civil service system, but that political appointees who were either personally or politically responsive fill sensitive or policy-making positions. Given the obvious need for politically responsive agency management, one might wonder why civil service systems pay so much attention to protection from political influence. The reason is that incidents frequently indicate that elected officials consider political loyalty the most important criterion for selection, regardless of the applicants' qualifications (Hamilton 1999). Merit-based civil service systems were adopted by most states by the 1930s and 1940s.

Under collective bargaining, which began in earnest in the public sector in the 1960s and 1970s, the terms and conditions of employment are set by direct contract negotiations between agency management and unions (or employee organizations). This is in contrast to the patronage system, where they are set and operationally influenced by elected officials, or the civil service system, where they are set by law and regulations issued by management and administered by management or an outside authority (such as a civil service board). Public sector collective bargaining has many of the same procedures as its private sector counterpart, such as contract negotiations and grievance procedures. But fundamental differences in law and power outweigh these similarities. Public-sector unions never have the right to negotiate binding contracts with respect to wages, benefits or other economic issues. The right to approve (or disapprove) negotiated contracts is reserved to the appropriate legislative body (such as the city council, school board, or state legislature) because only legislatures have the authority to appropriate money to fund contracts. Both labor and management realize that ratification of negotiated contracts is more critical than negotiation of them, and set their political strategies accordingly. In chapter 4 of this book, Richard C. Kearney offers an assessment of organized labor's perspective on civil service reform in the states.

Affirmative action systems arose as a direct result of the civil rights movement of the 1960s and the women's rights movement of the 1970s. They were supported by the fundamental beliefs that a representative bureaucracy was essential for our government to function as a democracy; and that other personnel systems had not been effective at ensuring proportional representation (Mosher 1982). State and federal compliance agencies control affirmative action systems by public agencies or contractors. This system takes effect when a gross disparity exists between the percentage of minority or female employees in an agency and their percentage in a relevant labor pool (such as the community served by that agency, or the percentage of applicants qualified for the position), and when the agency has resisted the voluntary adoption of techniques (such as recruitment, selection, training, or promotion) that would reduce this disparity. In such a case, the court can require an agency to hire or promote specific numbers or percentages of underutilized groups (qualified females or minority group members) until their representation in the agency workforce is more proportionate; and it can abrogate collective bargaining agreements that use seniority rules to perpetuate racism or sexism.

The gradual shift in emphasis to market-based values and systems leaves the fundamental issue of the appropriate role of government unresolved (Kirlin 1996). But one thing is certain. Historically, it was assumed that civil service employees working in public agencies and funded through appropriations would carry out public programs. Today, public services are often provided by market mechanisms (rather than public agencies), staffed by contingent workers outside civil service and funded by user fees in addition to appropriated funds. So public personnel management in the United States today is a dynamic equilibrium among these competing values and systems, for allocating scarce public jobs in a complex and changing environment (Freedman 1994; Nalbandian 1981).

The experience of several states with civil service reform, either radical or piecemeal, reflects this dynamic equilibrium of interacting and conflicting values and systems. In states like New York (see chapter 13) whose civil service systems were heavily affected by a culture of restrictive work rules and collective bargaining agreements with powerful unions, there was general consensus that some specific reforms (such as broad banding, creation of a senior executive service, revision of the "rule of three," and abolition of traditional written exams) could make the system more effective. Some researchers felt that incremental change, beginning with agency-based pilot programs, was the appropriate strategy for initiating reforms, testing their effectiveness and defusing political opposition (Cohen and Eimicke 1994; Peters and Savoie 1994). However, political leaders in other states (and the New Public Management advocates who were frequently their ideological allies) often concluded that more radical reforms were a more likely solution. Georgia radically altered its civil service system in 1996, making all new hires after that date "at will" employees, and decentralizing traditional personnel decisions (such as classification, pay, recruitment, and selection) to individual agencies (Carnevale and Housel 2001; Condrey 2001; Nigro and Kellough, this volume). Florida began with incremental reforms to its civil service system in 1993 under Governor Chiles, but changed it dramatically several years later under Governor Jeb Bush (Berry, Chackarian, and Wechsler 1999; Bowman, West, Gertz, this volume). Despite some fears that radical reform of the civil service would result in increased political inter-

Figure 1.1 Evolution of Public Personnel Systems and Values in the United States

STAGE OF EVOLUTION	DOMINANT VALUE(S)	DOMINANT SYSTEM(S)	PRESSURES FOR CHANGE
One (1789–1828)	Responsiveness	"Government by elites"	Political parties + Patronage
Two (1828–1883)	Responsiveness	Patronage	Modernization + Democratization
Three (1883–1933)	Efficiency + Individual Rights	Civil Service	Responsiveness + Effective Government
Four (1933–1964)	Responsiveness + Efficiency + Individual Rights	Patronage + Civil Service	Individual Rights + Social Equity
Five (1964–1980)	Responsiveness + Efficiency + Individual Rights + Social Equity	Patronage + Civil Service + Collective Bargaining + Affirmative Action	Dynamic equilibrium among four competing values and systems
Six (1980–now)	Responsiveness + Efficiency + Individual Accountability + Limited government + Community Responsibility	Patronage + Civil Service + Collective Bargaining + Affirmative Action + Alternative mechanisms+ Flexible employment relationships	Dynamic equilibrium among four pro-governmental values and systems, and three anti-governmental values and systems

ference or a return to the spoils system, advocates of such approaches felt that piecemeal changes would not be effective at increasing management flexibility or employee accountability and performance.

The dominant values and systems that characterize these evolutionary stages in the history of public personnel management are shown in Figure 1.1; along with the pressures for change that affect their competition and interaction:

"Personnel" Has Different Functions under Different Systems and Values

While the basic personnel functions are the same under all systems, the relative emphasis among functions and how they are performed differ depending on the system. Under patronage systems, personnel management heavily emphasizes recruitment and selection. The personnel manager is a political advisor or party official responsible for identifying individuals who deserve or require a political position, screening them informally to make sure that their personal and political background does not include activities or associations that might embarrass or discredit their boss politically, and then recommending who should be hired in which position. The elected official then makes the appointment (or nominates the individual, if legislative confirmation is required) based on the candidate's competencies, political or personal loyalty, financial or campaign support for the elected official, or support by an influential interest group. Inclusion of women or minorities may be important as political symbolism, but affirmative action laws do not apply to these "exempt" appointments. The other functions (planning, development, and sanction) are simply irrelevant or deemphasized. Once hired, political appointees are subject to the whims of the elected official. Few rules govern their job duties, pay, or rights, and they are usually fired at will. Nor is development a priority: they are hired for a position, not a career.

Because civil service is a complete system, there is balanced emphasis on planning, acquisition, development, and sanction. With respect to planning, personnel is responsible for maintaining the position classification system. The pay system is usually tied to the classification system, with jobs involving similar degrees of difficulty being compensated equally. Personnel conducts job analysis updates to make sure that actual work corresponds with the duties outlined in the job description, and updates pay plans (based on changes in a position's level of responsibility) as part of budget planning or in anticipation of collective bargaining negotiations. Personnel is also responsible for developing and updating the agency's retirement and benefits programs, negotiating with benefit providers, and maintaining each employee's official time, leave, and benefit records. It also handles eligibility and processing of personnel action requests (transfers, promotions, retirements, and other changes in job status), including calculation of authorized retirement benefits, disability retirement determinations, and monitoring of workers' compensation claims for job-related injuries and illnesses. With respect to acquisition, personnel advertises vacant or new positions, schedules and administers written tests for jobs that are often vacant, and reviews applicants for basic eligibility. It compiles a list of eligible applicants, keeps the list current as job applicants secure other employment and provides a ranked list of "eligibles" to managers when vacancies occur. After the manager conducts interviews and selects one applicant, personnel processes the paperwork required to employ and pay the person. With respect to development, personnel is responsible for orienting new employees to the organization and its work rules and benefits. It keeps track of and distributes notices of training or transfer opportunities. It may conduct training to familiarize supervisors and employees with new personnel policies and programs. With respect to sanction, personnel advises supervisors of appropriate codes of employee conduct, establishes procedures to discipline an employee for violations of these rules, and designs the procedures to follow in the event the employee appeals this disciplinary action or files a grievance.

If employees are covered by collective bargaining, personnel is responsible for negotiating the agreement (or hiring an outside negotiator), bringing pay and benefits into accord with contract provisions, training supervisors on contract compliance, and representing the agency in internal or external grievance arbitration procedures. Civil service system rules and procedures cover most aspects of acquisition and development.

The personnel director and affirmative action director have shared responsibilities for implementing affirmative action policies and procedures, and working with compliance agencies. Once members of protected classes are hired or promoted, other personnel systems (civil service or collective bargaining) also influence development and sanction.

Personnel has different responsibilities for alternative mechanisms, depending on the situation. In general, reliance on nongovernmental organizations reduces the number of public employees, thereby reducing personnel's responsibilities. However, increased planning and oversight are usually necessary to estimate the type and number of contract employees needed to provide a desired level of service; develop requests for proposals to outside contractors; evaluate responses to proposals by comparing costs and services, and overseeing contract administration and compliance. This requires skills in recruiting, selecting, training, and motivating volunteers (Pynes 1997).

Personnel manages flexible employment relationships primarily by either hiring temporary employees or independent contractors. This generally means less emphasis on planning, at least for these employees. Typically, career employees meet minimum workload levels, and contingent workers are added or let go based on workload fluctuations. Development is largely irrelevant. Contingent workers are hired with the skills needed to perform the job immediately. Performance evaluation is unnecessary—if they do their jobs adequately, they get paid; if not, they are simply released at the end of their contract and not called back when workload once again increases. Nor is it difficult, at least from management's perspective, to maintain the terms of the employment relationship. Contingent employees can be discharged "at-will," and management's responsibility to independent contractors is limited to the terms of the contract.

Thus far we have discussed how personnel functions under uniform systems (pure or ideal examples of patronage, civil service, collective bargaining, affirmative action, alternative mechanisms, or flexible employment relationships). But because managers may need to compromise among competing personnel systems, the "real world" of contemporary public personnel management usually involves hybrid systems. For example, selection often involves the following hybrid decision rules:

1. Civil service/political appointment. Revise the minimum qualifications for the position to include the candidate with the most political support, and then pick that candidate from among the most qualified applicants for the position.
2. Civil service/affirmative action appointment. Target recruitment to make sure the applicant pool has sufficient representation of qualified women and minorities. Then pick either the most qualified applicant or the most qualified minority applicant, depending on political pressure or legal authority to appoint a minority
3. Civil service/collective bargaining appointment. Fill the position based on seniority among equally qualified applicants, per the collective bargaining agreement.
4. Civil service/"at will" appointment. Offer civil service employees the opportunity to compete for a vacancy that has been reclassified as an exempt position. The job has a significantly higher salary and an attractive benefit package, but no civil service protection or bumping rights back into a classified position in the event of a layoff.
5. Civil service/independent contractor appointment. Offer highly skilled (professional or technical) civil service employees the opportunity to compete for a vacancy that has been removed from civil service and re-created as a

temporary or part-time contract. The hourly pay rate increases considerably, but it does not include benefits or some employer payroll taxes (worker's compensation or Social Security) that legally are the contractor's responsibility. Civil servants often retire from their classified positions and are rehired as independent contractors to perform essentially the same duties, but through a distinctly different type of employment relationship.

The Structure of Public Personnel Management

The structure of public personnel management in the United States generally follows a pattern that is tied closely to the evolution of personnel systems. The first stage begins with a transition from patronage to civil service marked by passage of a civil service law and creation of a central personnel agency responsible for developing and administering policies and procedures related to the range of personnel functions.

Nationally, this process was represented by passage of the Pendleton Act and creation of the U.S. Civil Service Commission (1883). This in some cases followed and in others preceded the establishment of subnational state and local civil service agencies. As the central personnel agency tried to unify the opposing roles of civil service protection and management effectiveness, its organizational location and mission became increasingly significant. In some cases it remained an independent commission. In others, it split into two agencies like the U.S. Merit Systems Protection Board and the Office of Personnel Management, one responsible for protecting civil service employees against political interference, and the other responsible for administering and enforcing the chief executive's personnel policies and practices in other executive agencies.

As collective bargaining and affirmative action emerged, separate agencies were often created to focus on these responsibilities. For example, the Federal Labor Relations Authority regulates collective bargaining for federal employees; the U.S. Equal Employment Opportunity Commission enforces affirmative action; and the U.S. Department of Labor is responsible for regulating pay, benefits, and working conditions. Subnational governments usually have counterpart agencies with similar responsibilities.

The dilemma that arises over the comparative advantages of centralization and decentralization is another variable that affects the structure of public personnel management. As central civil service agencies mature, they tend to become larger and more specialized. This in turn can lead to inefficiencies or delays in providing services to other agencies when a dynamic environment of change renders universal rules more a hindrance than a help. And because these agencies have developed their own internal personnel departments that assist agency managers and link with the central personnel agency on all requisite functions, these agencies tend over time to exert pressure on the chief executive for more autonomy. The argument goes, now that civil service principles are firmly established within the political and administrative culture, it is more efficient and effective to decentralize operational control to these agencies. And in periods of limited hiring where economies of scale do not apply, or tight recruitment markets where fast action on available and interested candidates is essential, pressures for decentralization increase. Under such conditions, the role of the central personnel agency tends to transform from direct responsibility for personnel functions to indirect responsibility and oversight of agencies' planning, management, and evaluation efforts.

Organizational size also matters. In large subnational jurisdictions, personnel may be staffed by hundreds of employees and divided into divisions. In smaller ones, the personnel "department" may include only a few employees, or the chief administrative officer or an assistant may perform its responsibilities. There are many possible variants within these extremes

The structure of public personnel management also parallels private sector innovations, because both are responsive to the same changes in available technology, workforce characteristics, and other contextual variables (Sampson 1998). Personnel may subcontract some functions (such as training, pay and benefits administration, or recruitment and selection through "headhunters" or employment services) with specialized private companies. And as public services become increasingly privatized, related personnel management responsibilities pass from the public employer to the private contractor (Siegel 2000).

Role Expectations

Just as the structure of public personnel management changes in response to varying conditions, so role expectations vary over time for the three groups involved.

Because political responsiveness is the ultimate value for elected and appointed officials, their view of their responsibilities tends to reflect the impact of changing conditions on public personnel systems and values. For example, voter discontent with high taxes or inefficient civil service agencies is likely to generate political pressure to adopt policies that favor privatization, service contracting, and use of temporary or contracted employees. However, voter unease at reports of cost overruns at privatized prisons or sexual harassment of inmates by private contractors' employees is likely to make the pendulum swing the other way, resulting in increased political pressure in favor of retaining civil service systems and control mechanisms. And in any case, elected officials will probably ask managers and personnel professionals to achieve the advantages of each competing system while avoiding their respective disadvantages. After all, it is elected officials' prerogative to ask for solutions that represent good policy, while leaving it up to supervisors and personnel managers to implement them in practice. Under any circumstances, collective personnel policy decisions (whether made by courts, legislatures, or appointed officials) should reflect deliberate and unified (i.e., strategic) thinking about policies' cumulative impact on employee performance. For example, if a state legislature approved a tuition remission program for state employees, it would hopefully also provide sufficient funding for state universities to offer courses to meet this demand. These decisions should also send congruent messages regulating conflict among personnel systems. For example, it would be unfortunate if a governor approved an affirmative action plan to hire minority employees at the same time a state budget crisis led the governor to impose a hiring freeze, or even seniority-based layoffs.

Role expectations for public personnel managers and specialists have become more complex and contradictory over time, with new demands tending to supplement rather than replace their predecessors. Initially, public personnel managers were considered watchdogs, responsible for guarding applicants, employees, and the public against the evils of the spoils system. This required knowledge of civil service policies and procedures, and the courage to apply them in the face of political pressure. During Stage Four (1933–1964), it became the responsibility of public personnel managers to synthesize two distinct values, protection of employee rights and bureaucratic political neutrality through civil service, and bureaucratic compliance with the personnel policy objectives of political leaders (political responsiveness). During Stage Five (1964–1992), the focus again shifted (to consultation) as managers continued to demand flexibility and equity through performance-based reward structures; and employees continued to demand job security, development, and recognition. This change from compliance to consultation required public personnel managers to work with managers to increase productivity, with elected officials to increase the political responsiveness of public agencies, and with employees to maintain their rights (Klingner 1979; Nalbandian 1981).

Under the current constellation of values and systems, public personnel managers may legitimately feel that they have fewer options and less discretion than before as to how they balance conflicting values and systems. Given the common public and legislative presumption that the public bureaucracy is an enemy to be controlled rather than a neutral and professional tool to accomplish public policy objectives, the scope of their authority may be diminished by legislative micromanagement, or the value of cost control may be so dominant as to preclude concerns for employee rights, organizational efficiency, or social equity. Civil service and collective bargaining will continue to be important as viable systems, for many public employees (particularly school teachers and administrators, police and firefighters) are still covered by union contracts. Though "people skills" will continue to be important, personnel management may require other skills more directed to minimizing maximum loss (through risk management and contract compliance) than to maximizing human development and organizational performance for permanent employees. For personnel managers, success may mean the ability to develop divergent personnel systems for permanent employees and contingent workers, and to emphasize both asset development and cost control simultaneously despite their conflicting objectives, assumptions, and impacts on organizational culture. But substituting this calculated perspective for a more optimistic view that it is possible to simultaneously achieve organizational productivity and individual growth does lessen the importance of the public personnel manager's perspective.

Conclusion

Most public personnel departments have moved cautiously into the modern era because of their traditional reluctance to be identified with or become involved in "politics." Yet as their function is increasingly viewed as the development and management of human resource systems involving the reconciliation of value conflicts, they are overcoming this reluctance and working outside the confining environment of the civil service system. And they are finding that this expanded role brings benefits as well as risks. They are able to bring their expertise to bear on a range of critical human resource issues in a variety of contexts—issues traditional personnel managers might define as falling outside their area of responsibility. By continuing to assert their central role in the most critical issues of agency management, they are developing not only their own professional status but also the status of their profession.

References

Beckett, Julia (2000). "The 'Government Should Run Like a Business' Mantra." *American Review of Public Administration, 30* (2): 185–204.

Berry, Frances, Richard Chackarian, and Barton Wechsler (1999). "Reinventing Government: Lessons from a State Capitol," in H. George Frederickson and Jocelyn Johnston, *Public Management Reform and Innovation.* Tuscaloosa: University of Alabama Press, 329–355.

Brewer, Gene, and Robert A. Maranto (2000). "Comparing the Roles of Political Appointees and Career Executives in the U.S. Federal Executive Branch." *American Review of Public Administration, 30* (1): 69–86.

Carnevale, David, and Steven Housel (2001). "Human Resource Management Reform in the States," in Condrey, Stephen and Robert Maranto, eds., *Radical Reform of the Civil Service.* Lanham, MD: Lexington Books, 151–175.

Civil Service Reform Act of 1978. P.L. 95–454, October 13, 1978.

Cohen, S., and W. Eimicke (1994). "The Overregulated Civil Service." *Review of Public Personnel Administration, 15,* 11–27.

Condrey, Stephen (2001). "Georgia's Civil Service Reform," in Condrey, Stephen and Robert Maranto, eds., *Radical Reform of the Civil Service.* Lanham, MD: Lexington Books, 177–192.

Fischer, J. (October 1945). "Let's Go Back to the Spoils System." *Harper's, 191,* 362–368.

Freedman, A. (1994). "Commentary on Patronage." *Public Administration Review, 54,* 313.

Freyss, S.F. (Fall 1995). "Municipal Government Personnel Systems." *Review of Public Personnel Management, 16,* 69–93.

Hamilton, David K. (1999). "The Continuing Judicial Assault on Patronage." *Public Administration Review, 59* (1): 54–62.

Heclo, H. (1977). *A Government of Strangers.* Washington, DC: Brookings Institution.

Hsu, Spencer (September 4, 2000). "Death of 'Big Government' Alters Region: Less-skilled D.C. Workers Lose Out as Area Prospers." *Washington Post,* A1.

International City Management Association (1989). *Service delivery in the 90s: Alternative approaches for local governments*. Washington, DC: ICMA.

Kirlin, John J. (1996). "What Government Must Do Well: Creating Value For Society." *Journal of Public Administration Research and Theory, 6* (1): 161–185.

Klingner, Donald, and John Nalbandian (2003). *Public Personnel Management: Contexts and Strategies, 5th ed.* Upper Saddle River, NJ: Prentice Hall/Simon & Schuster.

Klingner, D. (September 1979). "The Changing Role of Public Personnel Management in the 1980s." *The Personnel Administrator, 24,* 41–48.

Mahtesian, C. (April 1994). "Taking Chicago Private." *Governing,* 26–31.

Martin, Lawrence L. (1999). *Contracting for Service Delivery: Local Government Choices.* Washington, DC: International City/County Management Association.

Milward, H. Brinton (1996). "Introduction: Symposium on the Hollow State: Capacity, Control, and Performance in Interorganizational Settings." *Journal of Public Administration Research and Theory, 6* (4): 193–197.

Moe, R.C. (1987). "Exploring the Limits of Privatization." *Public Administration Review, 47,* 453–460.

Mosher, F. (1982). *Democracy and the Public Service,* 2nd ed. New York: Oxford University Press.

Nalbandian, J. (1981). "From Compliance to Consultation: The Role of the Public Personnel Manager." *Review of Public Personnel Administration, 1,* 37–51.

National Commission on the State and Local Public Service (1993). *Hard Truths / Tough Choices: An Agenda for State and Local Reform.* Albany: Rockefeller Institute of Government.

O'Looney, John (1998). *Outsourcing State and Local Government Services: Decision Making Strategies and Management Methods.* Westport, CT: Greenwood.

Peters, B.G., and D.J. Savoie (1994). "Civil Service Reform: Misdiagnosing the Patient." *Public Administration Review, 54,* 418–425.

Pynes, Joan (1997). *Personnel Administration in Non-Profit Agencies.* San Francisco: Jossey-Bass.

Roberts, Alasdair (2002). "The Subscriber State," paper presented at the annual conference of the American Society for Public Administration, Phoenix, March 2002.

Sampson, Charles (1998). "New Manifestations of Open Systems: Can They Survive in the Public Sector?" *Public Personnel Management, 27*(3): 361–383.

Sayre, W. (1948). "The Triumph of Techniques over Purpose." *Public Administration Review, 8,* 134–137.

Siegel, Gilbert B. (2000). "Outsourcing Personnel Functions." *Public Personnel Management, 29* (2): 225–236.

Siegel, Gilbert B. (March 1999). "Where Are We On Local Government Service Contracting?" *Public Productivity and Management Review*, 22 (3): 365–388.

Thompson, Frank (1994). "Symposium: The Winter Commission Report: Is Deregulation the Answer for Public Personnel Management?" *Review of Public Personnel Administration,* 14 (2): 5–9.

United States Census Bureau (2000). *Compendium of Public Employment: 1997.* Series GC97 (3)-2. Washington, DC: U.S. Department of Commerce, 2.

United States Merit Systems Protection Board (1994). *Temporary federal employment: In search of flexibility and fairness.* Washington, DC: U.S. Merit Systems Protection Board.

CHAPTER 2

Reform Trends at the Federal Level with Implications for the States: The Pursuit of Flexibility and the Human Capital Movement

Hal G. Rainey

As Paul Light (1997) has pointed out, reforms in government flow and ebb like tides. As with tides, some reforms and changes are small, some are like tidal waves. Some, large, long-running streams of reform amount to movements, such as the progressive movement in the United States in the early twentieth century, and perhaps such as the "new public management" movement that has swept across many nations in the last two decades (Barzelay 2001; Kettl 2000). Others come in smaller, more compact forms with shorter life spans, such as the "reengineering" initiatives that had some cachet in business firms and then in government during the 1990s (Hammer and Champy 1993) and then faded to the point where one would have to search to find current applications of them. These brief spates of activity strain the definition of reform. Is a short-term change initiative, that seeks to apply some new administrative procedure in an organization, a reform, especially if it is not particularly successful or influential? These brief and rapidly fading change initiatives have made the rounds in organizations of all types for many years. Their frequency and turnover has apparently accelerated in the last several decades, to the point where discussions of faddism have begun to appear in the management literature. People in some government agencies have complained that politically appointed executives chase these fads and engage in "flavor of the month" management.

The reforms come and go, usually with uncertain results, and create an ongoing instability in the working context of many people in government organizations. Often stereotyped as change resistant because of inherent cautiousness, public employees actually have good reason to respond with care to new reforms and change proposals. It makes sense to move carefully and to try to determine if a new initiative will really have staying power and will justify committing time and resources to it. In that vein, but also because it will raise important points about change and reform in public personnel administration, this chapter will examine two recent trends in reforms of human resource management in the public sector. These trends do not constitute reform packages in themselves, but rather themes in reform. The first theme involves the pursuit of flexibility in public sector human resources systems. These initiatives aim to loosen rules and constraints in personnel procedures that create delays and rigidities, and to allow participants in the system more opportunities to make decisions about the most effective and fastest way to carry out a step or an action. The second theme involves a recent emphasis on "human capital" in the federal government that may spread to state and local governments and in some ways already has.

The two themes relate to each other in important ways. The efforts to increase flexibility have taken many forms, some of which conflict with each other. Sometimes these efforts have involved providing more opportunity for rapid hiring of crucial personnel. In other instances they have taken the form of increasing the authority of managers to control subordinates through more control over their pay and more authority to discipline and fire them. These control-oriented steps do not necessarily coincide with much of contemporary management thought about how to get the most out of employees, especially those who are highly skilled and professionalized. The "human capital" theme, on the other hand, although it has received some ridicule because it sounds dehumanizing, actually has the opposite implication since it calls for recognizing the value of the knowledge and skills of the people in an organization. It actually reflects and represents much contemporary thought on the way to deal with highly skilled personnel in organizations. The flexibility theme has already been disseminated widely to all levels of government in the U.S. and across many other nations, but state and local governments will be likely to consider new forms of it now appearing at the federal level, and to reconsider older forms of it in light of their history. The human capital theme will disseminate in one form or another to state and local governments, and will have an interplay with the flexibility theme that has very important implications. Human resource management reforms in government have often had a negative and control-oriented cast, emphasizing as they have the need to force lazy bureaucrats out of their torpor through the use of carrots (pay for performance programs) and sticks (speeding up the firing process). If the human capital theme can move the quest for flexibility in directions that are constructive and supportive for the more educated and skilled employees that government needs—as well as for any employee, for that matter—the human capital orientation can lead personnel reform in very promising directions. At the same time, both the flexibility and the human capital themes can face tough going due to the political and social context of civil service reform. Both themes raise important issues about the challenges of mounting sophisticated modern reforms of governmental human resource systems.

The Quest for Flexibility in Governmental Human Resource Management Systems

At least by the 1970s a widespread conviction had developed about the need to reform governmental personnel systems because of their dysfunctional rules and procedural constraints. Reformers and critics claimed that in civil service systems at all levels of government it was too hard to fire or discipline bad employees and that it took too long to do so. Critics complained that the rules that had been put in place earlier in the 20th century to implement a merit system of employment in government and to defend against excessive political patronage had evolved into an excessively complex and rigid set of protections for employees. In addition, managers had too little authority to base their employees' pay on their performance. Pay raises were often based on longevity in the position rather than performance. Hiring procedures involved so many steps and requirements that managers in government agencies faced delays and difficulties in hiring the people they needed. Often a promising candidate for a job would have taken another job by the time the candidate had gotten through all the necessary procedures and approvals under the governmental hiring systems. Rigid systems of job and position classification made it hard to move employees around as needed, to adjust pay in relation to an employee's skills and value, and to hire. Similarly, at executive levels, when a new administration came into office and newly appointed executives would come in as heads of agencies, they would often find that their immediate subordinates at the heads of major subunits were entrenched in place by the rules of the civil service system.

One cannot easily locate the precise origins of these complaints about civil service systems, but during the 1970s periodicals such as the *Washington Monthly* were running articles with titles such as "Firing a Federal Employee: The Impossible Dream," and the *Public Interest* carried an article titled "The Civil Service: A Meritless System?" (Savas and Ginsburg 1973). Significantly, the critics and those calling for reform have included executives and managers in government, and groups representing them or sympathetic to them. For example, a report from the National Academy of Public Administration about the rules and constraints on public managers that hindered their ability to manage human resources, procurement, and other responsibilities, featured a picture of Gulliver on the cover, bound to the ground by thousands of small ropes that the Lilliputians had laced him in (National Academy of Public Administration 1986). Even recently, after various attempts at reform, many federal employees have expressed concern about the inadequate handling of poor performers in their agencies (e.g., U.S. Merit Systems Protection Board 1998; 1999). This report suggests that the rules and procedures protecting civil servants may contribute to lax management of poor performers, at least in the perception of many federal employees.

The continuing complaints about the rigidity of civil service personnel systems motivated a pursuit of flexibility that has followed many paths. One of the early targets was the purported protections of civil servants, and the supposed difficulties in firing even the most flagrantly awful government employee. The words "purported" and "supposed" in the previous sentence carry significant implications. Analysts at the U.S. Office of Personnel Management (hereafter, U.S.O.P.M. or OPM) searched for evidence of this problem and found little (U.S.O.P.M. 1999). One apparently faces great difficulty in proving that the federal civil service has a discharge rate lower than in private firms in the United States. Part of the difficulty comes from the failure of private firms to keep clear records of whom and how many they have fired. Often, managers in business firms will advise a person that they have no future at the firm and induce them to resign. This amounts to a dismissal, but does not get recorded as one. In addition, business firms have little incentive to keep careful records of their firings, and even less to disseminate those records.

In government, according to the OPM report, there appears to be little difficulty in getting rid of people who have done something seriously wrong, such as stealing government property. Often, however, rather than spending the taxpayers' money on a time-consuming and expensive prosecution, the managers involved may show the person the evidence and allow the person to resign immediately. Such a resignation would not go into the records as a firing, even though it amounts to a dismissal for cause. The U.S.O.P.M. analysts (1999, 27) estimated that about 3.7 percent of federal workers could be classified as poor performers, and concluded that this did not indicate a serious problem with poor performers in the federal service. In addition, analysts found no convincing statistics on private sector dismissals for a conclusive comparison, but found references in the business management literature to annual dismissal rates of about 4 percent in business in the U.S., Europe, and Japan. If one assumes that these dismissal rates include both layoffs and dismissals for poor performance, they do not seem very different from the 3 percent rate for annual dismissals that the OPM analysts found when they examined federal data.

In spite of this lack of clear evidence, however, civil servants certainly think that there are problems in dealing with poor performers in their organizations. Surveys have found consistently that federal managers and employees feel that poor performers do not receive proper correction or dismissal in their agency (U.S. Merit Systems Protection Board 1999; hereafter, U.S.M.S.P.B.). For decades and at all levels of government, in comparisons of public managers' survey responses to those of private business managers, the largest differences have been in opinions about the ability to fire poor performers. Managers in government have shown a much higher tendency to express the opinion that the personnel rules governing their organizations make it difficult to dismiss a poor performer (Rainey 1983; Rainey, Pandey, and Bozeman 1995).

These opinions, shared widely by many journalists, politicians, and other critics of the civil service system, have had very practical impacts. The most significant reform of the U.S. civil service system in recent history, the Civil Service Reform Act (CSRA) of 1978, contained provisions aimed at streamlining discipline and dismissal of poor performers. Kettl (1989) described how the Carter administration came to emphasize this aspect of the CSRA in trying to build support for it, because the media paid little attention to "good government" aspects of the proposed reforms, but gave intense coverage to the topic of how hard it is to fire a federal bureaucrat. The purported problem of firing poor public employees appeals to the desire on the part of editorialists in the media and critics elsewhere to play the role of champions of the public interest and of governmental efficiency and performance, holding forth against slothful government employees who enjoy too much job security. As illustrated by the surveys mentioned above, however, managers and employees in government join in the expressions of concern. Significantly, those surveys show that the reform efforts at the federal level have apparently had little impact, since the concerns have continued (U.S.M.S.P.B. 1999). In addition to the implications of the surveys, we should note that the Clinton administration's National Performance Review initiative called for "reinventing human resource management" in the federal government. One of the main objectives of this reinvention involved "strengthening systems to support management in dealing with poor performers" (Gore 1993). It may be difficult to prove that constraints on firing poor performers is a major problem in the federal government, but that has not eliminated a widespread consensus that a serious problem exists, which has led to continuing proposals and efforts to address the problem.

At the state government level this concern over excessive protection and job security for public employees has manifested itself in efforts to reduce or terminate those protections. Several states have tried to eliminate "property rights" in positions for state government employees, and to substitute "at-will" employment. This trend may spread to other states, depending on outcomes in these states attempting this change.

Reforms in the State of Georgia

In Georgia, then-Governor Zell Miller announced his determination to reform the state's civil service system in his 1996 State of the State address, proclaiming that ". . . The problem is governmental paralysis, because despite its name, our present Merit System is not about merit. It offers no reward to good workers. It only provides cover for bad workers" (Walters 2002, p. 15).

As Nigro and Kellough describe in more detail in chapter 6, Miller then advanced legislation that substantially reformed the Georgia civil service system (Walters 2002; West 2002). The legislation required that employees hired by the state after July 1, 1996, would have no civil service protections. They would serve at-will and would have no formal rights to appeal disciplinary actions, including dismissal. Employees hired after July 1996 could be transferred, demoted, promoted, and removed from state employment at the discretion of management. The legislation also gave Georgia's state agencies authority to do their own recruiting, hiring, and firing without going through the Georgia Merit System of Personnel Administration (the agency that had authority over the merit system).

The developments in Georgia illustrate the point that reforms always affect more than one dimension of personnel administration, such as the ability to fire an employee. Eliminating property rights in jobs and decentralizing personnel decisions to the state agencies also affects recruiting, hiring, transferring, and defining job responsibilities for an employee, and removing that employee during a reduction in force. In addition, reforms typically come as part of a reform movement and package of reforms. As Nigro and Kellough describe in chapter 6, during this period, for example, the Georgia legislature also passed GeorgiaGain, a reform of the individual performance evaluation and compensation system aimed at increasing the linkage between an employee's performance and pay raises. These multiple influences of the reforms, and multiple parts of reform complicate the evaluation of a reform process. Walters (2002), however, from interviews and other sources, finds beneficial effects of the changes in Georgia, which might increase the likelihood that the reforms there will spread to other states. He finds that personnel directors in the state agencies have welcomed the reforms, as an escape from a personnel system they regarded as unduly complicated and constraining. He also observes that personnel administrators and managers in the system feel that the reforms have improved the processes of recruiting, hiring, job classification, pay raises, promotions, downsizing, and discipline (including firing). No widespread abuses or pursuit of aggressive political patronage have occurred. The courts generally afford various protections against abusive or unfair treatment for employees in organizations of all types, and Georgia has strong anti-nepotism laws. Such provisions tend to restrain patronage and arbitrary or unfair treatment generally. On the other hand, Walters finds that some professionals and managers in the system point to a growing lack of uniformity in pay for similar work in different departments.

Other forms of evaluation find some more serious reservations. Nigro and Kellough (2000; Kellough and Nigro 2002; see chapter 6) report surveys of managers and employees in Georgia state government, in which the respondents tended to express little support for the reforms. Many respondents felt that the reforms removing employees from civil service protections had made little difference in improving the performance of individuals and agencies. Many respondents felt that GeorgiaGain had little or no beneficial effect on performance evaluation, linking pay to performance, training, development, and job satisfaction. Responses to other questions suggested that these unfavorable responses resulted from under-funding of the pay increases so that no significant increases were available even for good performers.

In addition, Condrey (2002) points to unique circumstances in Georgia that may limit the extent to which the reforms there will spread to other states. He points out that Georgia has weak labor unions, that the reforms were advanced by a popular, powerful governor who had a particular distaste for the state's elaborate personnel rules, and that the state's personnel agency was slow in reforming itself or unable to do so. Condrey therefore concludes that the reforms in Georgia represent "an anomaly, not a trend" (114). Kuykendall and Facer (2002) raise still more questions about the staying power of the Georgia reforms by pointing out that the Supreme Court has, in at least one decision, extended due process protections to employees in governments where statements in rules and employee manuals indicated a policy of firing only for cause. The Court interpreted this as an extension of a property right in the job, requiring due process prior to firing, and implying that state agencies in Georgia might fall under this precedent through statements they make to employees. In sum, there are many reasons to wonder whether the Georgia reforms will spread to other states. Kellough and Lu (1993), however, have described how government after government around the world sought to implement pay-for-performance systems, with little apparent success anywhere. Apparently governmental administrative reforms can disseminate as much because of their symbolic, ideological, and political attractiveness as because of their validated effectiveness at achieving their goals. During the period when the governor's administration was developing the reforms in Georgia, the newspapers quoted the governor's chief of staff as saying that the reforms included ". . . something never heard of in the public sector—pay for performance." The chief of staff thus showed no awareness of the many efforts at pay-for-performance systems around the nation and the world that had occurred prior to his statement, or he assumed that journalists and the public had no awareness of them.

The State of Florida and "Service First"

Civil service reforms in Florida may well illustrate this tendency to pursue reforms for their ideological and political attractiveness rather than their validated effectiveness (Walters 2002; West 2002; see Bowman, West, and Gertz' analysis of the Florida reforms in chapter 7). Governor Jeb Bush allied with a business council and a tax watchdog group to produce a report that lambasted the state's civil service system. Significantly, the report contained a few anecdotes about the dysfunctions of the system, but little systematic evidence of major problems (Walters 2002, p. 25; see Bowman, West, and Gertz in chapter 7). The report called for modernizing the Florida civil service system according to a "private sector model" by eliminating state employees' property rights in their jobs. These protections, the report complained, made it so that an employee could be removed only through a "complicated web" of due process restrictions.

The governor and his allies followed through, and in 2001 the Florida legislature passed the "Service First" program. The Service First initiative converted all state supervisory personnel to at-will employment, ended seniority for everyone in the state personnel system, and simplified the state's compensation and classification systems by broad-banding them (more on broad-banding below). The governor originally proposed converting all state personnel to at-will employment, but the Florida Senate ended up only converting 16,000 supervisory personnel, leaving 120,000 employees covered by civil service rules.

These changes have led to more flexibility in the system (Walters 2002). Recruitment and hiring had already been decentralized in Florida, but the reforms essentially made the state akin to a private business model for hiring. Managers in agencies could hire on the basis of their identification of the skills and abilities for the job, rather than going through a complex process of defining and justifying the job according to rules and procedures under the old civil service system. The changes in classification and compensation reduced the number of job titles in the system. Under the broad-banding of these systems, broad categories were substituted for more numerous smaller ones. This allows managers to move an employee's pay within these broader pay bands. Before, a manager would have to promote an employee up a complicated series of grades and steps, usually at one step per year, to provide a raise for a deserving employee, and this movement up the steps was often constrained by seniority and other limits. The new system also allows more flexibility in moving and reorganizing supervisory staff, and in dismissing supervisory staff.

On the more unfavorable side, in considering whether the Florida reforms will join those in Georgia to form a trend moving through the states, one must note that the new flexibilities in Florida provoked strong labor union opposition. Unions brought a court action against a downsizing in the Department of Juvenile Justice that removed 200 senior supervisory personnel. The unions vehemently protested that the gubernatorial administration was using the new situation to cut costs by laying off higher-salaried supervisors, even though this may actually do harm in the long term by depriving the agencies of their highly experienced and knowledgeable staff. In one of the disputes between the Bush gubernatorial administration and a major labor union, an impartial special master, a business professor from the University of Houston, came in to mediate. He disparaged Florida's reform initiative, labeling it "Service Worst." He rejected the assumption that only poor performers value the civil service protections that Service First removed, and argued that high-quality employees also valued the protections. Removal of the provisions, he said, could penalize the state in competing for employees, since job security and stable rewards represent some of the most critical benefits governmental employment can offer (West 2002, 84–85).

Bowman, West, and Gertz (see chapter 7) also sharply critique the reforms as ill-conceived and poorly designed. They point out that the reformers did little to take into account the history of problems that many of the sorts of reforms they proposed had encountered in efforts to implement them in other state and local governments. They also argue that the reforms are likely to weaken incentives for careers in the state's civil service, and will probably increase political patronage and other forms of opportunism that will damage the civil service in the long run. As with the case of Georgia, this situation raises the question of whether such reforms can spread to states with stronger unions, and with a less anti–civil service political culture.

The State of Texas: A Longer Experience with Flexibility

Texas provides still another example to review in assessing the potential for the spread of "flexibility" reforms, because Texas has long been known among public sector human resource professionals as a state that never had a highly centralized civil service system (Walters 2002; Barrett and Greene 1999; see Coggburn's analysis of Texas' approach to human resource management, in chapter 9). Texas agencies have much leeway to recruit and hire as they see fit. Discipline and firing also follow more of a private sector model, although significantly, most of the agencies follow clear, written policies involving warnings and other careful steps to avoid legal challenges. Compensation and classification in Texas are centralized, but without an oppressively complex set of job titles. The state auditor's office oversees a set of compensation categories, but with less emphasis on seniority than in other states and more opportunities and requirements to base pay raises on performance. While observers and people in the system point to the advantages of the system's decentralized patterns, such as the flexibility the agencies have in recruiting and hiring, they also note less desirable aspects of the Texas situation (see Coggburn, chapter 9). The decentralization impedes statewide human resource planning and has weakened statewide personnel information collection and analysis. In addition, while people in the Texas system report little political abuse in the form of demands for hiring someone's political crony, politics influence the system. Law enforcement personnel have been placed in a more structured personnel system where seniority plays a stronger role than for other state employees. Critics suggest that this is due to the political clout of the law enforcement groups. In addition, the legislature reportedly intervenes and micromanages a great deal. For example, they impose salary caps in some years and otherwise meddle with the system. In sum, Texas represents another example of flexibility provisions in state governments, and the pros and cons that will influence other states' adoption of similar provisions.

Examples of Other Flexibilities: Broad-Banding

As the preceding examples show, the long-running attack on civil service protections, property rights in civil service jobs, and attendant due process procedures in discipline and removal has not and cannot occur in a vacuum. Reforms aimed at such provisions become entwined with other reforms and changes such as compensation systems, and cannot be extricated from their relations to other elements of the systems such as court decisions independent of what some governor or state legislature aims to put in place. Compensation or pay systems, of course, logically should be considered jointly with such issues as due process protections, because both types of provisions can jointly influence motivation and productivity of the workforce. The examples of the states described above show that, as with the civil service "protections," reformers have attacked rigid classification systems and pay systems in government. They have argued that requiring supervisors to raise employees' salaries only by moving them up through a strict set of job steps and categories, often with this movement based largely on seniority in the job, weakens the connection between an employee's pay raises and his or her performance. Just as a person's job may be protected by due process requirements prior to removal, a person's pay can be protected, in a sense, by a system that gives them pay raises regardless of their performance.

A first assault on rigid pay systems, in pursuit of more flexibility, came in the form of widespread touting of "pay-for-performance" or "merit pay" systems for the public sector. Governments at all levels in the United States and in many other nations attempted such initiatives, with so little evidence of successful implementation of them that the current debate about them centers not on the question of whether they succeeded but on the question of why they did not (Kellough and Lu 1993). Experts on pay-for-performance have pointed out for a long time that successful implementation requires a reasonable level of trust between management and employees, a reasonably credible performance evaluation system, and enough resources to provide for appreciable differences in pay for the better performers. Public sector applications have often gone forward in systems with dubious performance evaluation procedures, and legislative bodies have shown a strong tendency to underfund the systems, thus providing scant rewards for the better performers. The poor record of success for pay-for-performance initiatives had cast them into disfavor by the time of the Clinton administration. The Clinton administration's National Performance Review essentially disavowed them (Gore 1993, 31), and instead advocated adoption of various approaches such as gainsharing, and other flexible approaches, ultimately moving to a strong advocacy of "pay-banding" or broad-banding.

A broad-banding system collapses numerous pay grades into fewer, broader pay bands. Thus a set of very wide pay classes is established with a correspondingly wide range of jobs and salaries. As a consequence, managers may exercise considerable discretion in determining compensation levels for particular positions within each band, provided, of course, that they stay within their overall budget ceiling. As suggested in the description earlier of the three states, this approach gets away from the tight restrictions of numerous job classifications and pay steps and grades, and allows a supervisor much more discretion to set a subordinate's pay at a higher or lower level within a much broader range, or band. The supervisor, of course, is expected to make this assignment on the basis of the performance and value of the subordinate.

Some federal agencies and other government organizations have implemented the broad-banding approach, and as noted earlier, the

Florida reforms involved a variant of it. The U.S. Internal Revenue Service (IRS), for example, received authority to create pay bands under the IRS Restructuring and Reform Act of 1998 (hereafter, RRA '98), and established a senior management pay band by 2001 (U.S. Internal Revenue Service 2001). The senior manager pay band collapses 10 pay steps in each of two pay grades, GS 14 and GS 15, into ten pay levels for senior managers. That is, the twenty steps for GS 14, 1 through 10, and GS 15, 1 through 10, collapse into the ten levels SM-1 through SM-10 spanning the same low and high levels of pay across the levels. Within one of the SM levels, a manager receives a base pay rate of fixed annual pay, and an annual, noncontinuing performance bonus based on the manager's summary performance rating for that year. RRA '98 also mandated a restructuring of the IRS, and the service reorganized into four major new operating divisions. Each division receives a "point budget" of 4 points per senior manager (SM-1 to SM-10s). Each proposed rating for a manager in the division requires the expenditure of some of these points. (An "outstanding" rating equals 6 points, "exceeded expectations" equals 4 points, and "met expectations" equals 2 points). This point budget serves to control and regulate the level of ratings given out, but not in a rigid fashion. Obviously, the highest annual, noncontinuing bonuses go to the outstanding ratings, and so on.

Once every two years a senior manager is eligible for movement up to the next level (from SM-4, for example, to SM-5), which will mean an increase in continuing base pay. To move up, a manager must have received a certain minimum level of performance rating in the two previous periods. For this purpose, the ten SM levels are further grouped into four levels, and at each higher one of these four levels, the required performance ratings for movement upward increase. That is, to keep moving up, one has to meet higher and higher expectations for the performance ratings one achieves.

Each of the new operating divisions in IRS has a Performance Review Board comprised of senior executives and managers. These boards review the annual ratings and bonuses to ensure consistent application across the division by, among other procedures, examining the allocation of the "point budget." They also evaluate the ratings against information about organizational performance, and forward a report to the Division Commissioner. RRA '98 also established a general Oversight Board for the IRS as a whole, which, among many other matters reviews executive and managerial compensation, and can serve as a check on excesses or misapplications of the pay-banding system. In sum, the IRS approach represents a very well-developed one, with substantial provisions for oversight and review.

Pay-banding or broad-banding offer an attractive idea for those interested in increasing managerial flexibility to enhance perform-ance and tie rewards to it, and to escape rigidities of traditional civil service systems. So was pay-for-performance, of course, and the checkered history of those initiatives illustrates a general truism about organizational reform and change. No matter how attractive the idea, a good idea badly or improperly implemented amounts to a bad idea. Proper implementation usually requires incentives, resources, commitments, and sound planning and thinking, so in a complex political and organizational system good ideas often go bad (not to mention the ideas for reform and change that were no good to begin with). We need, then, to consider the potential difficulties that a reform may encounter, as part of assessing its vulnerability to this evolution from a good idea to a bad one.

As with other ideas designed to decentralize authority and increase managerial flexibility, broad-banding may cause employees to feel that rewards are based on factors other than actual meaning-ful differences in work. Within each "broad" pay-band, for example, one can find a larger array of different jobs then would have existed previously in more narrowly defined pay grades. "Managerial flexi-bility" will likely lead to differences in pay levels for jobs that had pre-viously had very similar pay levels. Conversely, jobs that had been treated differently in the past may be treated similarly. Unless man-agement proceeds very carefully, perceptions of inequity and actual instances of inequity may increase. So far, federal experiments with broad-banding have found mixed evidence about levels of perceived inequality in compensation under that approach, as compared to tra-ditional classification systems (Schay, Simons, Guerra, and Caldwell 1992). When employees involved in broad-banding experiments were asked whether they perceived that individual differentials in pay reflected real differences in levels of responsibility and job difficulty, approximately one-fifth to one-third (depending on the experimental site) agreed that they did as compared to one-fifth to one-fourth of the control site employees classified in traditional pay systems. Of course, the most striking observation is that large majorities of employees under both approaches found pay differentials generally inequitable, and the potential for perceived inequity remains if reforms mandating wide and rapid implementation of broad-banding systems are implemented. Such perceptions will erode employee trust, satisfaction, and motivation.

These results by no means justify aggressive condemnation of broad-banding or efforts to decentralize personnel authority. Indeed, the demonstration projects and experiments with broad-banding represent commendable efforts to proceed carefully with assessment of such reforms rather than immediate across-the-board implementation. They have contributed to the development of the better-designed systems, such as the one implemented at IRS. The main point involves emphasizing the need to implement an approach such as broad-banding with attention to potential pitfalls, rather than as a surefire cure-all, and to recognize that successful implementation will require substantial planning, review, and study of successful and well-designed programs, and sufficient commitment and resources.

Critical Pay Authorities and
Other Special Hiring Provisions

Another development in pursuit of flexibility at the federal level that state government decision makers may consider involves special authorities for hiring critically needed personnel outside the normal hiring procedures and at higher salaries than other professionals and executives in the system. Some states have already begun to offer special pay arrangements for critical skills in such areas as information technology, but the critical pay authorities that federal agencies have used involve provisions beyond pay (Rainey 2001).

The RRA '98, mentioned above, gave the Internal Revenue Service the authority to hire forty people to positions critical to the mission of the agency. These people could be hired outside the normal civil service procedures, which included going through the Office of Personnel Management for authorization, and adhering to the "rule of three." The act authorized the IRS to pay these new hires salaries up to the level of the vice president of the United States. At the time, the Vice President's salary was more than $180,000, which exceed the top salaries for the highest level of the senior executive service. Thus, the people in the IRS working on carrying out the reforms required by RRA '98 received substantial authority and flexibility to decide on the positions these "critical" personnel would have, to search for them and recruit them, to hire them rapidly and independently of the civil service system and the Office of Personnel Management, and to decide what to pay them.

Executives leading the change process in the IRS used these positions to hire a variety of top executives—heads of major new divisions—and some middle-level professionals and managers. The IRS faced huge challenges in developing and updating its computer and information systems, because of the obvious massive load of information processing involved in collecting taxes for the nation. IRS executives regarded the critical pay authority as particularly helpful in hiring talented people they felt they needed. For example, they hired executives who had not just information technology knowledge, but experience in high-level leadership of large information technology projects, and executives who had experience in running large-scale auditing activities in the private sector, who had the potential to bring new ideas about auditing processes into the agency.

Also as part of the reforms at IRS, the leaders of the change process sought to improve the way the agency facilitated taxpayers' efforts to pay their taxes. The reforms sought to move the agency away from a heavy emphasis on enforcing tax laws, toward more emphasis on helping honest taxpayers fulfill their duty to pay their taxes. As part of this strategic orientation, they hired individuals with backgrounds in conducting public relations with large professional and business associations. The members of an association of businesses and professionals usually have very similar tax issues, and persons with experience in dealing with such associations could work with them to use them as a way of disseminating tax information to their members. As these examples suggest, leaders at IRS regarded the "critical pay authorities" as valuable in finding and hiring the talent they needed to carry out reforms and address major challenges in such areas as computerization and information technology.

The critical pay authorities sparked some criticism and controversy. Leaders in IRS would mention in interviews that some IRS employees resented the implication that outsiders had to come in to fix the agency (but most of the executives and the critical pay hirees indicated that such opposition was rare and quiet, if it existed; Rainey 2001). A segment on the *Prime Time* television show lambasted the IRS over their use of the authorities, targeting for criticism high relocation costs for some of the people hired under the critical pay authorities, who came from the private sector with high levels of wealth. This segment drew largely on distortions of the facts of the situation, aimed at dramatizing it as an instance of squandering the taxpayers' money on rich business executives, and it had little effect on the program at IRS because representatives of the agency could so easily refute the criticisms. Still, the episode illustrates potential problems with the dissemination of this practice to other levels of government.

More seriously, some representatives of the Senior Executives Association, an association representing members of the Senior Executive Service (SES) in the federal government, attacked the critical pay authorities as unfair to SES members. A career senior executive in the SES might labor for years in government, working his or her way up, only to be closed out of a senior position by an executive brought in from the private sector at a much higher salary and without equivalent government experience. This amounted to something like union opposition to these critical pay authorities, and public sector unions have tended to oppose "flexibilities" that erode protections for civil service employees, so that this form of opposition may build up at state and local levels.

Still, the general idea behind the critical pay authorities at IRS has been proposed and used in various ways in the federal government that will continue its availability as an alternative for state governments. Actually, the federal personnel laws and rules have included a critical pay authority for years, but one that involved a lot of difficulty in attaining and using the authority. An agency that wanted to use the authority had to get approval from the Office of Management and Budget and from the Office of Personnel Management, and this took a lot of time and effort. Significantly, by 2002 this authority had only been used twice in the entire federal government. Hence, IRS leaders placed great value on the flexibility that Congress gave to the IRS. Congress also gave a somewhat similar grant of authority to the Office of Student Financial Assistance (SFA) in the Department of Education, an agency that works on providing students with financial support for higher education, and which announces in its publications that with partner organizations it channels more than $54 billion in such aid to students each year. Congress authorized SFA about two dozen "unclassified" positions and considerable flexibility in setting salaries for those positions. Representatives of SFA report similar satisfaction with the way the agency has used these positions to hire specially needed and valuable talent (Rainey 2001).

Senator George Voinovich of Ohio, along with some other members of the Senate Governmental Relations Committee, has emphasized the need to attend to the "human capital crisis" facing the federal government. He has advanced legislation designed to address the crisis that includes proposals to extend more widely in the federal government critical pay authorities of the sort given to IRS. Similarly, representatives of the Partnership for Public Service, an organization recently formed to support the public service in the United States (see www.ourpublicservice.org) have proposed a program of mid-level management fellows to be brought into federal agencies from the outside. They have also proposed various ways of ending barriers to hiring for the federal government from outside sources. These proposals generally support efforts to open up recruiting and hiring in the way the IRS critical pay authorities did, and make it more likely that reformers in state governments will bring up such proposals.

The Human Capital Crisis and the Human Capital Movement

These proposals for more flexibility in bringing people into the federal service relate to a growing emphasis on "human capital" in the federal government, which has origins and imperatives similar to those in many state governments (e.g., Abramson and Gardner 2002). This emphasis amounts to a movement at the federal level that responds in part to a purported crisis. These developments have very important potential relations to how the quest for flexibility may continue to spread among the states and how it may play out.

The term "human capital" has attracted its share of ridicule. A Dilbert cartoon in 2002 portrayed Dogbert, one of the usual characters, talking to Dilbert's boss, who is always insensitive and inept, about human capital. Dogbert asks if the boss prefers to refer to the employees as "human capital" or "livestock." The boss says he prefers human capital because if they use the term livestock, the employees may demand hay. Human capital may sound somewhat dehumanizing since it conjures up the use of human beings like machines or other capital stock. Proponents of this movement, however, intend totally opposite implications. They call for leaders to regard the human beings in their organizations as the most valuable asset. They argue that in the information age when human knowledge and intellectual skills play such a crucial role in organizational success, leaders need to realize the value of investing in human beings in their organizations, to help people develop their knowledge and skills. Moreover, organizations need to strategize, plan, and invest in making sure that this human capital emphasis infuses the organization's operations and its long-term development.

Various agencies and individuals have contributed to this movement at the federal level. President Bush has issued a "President's Management Agenda" through the Office of Management and Budget, hereafter, OMB (Executive Office of the President 2002).

This agenda announces five main "government-wide initiatives," one of which is "strategic management of human capital." OMB has further published "agency scorecards" for all the major federal agencies, purportedly based on an assessment of how well the agency is pursuing the five government-wide initiatives. The scorecard employs a simple "traffic light" grading system, which the OMB Web site describes as "common today in well-run businesses." The grading system awards a green light for success, yellow for mixed results, and red for unsatisfactory. OMB further announces that scores are based on five standards for success defined by the President's Management Council and discussed with experts throughout government and academe, including individual Fellows from the National Academy of Public Administration. (Executive Office of the President, OMB, 2002, www.omb.gov). So far, at the time of this writing, most of the agencies have red lights on all five initiatives, probably as a tactic the administration is using to get the agencies to take the President's initiatives seriously. Obviously, the long-term influence of this agenda and the traffic light exercise remains unclear, but emphasis on strategic human capital management, coming from the Executive Office of the President, clearly raises the salience of the topic in the federal government.

David M. Walker, Comptroller General of the United States, has served as one of the main proponents of the human capital focus. As an executive in one of the large consulting and accounting firms in the private sector, Walker had a strong interest in human capital prior to coming to the General Accounting Office as the Comptroller General (e.g., Freidman, Hatch, and Walker 1998). At GAO, Walker continued to press this issue (Walker 2001; U.S. General Accounting Office 1999). As mentioned above, Senator Voinovich of Ohio has advanced legislation on human capital issues that was included in the Homeland Security bill that Congress passed in 2003, with the provisions applying to all federal agencies and not just the Department of Homeland Security. The legislation requires that each federal agency appoint a chief human capital officer, who would be responsible for strategic planning for human capital, aligning the strategic planning with the agency's mission, and fostering a culture of performance and improvement. The legislation also establishes a chief human capital officers council in the federal government, and provides for various other changes and reforms that would support the development of human capital in the federal government.

The human capital movement has been driven in part by concerns over a growing crisis in human capital in the federal government, one that the situation in the states tends to mirror. The Senate Governmental Affairs Committee (U.S. Senate 2001) and the National Partnership for Public Service (2002), as well as other sources, described the growing crisis as involving several developments. As of 2002, 53 percent of the federal workforce would be eligible for retirement within several years, 71 percent of the senior managers would be eligible for retirement in four years, and 58 percent of the GS-15 managers could retire in five years. At the same time, a survey found that good students in universities tended to have an unfavorable view of the federal government as an employer. In the survey, only one out of ten members of Phi Beta Kappa rated the federal government as a good place to work. In addition, the federal workforce had been downsized by about 325,000 between 1993 and 2000, with new hires decreasing sharply during that period also, and with critics complaining that the downsizing was nonstrategic, or poorly planned and executed in relation to long-term human resource needs (Partnership for Public Service 2002; Executive Office of the President 2002). As still another challenge, the rapid changes in information technology and other areas force changes in the sorts of skills and personnel needed in all types of organizations. These changes usually involve imperatives for bringing in more highly educated, trained, and skilled employees, for which organizations in the public, nonprofit, and private sectors compete aggressively.

In response to these developments, the players in this movement have so far concentrated on exhorting or pressuring federal agencies to take human capital seriously, advising them on how to do it, and recommending or crafting legislation to set in place some of the structures and requirements to support it (such as chief human capital officers). GAO, for example, has issued frameworks, checklists, and a model to guide agency efforts (U.S. General Accounting Office 1999, 2002a, 2002b). The GAO model provides a conceptual framework and guidelines and pointers on how to achieve success in establishing four human capital cornerstones:

- Leadership, to establish a commitment to human capital management and to establish the role of the human capital function.
- Strategic human capital planning, to achieve integration and alignment of the human capital function with the organization's strategy, mission, and operations, and to produce data-driven human capital decisions.
- Acquiring, developing, and retaining talent, through making

targeted investments in people, and to ensure that human
capital approaches are tailored to meet organizational needs.
- Results-oriented organizational culture, involving empowerment and inclusiveness, and to ensure that unit and individual performance are linked to organizational goals.

Obviously, the long-term influence of the legislation, admoni-
tions, traffic lights, frameworks, and guidelines coming from the
human capital movement remains to be seen. The imperatives moving this activity along, however, manifest themselves at the state and
local levels. According to recent analyses, 42 percent of the 15.7 million state and local government employees in the United States in
1999 were 45 to 64 years old. Between 2000 and 2015, two-fifths of
state and local government employees will be eligible to retire. This
outflow of talent and knowledge has disastrous potential for numerous reasons. Among many other reasons, state and local governments need to play a major role in homeland security, and they face
increasing pressures to upgrade information and communication
systems for improved service delivery in many areas. Thus, state governments face pressures to develop and improve human capital, and
to consider ways to respond flexibly and rapidly to this imperative,
including the possibility of bringing in people who have not moved up
through the state civil service system.

When Congress deliberated over the legislation for the Department of Homeland Security, a key point of conflict in the debate concerned an issue in human resources and personnel administration.
The administration wanted extensive flexibilities in personnel administration in the new department, while public employee unions
strongly opposed any provisions that would deprive the employees of
civil service protections. This conflict echoed the union opposition in
Florida to the efforts of another Bush to expand certain types of flexibility in the state's system of personnel administration. It may fore-
shadow similar conflicts to play out in states around the nation if
governors or other political leaders seek to extend flexibilities, and the
conflicts represent a dramatic confrontation between two sides that
each espouse important values and priorities.

Depending on how the human capital movement plays out, and
on whether and how it spreads to the level of the states, it has the
potential to serve as a source of compromise or at least as an alternative perspective on this conflict. The reforms seeking "flexibility"
at the federal and state levels have often taken a negative cast
toward public employees and public personnel systems. Reformers

advancing these initiatives have claimed their necessity because of the slothfulness of government employees and the need to make it easier to get rid of them. They have called for pay-for-performance systems, often on grounds that the slackers get paid as well as the hard workers. Implicitly or explicitly, they have assumed that the fear of being fired and the desire for pay increases play primary roles in the motivation and productivity of public employees. Reformers have also attacked the allegedly dilapidated, ossified civil service rules and procedures that tend to hold these dysfunctional circumstances in place. These reform initiatives do have justifications and often the people in the system are the ones complaining most loudly about it, but this approach to reform faces problems. It tends to understate and underestimate the strengths of the existing system and the often excellent performance of many government entities operating under these same, supposedly abysmal personnel systems. It tends to overestimate what some changes in firing and pay procedures, and some loosening of rules, can accomplish. It also tends to underestimate the difficulties in the long run of following through on the reforms, and the potential to damage valuable institutions in trying to improve them.

For example, excessive decentralization of personnel policy authority may give rise to important legal questions. The constitutional guarantee of equal protection of the law will tend to require some degree of centralization and the application of consistent standards across government organizations. When agencies or bureaus are given authority to determine for themselves the compensation levels for jobs within their boundaries, significant pay discrepancies between similar jobs across different organizations could easily emerge. Employees might press questions of equal protection through legal channels. In addition, the elimination of civil service rules will necessarily be limited by the constitutional imperative that procedural due process be afforded employees who have property interests in their jobs because of statutory merit system provisions or implied contracts based on promises made in personnel procedure manuals.

These constraints on the prospects for reforming certain aspects of civil service systems, however, do not represent as great a problem with many of the reform initiatives as does a more fundamental problem. The reformers have generally lacked a viable framework, ideology, and guidelines as to how their alternative vision is supposed to work. What is supposed to happen when we give government managers more freedom and flexibility to control pay, discipline, and dismissal of their subordinates? Those managers, who were bungling bureaucrats yesterday, will, through the magic of managerial flexibility, become efficient business magnates today, skillfully employing their new authority to attain ever-increasing value for the taxpayers' moncy? The mantra of making government systems more like those in business conveniently overlooks the problem that the systems used in business corporations often blunder and fail, and overlooks the problem that the institutional context and incentives tend to differ between tax-funded government agencies and business firms.

This is where the human capital movement may have the potential to provide an enlightened alternative to support reforms moving in the direction of more flexible systems. If that movement simply becomes aligned with conservative ideologues and politicians looking for a rationale to make further cuts in government agencies that have already had their budgets and workforces cut, and simply to erode public employees' rights on the grounds that respecting an employee's rights breeds laziness in that employee, then the movement will offer little in the way of a useful alternative. If, on the other hand, the movement can foster a genuine movement in the direction of investing in people and their development and empowerment, with frameworks, guidelines, and supportive resources to bolster that potential, it can offer a constructive alternative to personnel systems as usual. It could, for example, offer an alternative to the long-running underinvestment in personal and professional development in the public service at all levels. Of course it sounds naive to hope that unions will not be suspicious and oppose such a movement, or to hope that such a movement will not play out, as many of them do, into a blizzard of buzzwords, memoranda, directives, training sessions and committee meetings, only to fade as other fads have. The human capital movement, nevertheless, does raise the hope for a reform alternative that could attract the support of public employees and their associations through offering positive incentives of constructive development of people in pursuit of public missions.

References

Abramson, Mark A., and Nicole W. Gardner, eds. (2002). *Human capital 2002*. Lanham, MD: Rowman & Littlefield.

Barrett, Katherine, and Richard Greene (1999). "Grading the States: A Management Report Card." *Governing*. February: 17–90.

Barzelay, Michael (2001). *The New Public Management*. Berkeley CA: University of California Press.

Executive Office of the President, Office of Management and Budget (2002). *The President's Management Agenda*. Washington, DC: U.S. Office of Management and Budget. www.omb.gov.

Friedman, Brian, James Hatch, and David M. Walker (1998). *Delivering on the Promise: How to Attract, Manage, and Retain Human Capital*. New York: Free Press.

Gore, Vice President Al (1993). *From Red Tape to Results. Creating a Government that Works Better & Costs Less: Reinventing Human Resource Management*. Washington, DC: Office of the Vice President, Accompanying Report of the National Performance Review, September.

Hammer, Michael, and James Champy (1993). *Reengineering the Corporation*. New York: HarperCollins.

Kellough, J. Edward, and Lloyd C. Nigro (2002). "Pay for Performance in Georgia State Government: Employee Perspectives on GeorgiaGain After 5 Years." *Review of Public Personnel Administration* 22 (2): Summer: 146–166.

Kellough, J. Edward, and Huran Lu (1993). "The Paradox of Merit Pay in the Public Sector: The Persistence of a Problematic Procedure." *Review of Public Personnel Administration* 13 (2): 45–64.

Kettl, Donald F. (2000). *The Global Public Management Revolution: A Report on the Transformation of Governance*. Washington, DC: Brookings Institution Press.

Kettl, D.F. (1989). "The Image of the Public Service in the Media." In Volcker Commission, *Leadership for America: Rebuilding the Public Service*. Lexington, MA: Heath.

Light, Paul C. (1997). *The Tides of Reform: Making Government Work, 1945–1995*. New Haven, CT: Yale University Press.

Nigro, Lloyd C., and J. Edward Kellough (2000). "Civil Service Reform in Georgia: Going to the Edge?" *Review of Public Personnel Administration* 20 (Fall): 41–54.

Partnership for Public Service (2002). *News from the Partnership,* vol. 1, Issue 2, May. Washington, DC: Partnership for Public Service, 1725 Eye Street NW, Suite 900, Washington, DC 20006. www.ourpublicservice.org.

Rainey, Hal G. (2001). *A Weapon in the War for Talent: Using Special Authorities to Recruit Crucial Personnel*. Arlington, VA: PricewaterhouseCoopers Endowment for the Business of Government. (Monograph).

Rainey, Hal G. (1983). "Public Agencies and Private Firms: Incentive Structures, Goals, and Individual Roles," *Administration and Society*, Vol. 15, No. 2, (August): 207–242.

Rainey, Hal G., Sanjay Pandey, and Barry Bozeman (1995). "Public and Private Managers' Perceptions of Red Tape," *Public Administration Review*, Vol. 55, No. 6 (November/December): 567–574.

Savas, E.S., and S.G. Ginsburg (1973). "The Civil Service: A Meritless System?" *The Public Interest* 32 (Summer): 72–84.

Schay, Brigitte W., K. Craig Simons, Evelyn Guerra, and Jacqueline Caldwell, *Broad-Banding in the Federal Government: Technical Report* (Washington DC: Government Printing Office 1992), 31–33.

U.S. General Accounting Office (2002a). *Managing for Results: Using Strategic Human Capital Management to Drive Transformational Change.* Washington, DC: U.S. General Accounting Office, July 15, 2002. GAO-02–940T.

U.S. General Accounting Office (2002b). *A Model of Strategic Human Capital Management.* Washington, DC: U.S. General Accounting Office, March, 2002. GAO-02–373SP.

U.S. General Accounting Office (1999). *Human Capital: A Self-Assessment Checklist for Agency Leaders.* Washington, DC: U.S. General Accounting Office, September. GAO/GGD-99–179.

U.S. Internal Revenue Service (2001). "Senior Manager Payband." IRS Office of Strategic Human Resources, Personnel Policy Division, Office of Compensation, February 16, 2001.

U.S. Merit Systems Protection Board (1998). *The Changing Federal Workforce: Employee Perspectives.* Washington, DC: U.S. Merit Systems Protection Board, March.

U.S. Merit Systems Protection Board (1999). *Federal Supervisors and Poor Performers.* Washington, DC: U.S. Merit Systems Protection Board, July.

U.S. Office of Personnel Management (2002). *Human Resources Flexibilities and Authorities in the Federal Government.* Washington, DC: U.S. Office of Personnel Management, Office of Merit Systems Effectiveness, Center for HR Innovation, http://www.opm.gov.

U.S. Office of Personnel Management (1999). *Poor Performers in Government: A Quest for the True Story.* Washington, DC: Office of Merit Systems Oversight and Effectiveness, U.S. Office of Personnel Management, January.

U.S. Senate. (2001). Committee on Governmental Affairs. Subcommittee on Oversight of Government Management, Restructuring, and the District of Columbia. *High Risk: Human Capital in the Federal Government*: Hearing before the Oversight of Government Management, Restructuring, and the District of Columbia Subcommittee of the Committee on Governmental Affairs, United States Senate, One Hundred Seventh Congress, first session, February 1, 2001. Washington, DC: U.S. Government Printing Office.

Walker, David M. (2001). *Human Capital: Taking Steps to Meet Current and Emerging Human Capital Challenges*: Statement of David M. Walker, Comptroller General of the United States, before the Subcommittee on Oversight of Government Management, Restructuring, and the District of Columbia, Committee on Governmental Affairs, U.S. Senate.

Washington, DC: United States General Accounting Office. GAO-01-965T

Walters, Jonathan (2002). *Civil Service Reform in Texas, Georgia, and Florida.* Washington, DC: PricewaterhouseCoopers Endowment for the Business of Government.

West, Jonathan P. (2002). "Georgia on the Mind of Radical Civil Service Reformers." *Review of Public Personnel Administration* 22, No. 2 (Summer): 79–93.

CHAPTER 3

Classifying and Exploring Reforms in State Personnel Systems

Sally Coleman Selden

Public personnel reforms have been wide spread in state governments since the early 1990s (Selden, Ingraham, and Jacobson 2001; Ingraham and Selden 2002). Some states, such as Maryland and Georgia, passed legislation that significantly altered public employment practices, while other states implemented changes to the personnel processes and procedures. In the state of New York, Governor George E. Pataki launched a sweeping reform plan to revolutionize its civil service system without eliminating the core of its civil service legislative platform. Pressures and momentum for reform continues with recent activities in Hawaii, Idaho, Ohio, Texas, and Washington (National Council on State Legislators 2002). For example, in Washington, the state passed civil service reform in 2001 that provides state workers the right of collective bargaining. Currently, there are efforts underway to overturn this reform (National Council on State Legislators 2002).

This purpose of this chapter is threefold. First, it seeks to classify public personnel reforms. Second, it identifies recent reforms falling within each category. Finally, it explains what factors are associated with implementing those reforms in 1999 and 2000.

Approaches to Public Personnel Reforms

Current personnel reforms and innovations are taking place during a period of considerable dialogue and debate about the appropriate role and shape of government organizations. Some states have attempted to completely overhaul their civil service system, while others make incremental changes to particular personnel functions. Georgia implemented sweeping changes by dismantling

59

its civil service system. In a similarly bold fashion to Georgia, Florida passed "Services First" in 2001, which removed career civil service protections from parts of the workforce thus affecting supervisors, managers, and confidential employees by placing them into the Selected Exempt Service (SES). SES employees serve at the pleasure of their department head and do not have appeal rights in adverse personnel actions (Bowman, West, and Gertz 2002).

The litany of changes adopted by state governments is extensive, from minor improvements, such as revising application forms, to major changes, such as overhauling a state's compensation system. Regardless of the approach taken, states hope to improve how government works by revamping state personnel systems, adopting innovative personnel techniques and updating and streamlining personnel practices (Selden, Ingraham, and Jacobson 2001). One purpose of this chapter is to put forth a framework for classifying changes or reforms to state personnel systems. The categories are broadly based on two dimensions: scope of reform and locus of control over the change. Reforms are classified as follows:

- Systemwide: The scope of these reforms impacts the entire state civil service system and must be approved by voters, the executive, and/or legislature, such as in the passage of civil service reform in Georgia.
- Structural: The scope of these reforms impacts multiple agencies by changing the structural configuration of the state central personnel office (CPO), such as the reporting relationship between the CPO and the executive branch, or how personnel authority is allocated between the CPO and other state agencies. These reforms do not necessarily alter current personnel management practices, rather they alter who has implementation authority and who is held accountable for implementing those practices.
- Policy/ Rules/Regulations: Policy reforms impact how personnel functions are implemented and involve changes to state policies, rules, or regulations, such as hiring rules (Rule of 3) and residency requirements. The decision to adopt or to repeal a policy falls outside the authority of agencies or individuals tasked with their implementation and often require executive or legislative passage or approval.
- Activity/Techniques: Activity reforms also impact how personnel functions are implemented but are determined by those with responsibility for implementation. Activity

reforms might require the adoption of new technologies or techniques to improve the operational efficiency of a specific personnel function or set of functions, such as adoption of workforce planning or a human resource management information system.

Since several of the major civil service reform efforts are discussed in other chapters in the book, this chapter focuses on classifying and explaining factors associated with structural, policy, and activity changes. These types of reforms are much more common in public organizations than systemwide civil service changes (Selden 2002; Selden, Ingraham, and Jacobson 2001; Selden and Ingraham 2002). Specifically, using data collected as part of the Government Performance Project in 1998 and 2000, the chapter will examine one set of changes in each of the following categories: structural, policy, and activity. Specifically, it will examine whether a state's structure of personnel authority in five personnel functions shifted during 1999 and 2000 (structural), it will classify policy changes to a state's hiring system in 1999 and 2000 (policy), and finally it will determine whether a state adopted formal workforce planning in 1999 and 2000 (activity).

Personnel Reforms: Personnel Authority, Hiring, and Workforce Planning

As mentioned previously, reforms impact the organizational structure of the state personnel system and how authority for personnel functions is allocated. An important dimension of personnel structure, and the one examined in this analysis pertains to whether the authority for different personnel functions are centralized in one central personnel office or decentralized among state agencies (Cayer 1996). Many states combine both approaches. The structure of personnel authority for different functions varies from state to state, with the flow of authority ranging from centralization to shared authority to decentralization. In recent years, scholars have began to focus and examine this concept, with much interest being focused on understanding how and why states are decentralizing personnel authority (Hou et al. 2000; Kellough and Selden, 2003). Changes in personnel authority are particularly important because of the profound implications of these decisions for the day-to-day operation of the state personnel system and for the identification of appropriate mechanisms of accountability.

When many state civil service systems were created during the reform movement following the 1883 Civil Service Act, there was a strong belief that rigidly, centrally controlled systems were the only way to exclude partisan pressure on public employment systems (Ingraham and Selden 2002). Most state governments developed central personnel offices during the first half of the 20th century. Many of the components of the personnel systems that emerged during the mid-1900s contributed to increasingly centralized, standardized, and rule-based state civil service systems that provided great job protections to employees. Today, the legacy of this period remains evident in some states' civil service systems. Rhode Island and Pennsylvania, for example, still centrally manage most of their personnel management functions.

At the other end of the continuum is a totally decentralized system, such as Texas, where personnel authority rests primarily with the state agencies. Each agency has its own personnel director and most personnel functions are not uniform across the state agencies, with the exception of job classification. Texas neither has a central personnel agency nor does it provide merit protections to its employees. Job classification is a central function but falls within the purview of the state auditor's office, which reports to the legislature. The Texas governor has little centralized influence over the systems that govern state employment.

The majority of states have created personnel systems that balance or share responsibility and authority between the central personnel agency and the other agencies of government. Within this "middle ground" there can be wide variation in the extent to which authority is formally delegated away from the center or the extent to which it is shared with state agencies and managers. Some central personnel agencies are responsible for developing policies and ensuring agency compliance with policies, leaving the state agencies to operate the day-to-day personnel activities associated with that policy. Such sharing allows continued consideration of broad governmental concerns, such as equity, but combines them with the human resources (HR) customization necessary for better agency performance. For example, in South Carolina, agencies are given substantial flexibility in creating reward and recognition programs and are given broad discretion in designing disciplinary policies.

Like the structural reforms discussed above, policy reforms impact the day-to-day operational practices of personnel officials. Policy, rule, or regulatory changes may substantially change the nature of different personnel processes, such as the recruiting process. Rather than changing who has responsibility or authority for personnel functions (that is, who is ultimately accountability for a personnel function), policy reforms are about changing the laws, rules, and regulations governing personnel policies. For example, eliminating the requirement that a candidate selected for a position must be a state resident could have a significant impact on the recruiting process. It would allow personnel staff to extend their target recruiting market from a state to a national focus. This allows personnel staff to take advantage of additional recruiting sources, such as a professional association meeting held in a different region. Previously, this source may not have proven cost-effective because it would not yield enough "state" qualified applicants to warrant the expense of sending recruiters. So the residency policy change directly impacts a state's recruiting plan that subsequently should impact the state's applicant pool for the position.

During the late 1990s many public officials were concerned about government's ability to recruit and retain high-quality employees (Ingraham, Selden, and Moynihan 2000). State governments were competing for labor in an economy with an extremely low unemployment rate and a culture where notions about work and organizational commitment were changing (Selden, Ingraham, and Jacobson 2000). Moreover, turnover rates and the number of open positions were growing (Selden and Moynihan 2000). In short, many states perceived that they were facing a crisis, particularly in specific areas, such as information technology and engineering (Barrett and Greene 1999). In 1998 many states noted in their narrative responses that hiring was an area they were investing resources to improve.

Changes in workforce planning can be implemented without requiring changes to legislative or executive rules and regulations. These reforms may involve engaging in a personnel practice that previously was not conducted or adopting new technologies or innovations that transform current practices. These reforms are aimed at improving the operational efficiency of a personnel function or set of functions. For example, adopting a new human resources management (HRM) information technology system may not only improve a state's training and development system, by improving the state's ability to track training, it may improve its workforce planning system by collecting and integrating data that previously was not accessible or located in disparate locations.

This chapter focuses on the adoption of formal workforce planning. This function was selected because relatively few states reported having a formal workforce planning process in place in 1998 and many national conferences, such as the National Association of State Personnel Executives and the International Personnel Management Association, highlighted the importance of workforce planning in the late 1990s. Workforce planning, defined as a strategy and set of procedures by which the state's future personnel needs are assessed, enables agencies to ascertain their need for and availability of human resources to meet their objectives. Moreover, it is an important tool that can be used to align human resource management needs with government and agency goals. Some governments have incorporated staffing projections into their budgets, while others have approached workforce planning much more systematically with a long-term focus, such as in Kansas. Without the knowledge gained from workforce planning, Cayer (1996) argues, agencies and their managers will have difficulty maintaining a highly productive workforce.

Explaining Personnel Reforms in the State

This chapter builds upon a model developed by Kellough and Selden (2003) to explain the diffusion of personnel reforms in state government. Like Kellough and Selden, it examines the impact of two sets of factors on reforms: organizational and environmental. This approach differs, however, in that it examines the adoption of different types of personnel to determine whether factors associated with different types of reform vary in a specific time period (between 1998 and 2000). Moreover, it expands upon the organizational factors utilized by Kellough and Selden to include additional organizational measures related to the management and leadership of the personnel system. This section discusses the rationale underlying the explanatory factors included in the model.

Organizational Context

Most public managers and scholars of public management assume that effective management is positively related to effective performance (or of promoting particular outcomes) (Ingraham and Kneedler 2000; Lynn 1997; Kettl and Milward 1996). Management is an important dimension of the organizational context. Since this study is concerned with personnel reform, it focuses on the management capacity of a state's personnel system (Ingraham and Selden 2002; Burke and Wright 2000). A well-designed personnel system will have an impact on the ability of state government to respond to stakeholder concerns and to implement reforms to address those needs (Arthur 1994; Delaney and Huselid 1996; Huselid 1995; Snell and Youndt 1992). Research has shown that organizations committed to their employees typically invest more in their employees and in progressive personnel practices (Arthur 1994; Huselid 1995). Because the Government Performance Project (GPP) graded each state's personnel system in 1998, this study uses it as its proxy measure of performance. There is no overlap between the 1998 GPP grade and the reforms examined in this study because the reforms explored as dependent variables must have been implemented in either 1999 and 2000 and therefore are not reflected in the 1998 grade.

Second, the study focuses on the organizational context of the central personnel department (CPO). The chapter includes two types of indicators. First, the study considers a structural measure—to whom the central personnel office reports. The study posits that states whose CPOs report directly to the governor possess more administrative influence and are able to cultivate more momentum and support for reform of the state's personnel system. Second, the study includes a measure of network activities of the central personnel director/executive. The study argues that personnel directors who interact more regularly with the Executive and Legislative branches are more likely to generate support for their efforts to change personnel policies, procedures, and practices. As Barrett and Greene (1999) found in their personal interviews, state civil service code changes cannot be made within the legislature's support. Lastly, the study posits that those personnel directors that seek out the advice of consultants are more likely to engage in activities to reform the state's civil service system.

Environmental Context

Unionization, economic conditions, and region form the environmental context examined here. Unionization is often mentioned as an impediment to public personnel reform (Babcock and Engberg 1997; Barrett and Greene 1999; Kellough and Selden 2003; Smith 1985). As protectors of employee interests, unions typically favor increasing benefits and oppose reform that increases managerial flexibility and authority over employees. In this sense, unions are big players in "seek[ing] influence over as many important decisions as possible, in ways that can impede the development of simplified and more flexible procedures" (Rainey 1994, 201–202). The rigidity and complexity produced by state personnel systems with well-developed union clout is likely a barrier to personnel reform. Kneedler, Selden, and Ingraham (2000) found, for example, that local workforce union-ization was associated with less innovated hiring and motivation systems in local government. Since decentralization of personnel authority is expected to increase the discretion and flexibility of managers, we expect the degree of unionization, as measured by the percent of state employees who are members of unions, to be negatively associated with personnel reform. Barrett and Greene (1999) found that unions were more problematic in some states with greater and stronger presences, such as Rhode Island and New York, than in other states, such as Georgia and South Carolina.

A state's economic conditions may influence the demands for services within a state and may have an impact on whether to adopt reforms. States with low unemployment are likely to be doing better financially and therefore have additional resources to implement new changes (Kellough and Selden, 2003). Moreover, some personnel professionals believe that tight labor markets have driven changes to personnel systems, particularly in the areas of planning, hiring, and compensation (Leonard 1998).

It is also likely that region is linked to efforts to reform personnel systems because cultural traditions often heavily influence political decisions (Elazar 1966; Lieske 1993). Studies have demonstrated the importance of regional and cultural differences on state policies and personnel practices (for example, McCurdy 1998; Sharkansky 1969). This study controls for the impact that region may have on a state's adoption of different types of personnel reform.

Data, Methods, and Measures

The analysis is based upon information collected by the Government Performance Project (GPP) in 1998 and in 2000.[1] In January 1998 surveys were mailed to state budget directors. Budget directors coordinated the completion of the personnel section with state personnel directors. Completed surveys and supporting documentation were received from 49 states. The gathered information includes quantitative data such as the extent of use of performance tools, as well as qualitative information describing policies, priorities, and procedures. In March 2000 the GPP administered a second survey that included a section about personnel to state governments. All states returned completed surveys. In this survey, respondents were asked 104 multipart, open- and closed-ended questions about an array of personnel activities. The open-ended questions were aimed at understanding the personnel reforms and barriers encountered by the government. Additional data were collected from a follow up telephone survey of state personnel directors (executives) in early 2001. In this survey, respondents were asked to specify the frequency of their contact with an array of stakeholders within and outside of state government based on their work in 2000 and to answer a few questions about the organizational structure of the state personnel office. Personnel directors were faxed a copy of the survey before the scheduled interview to promote careful assessment of these interactions. Forty-four state personnel directors participated in the telephone interview (88 percent response rate).

This analysis draws upon both the qualitative data and quantitative data. Changes in personnel authority were analyzed by examining who had primary responsibility or authority for the personnel functions of classification, compensation, performance appraisal, recruiting, and training in 1998 and 2000. Changes were noted and summed, creating a theoretical range of 0 to 5. In other words, the study did not place a valuation on whether structural authority was shifted toward decentralization, centralization, or shared authority. For each function, a state was assigned a value of 1 if it changed primary responsibility for that function during the two-year period. The actual range was 0 to 4, with a mean of 1.64 and standard deviation of .90 (see appendix).

The study measured policy changes to a state's hiring system by analyzing a state's response to an open-ended question regarding what changes or innovations had occurred in the hiring process in 1999 and 2000 using QSR NUD*IST—a qualitative data analysis tool. These responses were checked with the 1998 survey responses to ensure that they were adopted in 1999 or 2000. States implementing a policy change to its hiring system in 1999 or 2000 were assigned a value of 1. The mean value of the dependent variable, adoption of policy change in the hiring process, is .22, with a standard deviation of .42. That is, eleven states adopted policies impacting their hiring systems in 1999 and 2000, ranging from repealing residency requirements, eliminating hiring rules, repealing a law regarding patronage hiring, and passing a law that allows state agencies to use temporary employees.

Finally, adoption of formal workforce planning was determined by comparing the 1998 and 2000 survey responses to identify states that had adopted formal workforce planning. States that adopted a formal workforce plan in 1999 or 2000 were assigned a value of 1. The mean value of the dependent variable, adoption of a formal workforce plan, is .36, with a standard deviation of .48. That is, eighteen states adopted formal workforce plans in 1999 or 2000.

The Appendix discusses the measurement and presents descriptive statistics of the independent variables included in the analyses. The study uses Ordinary Least Squares (OLS) regression to analyze changes in personnel authority and logistic regression to analyze changes in the hiring policies and adoption of workforce planning.

Findings

As illustrated in Tables 3.1, 3.2, and 3.3, the independent variables included in the multivariate analysis explain a substantial degree of the observed variation in structural reform (R^2=.42), policy reform (Pseudo R^2=.51), and activity reform (Pseudo R^2=.33). Moreover, several patterns emerged across the equations and the

Table 3.1
Ordinary Least Squares Regression of Structural Reform:
Dependent Variable: Changes in Personnel Authority

Organizational	B	Standard Error
1998 GPP Grade	.43**	.21
HR director reports to Governor	.62**	.29
Level of interaction with Governor	.00	.09
Level of interaction with Legislature	.12	.10
Level of interaction with Consultants	.21**	.10
Environment	**B**	**Standard Error**
Percent of employees covered by union contract	−.00**	.00
Unemployment 2000	.46***	.17
Midwestern region	.63	.43
Southern region	−.71*	.39
Eastern region	1.19**	.51
Constant	−3.06***	1.18
R^2 = .42		
F = 2.4***		
N = 44		

*** = Significant at .01 level
** = Significant at .05 level
* = Significant at .10 level

Table 3.2
Logistic Regression Analysis of Policy Reform: Dependent
Variable: Rule Change in Hiring Process

Organizational	B	Standard Error
1998 GPP Grade	9.03[**]	5.6
HR Director reports to Governor	3.30	3.12
Level of interaction with Governor	1.89	1.56
Level of interaction with Legislature	−.90	1.34
Level of interaction with Consultants	3.36[**]	1.90
Environment	**B**	**Standard Error**
Percent of employees covered by union contract	−.01	.05
Unemployment 2000	4.00[*]	2.77
Midwestern region	−.88	4.05
Southern region	1.92	2.46
Eastern region	.75	8.06
Constant	−1.358[***]	.37

−2 Log Likelihood = 12.83
Model Child-Squared = 31.76[***]
Correctly predicted (%) = 79.5 %
Pseudo R^2 = .51 (Cox & Snell)
N = 44

[***] = Significant at .01 level
[**] = Significant at .05 level
[*] = Significant at .10 level

findings of the analysis are largely as expected, although with the exception of unemployment.

As shown in Tables 3.1, 3.2, and 3.3, a state's 1998 GPP personnel grade has a positive and statistically significant impact on its likelihood of adopting all three types of personnel reforms. While considerable research in the private sector has examined the impact of personnel performance on organizational performance, this is the first study that examines whether personnel performance, as measured by the 1998 GPP grade, is linked to future adoption of personnel reforms (Davidson 1998; Delery and Doty 1996; Fitz-enz 1994; Markowich 1995; Martinez 1996; Ulrich 1997). This research suggests that higher performing states are more likely to implement and to experiment with new personnel strategies, policies, and practices. There may be political and administrative reasons that entrench certain states and impede their ability to change their personnel systems. States that are higher performing are engaging in more strategic human resource

Table 3.3
Logistic Regression Analysis of Activity Reform: Dependent
Variable: Adoption of Formal Workforce Planning

Organizational	B	Standard Error
1998 GPP Grade	1.4**	8.0
HR director reports to Governor	−.42	.92
Level of interaction with Governor	−.34	.31
Level of interaction with Legislature	−.15	.40
Level of interaction with Consultants	.78**	.41

Environment	B	Standard Error
Percent of employees covered by union contract	−.01	.02
Unemployment 2000	.32	.62
Midwestern Region	1.23	1.73
Southern Region	2.58*	1.42
Eastern Region	4.72***	2.39

	B	Standard Error
Constant	−7.51*	4.62

−2 Log Likelihood = 39.04
Model Chi-Squared = 17.42**
Correctly predicted (%) = 65.9 %
Pseudo R ^{2} = .33
N = 44

*** = Significant at .01 level
** = Significant at .05 level
* = Significant at .10 level

management (SHRM) (Selden, Ingraham, Jacobson 2001). This approach is typically associated with planned changes to personnel systems that enable an organization to achieve its goals (Wright and Scott 1998). These findings suggest that states that are performing at higher levels are likely to continue by capitalizing and further developing synergies within the personnel system.

Surprising only one of the three network measures is statistically significant across the equations. The extent to which personnel directors interact with consultants has a positive and statistically significant impact on the likelihood of adopting structural, policy, and activity reforms. This finding may simply reflect that states that are interacting more regularly with consultants have made the strategic commitment to change, and are utilizing the services of a consultant to advance desired changes to the personnel system. The findings suggest that states that want to successfully adopt reforms should consider engaging the services of consultants to assist with the change process.

The final organizational context variable, reporting relationship, is significant in only one of the equations. Like Hou et al. (2000), the findings indicate that states where the CPO reports directly to the governor are significantly more likely to alter their configuration of personnel authority. The differences observed across the types of reform may reflect a governor's level of interest in the different types of reform. Governors may be more interested in reforms that alter the amount of control exerted by the central personnel office and the balance of power between the CPO and agencies than changes to how personnel processes are implemented.

Areas with more unemployment are significantly more likely to make changes to personnel authority and hiring policies. Contrary to expectation, the analyses suggest that states with higher unemployment rates have greater likelihood of changing their personnel authority structures and hiring policies. This relationship proved robust in the analysis despite a number of efforts to test its reliability.[2] This finding defies previous studies on reform and the apparently commonsense assertion that states may be driven to reform their personnel practices in tighter labor markets (Kellough and Selden 2003; Leonard 1998). The findings may be a product of the general low level of unemployment in 2000 (see Appendix at the end of this chapter) but future research should explore this issue.

Finally, the study finds a significant negative relationship between the percent of employees unionized and changes in personnel authority. This finding suggests that the likelihood of making changes to how personnel authority is structured between the central personnel office and the agencies is likely to decline as the percent of employees unionized increases. This result is consistent with other studies (Kellough and Selden, 2003). However, the evidence is not overwhelming that unions create barriers to change. For the other two types of reforms—changes in hiring policies and procedures and adoption of workforce planning—greater unionization is not statistically related to the passage of policy and activity reforms. While unions may resist seeing greater managerial discretion over the implementation of different personnel functions, such as classification and compensation, they may not resist changes to processes, such as workforce planning, that have little direct impact on the employee-employer relationship. Similarly, while unions might place great concern over changes to promotional policies and procedures, they may act less fervently to changes related to hiring policies.

These findings suggest that unions, like administrators, have agendas and they may not as a practice impede the passage of all personnel reforms. Rather, they are likely to focus their energies toward influencing those changes that have the greatest impact on their current membership.

Conclusion

Understanding factors that are associated with personnel reform is important to the field of public personnel. This chapter seeks to further the field's understanding of what factors are associated with a state's decision to adopt different types of reforms. The model proposed and examined in this chapter was simple but important. The findings illustrate that personnel performance, as measured by the 1998 GPP grade, is an important predictor of different types of personnel reform. Moreover, states whose directors interact with consultants are more likely to experiment with new approaches. The study also shows that unions may work against some reforms but not necessarily all reforms.

This chapter makes two main contributions to the field of public personnel. First, it provides an empirical test of a set of factors to explain different types of personnel reform. Second, it examines two important organizational concepts that have not been previously linked to personnel reform—prior personnel performance and state director's level of interaction with specific stakeholders. While this study adds to our understanding of different types of personnel reform in the public sector, additional research is needed to explore other measures of personnel reforms and explanatory factors.

Notes

1. Details of Government Performance Project are available at the project's Web site: www.maxwell.syr.edu/gpp.

2. Because the relationship between unemployment and the different types of reform were not as expected, I explored a number of different models to determine its robustness. I examined the relationship between turnover and unemployment over a two-year period: 1998 and 1999. In both years the relationship remained positive and significant. I included the Gross State Product growth but it did not mitigate the original relationship between unemployment and reform.

References

Allison, G.T. (1983). "Public and Private Management: Are They Fundamentally Alike in All Unimportant Respects?" In J.L. Perry and K.L. Kraemer, eds. *Public Management.* Mountain View, CA: Mayfield.

Babcock, L.C., and J.B. Engberg (1997). "A Dynamic Model of Public Sector Employer Response to Unionization." *Journal of Labor Research,* Vol. 18, No. 2 (August): 265–286.

Barrett, K., and R. Greene (1999). "Grading the States." *Governing Magazine,* February. Available: http://www.governing.com/gpp/gp9intro.htm (printed 11/20/02)

Bowman, J.S., J.P. West, and S.C. Gertz (2002). "Florida's 'Service First'; Radical Reform in the Sunshine State." Paper presented at 2002 annual meeting of the American Political Science Association.

Burke, B.F., and D.S. Wright (2000). "Reviewing, Reassessing, Reconciling, and Reinterpreting Performance Indicators in the American States: Exploring State Administrative Capacity" Discussion Paper, University of North Carolina, Chapel Hill, NC.

Cayer, N.J. (1996). *Public Personnel Administration in the United States.* 3rd edition. New York: St. Martin's Press.

Coggburn, J. (2002). "Lone Star HR: Texas' Decentralized, Deregulated Approach to State Human Resources." Paper presented at 2002 annual meeting of the American Political Science Association.

Davidson, L. (1998). "Measure What You Bring to the Bottom Line." *Workforce,* Vol. 77, No. 9 (September): 34–40.

Delaney, J.T., and M.A. Huselid (1996). "The Impact of Human Resource Management Practices on Perceptions of Organizational Performance." *Academy of Management Journal,* Vol. 39, No. 4 (August): 949–969.

Elazar, Daniel J. (1984). *American Federalism: A View from the States* (3rd edition, 1st edition 1966). New York: Harper and Row.

Fitz-enz, J. (1994). "HR's New Score Card." *Personnel Journal,* Vol. 73, No. 2 (February): 84–91.

Hou, Y., S.C. Selden, P.W. Ingraham, and S.Bretschneider. (2000). "Decentralization of Human Resource Management: Driving Forces and Implications." *Review of Public Personnel Administration,* Vol. 20, No. 4 (Fall): 9–23.

Huselid, M.A. (1995). "The Impact of Human Resource Management Practices on Turnover, Productivity, and Corporate Financial Performance." *Academy of Management Journal,* Vol. 38, No. 3 (June): 635–672.

Ingraham, P.W., and S.C. Selden. (2002). "Human Resource Management and Capacity in the States." In *Public Personnel Management: Current Concerns, Future Challenges,* edited by Carolyn Ban and Norma M. Riccucci, eds. New York: Longman, 210–224.

Ingraham, P.W., and A.E. Kneedler. (2000). "Dissecting the Black Box: Toward a Model and Measures of Government Management

Performance." In Jeffery L. Brudney, Laurence J. O'Toole, and Hal G. Rainey, eds. *Advancing Public Management: New developments in Theory Methods, and Practice.* Washington, DC: Georgetown University Press.

Ingraham, P.W., S.C. Selden, and D. Moynihan. (2000). "People and Performance: Challenges for the Future Public Service." Public Administration Review, 60.

Kellough, J.E., and S.C. Selden. (2003). "The Reinvention of Public Personnel Administration: An Analysis of the Diffusion of Personnel Management Reform in the States." *Public Administration Review,* Vol. 63, No. 2 (March/April): 165–176.

Kettl, D.F., H.B. Milward, eds. (1996). *The State of Public Management.* Baltimore: Johns Hopkins University Press.

Donahue, A.K., S.C. Selden, and P.W. Ingraham (2000). "Measuring Government Management Capacity: A Comparative Analysis of City Human Resources Management Systems." *Journal of Public Administration Research and Theory*, Vol. 10, No. 2 (April): 381–411.

Leonard, B. (1998). "What Do HR Executives Want from CEOS?" *HR Magazine*, Vol. 43, No. 13 (December): 92–98.

Lieske, J. (1993). "Regional Subcultures of the United States." *Journal of Politics*, Vol. 55, No. 4 (November): 888–913.

Lynn, L.E. (1997). "In Government, Does Management Matter? Explain." Panel presented at the Fourth National Public Management Research Conference, The University of Georgia, Athens, GA, October 30–November 1.

Markowich, M.M. (1995). "HR's Leadership in the Third Wave Era." *HRMagazine*, Vol. 40, No. 9 (September): 92–100.

Martinez, M.N. (1996). "Three Strategies for Successful Business Partners." *HRMagazine*, Vol. 41, No. 10 (October): 1–5.

McCurdy, A.H. (1998). "Political Culture, Local Government and Progressive Personnel Practices: The Case of Collective Bargaining Provisions and a Test of Elazar's and Lieske's Measures of Political Culture." *Review of Public Personnel Administration*, Vol. 18, No. 1 (Winter): 23–38.

National Council of State Legislators (2002). Employment Issues Report for 2002. Available: http://www.ncsl.org/programs/employ/empoutlook.pdf (Printed November 23, 2002).

Rainey, H.G. (1997). *Understanding and Managing Public Organizations*, 2nd edition, San Fransico: Jossey-Bass.

Selden, S.C. (2002). *Human Resource Management in the American Counties*. Working paper.

Selden, S.C., and D.P. Moynihan (2000). "A Model of Voluntary Turnover in State Government." *Review of Public Personnel Administration*, Vol. 20, No. 2 (Spring): 63–74.

Selden, S.C., P.W. Ingraham, and W. Jacobson (2001). "Human Resource Practices: Findings From a National Survey." *Public Administration Review*, Vol. 61, No. 5 (September/October): 598–607.

Sharkansky, I. (1969). "The utility of Elazar's Political Culture." *Journal of Politics 2.*

Smith, B.C. (1985). *Decentralization—the Territorial Dimension of the State.* London: George Allen & Unwin.

Snell, S.A., and J.W. Dean, Jr. (1992). "Integrated Manufacturing and Human Resource Management: A Human Capital Perspective." *Academy of Management Journal*, Vol. 35, No. 3 (August): 467–504.

Ulrich, D. (1997). "Measuring Human Resources: An Overview of Practice and a Prescription for Results." *Human Resource Management*, Vol. 36, No. 3, (Fall): 303–320.

Appendix

Construction of Human Resources Indices and Descriptive Statistics for Variables Contained in Final Analyses

1998 GPP Grade (HRM Performance Indicator)
- Letter grades translated to 4 point scale, with A= 4.0, A-=3.7, B+ =3.3, B=3.0, B-=2.7, etc.
- Mean=2.52; Standard Deviation=.70

Level of Interaction with Executive *(Theoretical Range: 0–9)*
- Summative index of the frequency of contacts the HRM director has with the Governor, his staff., agency heads, and other executive branch directors (Range, 0 (never) to 9 (more than 1 daily); divided by 4).
- Alpha=.87
- Mean=5.53; Standard Deviation=1.76

Level of Interaction with Legislature *(Theoretical Range: 0–9)*
- Summative index of the frequency of contacts the HRM director has with State Legislators, State legislative committees, and Legislative staffers (Range, 0 (never) to 9 (more than 1 daily); divided by 3).
- Alpha=.88
- Mean=4.43; Standard Deviation=1.58

Level of Interaction with Consultants *(Theoretical Range: 0–9)*
- Summative index of the frequency of contacts the HRM director has with consultants (Range, 0 (never) to 9 (more than 1 daily))
- Mean=3.19; Standard Deviation=1.39

Other Variables Included in the Analysis

Independent Variables	Mean	Std. Deviation
HR director reports to Governor	.42	.50
Percent of employees covered by union contract	43.06	39.14
Unemployment 2000	4.22	.88
Midwestern region	.26	.44
Southern region	.26	.44
Eastern region	.24	.43
Dependent Variables	*Mean*	*Std. Deviation*
Change in personnel authority	1.64	.90
Adoption of policy change in hiring process	.22	.42
Adoption of formal workforce planning	.36	.48

CHAPTER 4

The Labor Perspective on Civil Service Reform in the States

Richard C. Kearney

The dance of state civil service reform may feature many complicated and often interrelated steps, including decentralization of human resource management structures and responsibilities, privatization of certain personnel functions, and debureaucratization and streamlining of personnel strategies and activities. When the music fades and the dance is done, after politicians and top-level public administrators have applauded, declared it to be a success, and walked off the floor, public employees remain to clean up the mess and go on with their work lives. But the state dance club may look dramatically different, with new organizational structures, modernized recruitment and selection systems, altered incentive systems, and modified position classification and compensation plans, among other changes.

Whether state employees and their unions or associations choose to be willing partners in the dance of civil service reform, sit it out, or break up the orchestra, depends on how they answer the critical question of what the likely impacts will be on the organization and its members. Where unions and collective bargaining exist, and the perceived effects of reform are negative, unions will likely be staunch opponents of reform. Often such reforms, particularly privatization or outsourcing, potentially threaten their membership bases as well as their capacities to influence personnel policy in virtually all areas of the employment relationship. But if the unions have participated meaningfully in the dance and ensured that the outcomes will not seriously damage the pay, benefits, and working conditions of their members, they may help facilitate the design and implementation of civil service reform. That is the major conclusion of this chapter.

Following a brief examination of the extent of unionization and collective bargaining among state employees, I will discuss the

77

perspectives and impacts of unions on state civil service reform in the 1990s and early 2000s. Where possible, I will offer examples of specific cases of union opposition or support for major changes in human resource management structures and processes.

State Employee Unionization and Collective Bargaining

The role of unions is ignored or given short shrift in much of the scholarly and practitioner literature on civil service reform. Yet unlike their counterparts in the private sector, where union membership has steadily declined to only 9 percent of the nonagricultural labor force, public employee unions remain robust, powerful fixtures in the majority of state governments. Altogether, 37.4 percent of government employees belonged to labor unions in 2001. The highest unionization rate was among local government workers, at just over 43 percent. The membership rate for state employees was 30.5 percent (U.S. Bureau of Labor Statistics 2002). Union representation of state employees through collective bargaining was slightly higher at 34.5 percent, reflecting the fact that some members of the bargaining unit choose not to join the union.

Table 4.1 indicates which state employees enjoy collective bargaining rights and the percentage of state employees that belong to unions. Thirty-two states provide for collective bargaining or meet and confer[1] for state employees. The majority of states have done so through legislation, but in some cases collective bargaining has been extended through court order, attorney general opinion, or gubernatorial executive order. The most recent states to grant collective bargaining rights were Kentucky and Missouri in 2001, in both cases through executive order. The 2001 membership statistics are 1994–1996 averages and thus do not incorporate the influx of newly represented employees in these two states. The last column in Table 1 reports the 2001 state ratings on quality of human resource management as calculated by the Government Performance Project.[2] A glance at the column indicates that collective bargaining is not necessarily associated with low ratings on human resources management (HRM) (as commonly believed), and, similarly, that the absence of collective bargaining is not necessarily associated with high ratings.

Public employees join unions for the same reasons as private and nonprofit sector workers: they are dissatisfied with one or more salient aspects of their jobs. Discontent may result from perceived pay and benefits disparities, hazardous or repetitive tasks, arbitrary

Table 4.1
State Employee Collective Bargaining Status, Union Density, and Human Resources Management Performance Ratings

STATE	BARGAINING STATUS	% UNION	HRM RATING
Alabama	—	28.5%	D+
Alaska	X	61.1	C
Arizona	—	14.1	C
Arkansas	—	13.8	C
California	Y	55.7	C
Colorado	—	16.4	B-
Connecticut	X	75.3	C
Delaware	X	38.5	B
Florida	X	73.2	B-
Georgia	—	14.6	B-
Hawaii	X	71.4	C
Idaho	—	17.9	B
Illinois	X	43.1	B
Indiana	X	20.5	B
Iowa	X	19.8	B+
Kansas	Y	14.4	B+
Kentucky	X*	15.3	B+
Louisiana	—	18.2	B
Maine	X	61.2	B-
Maryland	X	34.0	B
Massachusetts	X	58.4	B-
Michigan	X	52.9	B+
Minnesota	X	61.1	C+
Mississippi	—	11.8	B-
Missouri	X*	16.4	B+
Montana	X	47.3	C+
Nebraska	X	28.1	C
Nevada	—	30.6	D+
New Hampshire	X	55.6	C-
New Jersey	X	64.1	C-
New Mexico	—	17.4	B-
New York	X	73.8	C+
North Carolina	—	16.7	B+
North Dakota	Y**	23.9	B
Ohio	X	47.3	B
Oklahoma	—	18.9	C-
Oregon	X	60.4	C
Pennsylvania	X	63.4	B+
Rhode Island	X	68.1	C-
South Carolina	—	13.3	A
South Dakota	X	13.7	B-
Tennessee	—	16.0	B-
Texas	—	11.5	B
Utah	—	20.1	B-
Vermont	X	45.5	C
Virginia	—	7.6	B+
Washington	X	46.4	A-
West Virginia	Y**	14.1	C+
Wisconsin	X	39.9	A-
Wyoming	—	14.3	C+

*Collective bargaining extended by executive order in 2001.
**Meet and confer extended through attorney general opinion

Sources: Bargaining Status is from Kearney 2001: 60–61 (updated); Union Density from AFL-CIO, 1997:3–4 (average union density, 1994–1996); Human Resource Management Ratings are from the Government Performance Project at www.governing.com/gpp/gp1glanc.htm (July 21, 2002)

or unfair management actions, or any number of other causes. But mere dissatisfaction is not enough. State employees in the Carolinas and Utah, for instance, may be deeply unhappy with pay and working conditions, but because the state-as-employer does not have the legal authority to recognize unions and negotiate with them, their joining a labor organization may be an empty gesture. North and South Carolina and Virginia explicitly prohibit the recognition of public employee unions for purpose of collective bargaining.

Indeed, the most important determinant of state employee unionization is whether the state has a legal environment that permits or mandates collective bargaining (Kearney 2001, 28–34). A distinct regional pattern indicates that the socioeconomic environment and political culture of sunbelt states are generally antagonistic to organized labor. If the sunbelt is defined as south of the Mason-Dixon Line extended to the Pacific, all except Florida, New Mexico, and California are Right-to Work states; only California, Florida, and Maryland permit collective bargaining by state employees (New Mexico's collective bargaining statute was sunset in 1999). Because few sunbelt states authorize collective bargaining, relatively low proportions of their employees belong to labor unions (see Table 1).

In the nonunion states, employees typically are offered membership in a state employee association. These organizations, such as the Texas Public Employees Association and the State Employees Association of North Carolina, offer various member benefits and programs. They also engage in electoral activities intended to benefit their legislative and gubernatorial supporters and punish their perceived enemies, and when provoked, may picket or demonstrate, as Texas state employees did across the state in July 2002. State employee associations employ professional lobbyists to favorably influence legislative decision making on wages, benefits, working conditions, and other matters of importance to state employees. However, the effectiveness of these associations is severely limited by the absence of the right to negotiate collective bargaining contracts. Without bargaining rights, associations are essentially relegated to the status of large, and occasionally loud, interest groups. Civil service reformers may take into account the views expressed by an association, and association representatives may participate in study commissions or other reform groups, but in the end, the positions of the association can be ignored. This would certainly appear to be the case in Georgia's dismantling of its civil service system in 1996 (West 2002; Gossett 2002).

How Unions Influence Policy Outcomes

Collective bargaining laws either require or permit bilateral negotiations over pay, benefits, and the terms and conditions of employment. Union and management representatives sit at the bargaining table as equals to negotiate a binding contract that will govern the employment relationship for, typically, the next two to three years. In most bargaining states, an impasse over one or more issues results in some combination of mediation, fact-finding, and binding arbitration (seven states—Alaska, Hawaii, Illinois, Minnesota, Ohio, Oregon, and Pennsylvania—permit state workers to strike; see Kearney 2001, 236–237). What unions are unable to secure at the table, they might obtain through a favorable arbitration decision. Although the state legislature has final authority over spending and in theory, at least, can overturn a negotiated contract or arbitration decision, this is extremely rare. What emerges from the collective bargaining or arbitration process nearly always stands. Thus, penurious legislative bodies are taken out of the pay and benefit determination equation in bargaining states.

State employee unions are also effective in the political arena. Their political action committees provide endorsements and reward union-friendly candidates with campaign donations. Union members vote and provide human resources for campaign activities. Union lobbyists are busily engaged in the legislative process and in cultivating trust and cooperation among state elected officials. These activities can have both immediate and long-term payoffs, varying from a successful end run to powerful legislative or executive branch allies to secure a raise denied at the bargaining table, to support for union positions on civil service reform.

The relationship between collective bargaining and state employee compensation provides some indication of union influence on policy outcomes. Generally speaking, when union and nonunion states are compared, unions have been successful in producing pay and benefit advantages for members of the bargaining unit. At the state level, however, the effects on pay and benefits have been moderate and not as substantial as the monetary impacts of private sector unions. Although the empirical research is sparse, the magnitude of the union pay impact in state government appears to have varied over time and jurisdiction, ranging from 4 percent to 7.4 percent as of the early 1990s (Kearney 2001, 156–166; Belman et al. 1997). Because of the almost unlimited variety of state benefits possibilities and the epic difficulty of comparing health insurance plans, little systematic research has appeared on the union impact on benefits. But according to one recent study, the benefits in collective bargaining states are generally far more generous than those in nonbargaining states, particularly employee and dependent health insurance and pensions (Kearney 2003).

Unions and State Civil Service Reform: General Principles

Collective bargaining states have dual, and sometimes conflicting, personnel systems. The traditional merit system is a legacy of the civil service reform movement that swept the states during the late nineteenth and early twentieth centuries. The purpose was twofold: to ensure the political neutrality of civil servants by protecting them from partisan political pressures and spoils politics, and to instill merit as the dominant criterion for selecting, promoting, and retaining employees. With the passage of time, according to their critics, merit systems have become rule bound, rigid, ponderously slow, and excessively protective of public employees. These traditional merit systems are now under attack by reformers.

Collective bargaining contracts and state labor relations law compose the second personnel system. Elements of traditional merit systems that fall within the scope of bargaining, such as union rights, union security, discipline and discharge, grievance procedures, hours and conditions of work, layoffs, bumping and recall rights, seniority, various forms of leave, position classification, employee health and safety, privatization, and the use of new technology may be modified through collective bargaining, thereby creating a second personnel system. Collective bargaining personnel systems, too, have experienced criticism along many of the same lines as traditional systems. However, few efforts to reform collective bargaining systems have progressed beyond rhetoric. Reform of key elements of a collective bargaining system usually must take place within the framework of the system itself, as a product of bargaining, arbitration, or agreements constructed by labor-management committees. Unilateral management action is not feasible unless management authority to decide an issue is formally housed in statute or a management rights clause. Even when management authority is reserved, for instance, to make promotion decisions, the contract may call for seniority to play the determining role. Similarly, position classification may be reserved as a management right, but the *process* for classifying and reclassifying positions may be specified in the contract.

In a nonbargaining state the only major impediment to civil service reform, besides a pronounced legislative disposition in favor of inertia, may be a vociferous but essentially punchless employee association. An association acting in the political arena has some degree of leverage with elected officials, but little else in terms of fields of influence. Unions, on the other hand, have multiple arenas for halting or otherwise influencing the direction of reform.

Can significant civil service reform take place in a union environment? The short answer is yes, but the posture of state employee unions may be the determinative factor in success or failure. If reform is perceived to threaten or damage the union or members of the bargaining unit, the union is certain to resist and obstruct change. If unions are incorporated into the reform planning and implementation processes, they are more inclined to cooperate and even facilitate reform. Finally, if the unions discern that reform will advantage or advance their interests, their support is likely to be forthcoming.

Resistance and obstruction are nearly certain, for example, if the union is threatened by a loss of fair share or dues check-off arrangements. If reform would weaken union or state employee rights, pay, or benefits, or threaten to make work more dangerous or demanding without adequate compensation, then opposition is assured. Proposals to contract out work presently being performed by state employees will be fiercely resisted unless jobs are protected. Adoption of labor-saving technology or other productivity enhancements that presage a reduction in force will be impeded unless acceptable accommodations are offered to disadvantaged workers.

The bottom line is that a union wants to protect itself and the members of the bargaining unit from negative aspects of reform and, other things being equal, it wants to do this through limiting management discretion. This posture is clearly antithetical to many initiatives that seek to reduce red tape, streamline agency operations, or increase productivity by providing managers with more decision-making flexibility. In the next section, union reactions to specific reforms in human resource management are considered.

The Union Response to Reinventing Human Resource Management

Although the scope of civil service reform today is very wide, the principal human resource management reforms can be categorized into recruitment, testing, and selection; position classification and broad-banding; compensation; retention; and privatization.

Recruitment, Testing, and Selection

Widespread concern over the quality and diversity of new entrants into state government employment is shared by states across the country. The tenor of reform is to expand the scope of recruitment, streamline and decentralize selection processes, and provide greater management flexibility to make hiring decisions. In principle, staffing has always been a management right. But unions have resisted changes in job qualifications, opposed written examinations, and favored restrictive rules on how many certified applicants managers may consider for a job (e.g., preferring a Rule of One to a Rule of Ten). Unions also favor giving members of the bargaining unit first shot at filling a position opening through promotion, with seniority given proper consideration (Kearney 2001, 196–198).

Perhaps the most celebrated staffing reforms have occurred in Wisconsin, through partnerships between the state and the Wisconsin State Employees Union and other state employee unions that have streamlined recruitment and testing. Applicants for selected jobs can qualify online; specially tailored job searches are developed for hard-to-fill positions; walk-in-testing is available at various sites around the state; and agency managers are authorized to make on-the-spot hiring decisions in certain cases (Walters 2000; Beil and Litscher 1998). Limited certified lists, which restricted selection to the top five or ten test scorers, have been eliminated as well.

Other collective bargaining states have implemented their own reforms to streamline and decentralize staffing, including Kansas, Washington, Alaska, Iowa, Massachusetts, Nebraska, Hawaii, and Ohio. Even traditionally rule-bound and union-strong Rhode Island and New York have made changes. In Rhode Island, the time required to fill an ordinary vacancy has been cut from six months to 60 days. And New York, "the king of the calcified and recalcitrant (states)" (Walters 1998), with one of the most antiquated and cumbersome staffing systems of all the states, has made improvements through aggressive recruiting, online job listings and applications, the testing of provisional employees, and increased management hiring flexibility. New York's nine unions opposed some of the staffing reforms, particularly the substitution of band or zone scoring for the rule of three (as noted by Riccucci in chapter 13 in this book), but they cooperated with others (Walters 1998, 22).

This is not meant to suggest that unions are usually supportive of staffing reforms. Keeping patronage and other nonmerit considerations out of the selection process remains a paramount concern. Also, when proposed staffing reforms threaten to eliminate civil service hiring protections wholesale, unions will lead the counterattack as they did successfully in Massachusetts in 1993 but unsuccessfully in Florida in 2001. What I do mean to suggest is that when unions are brought into the reform process, as they were in Wisconsin, New York, and other states, resistance may be attenuated and cooperation becomes a possibility.

Position Classification and Broad-Banding

A traditional prerogative of management, position classification is criticized by unions for its allegedly pseudo-scientific approach to categorizing jobs by similarities and differences. Unions consider position classification to be inherently subjective and arbitrary, but they generally accept its existence and would prefer to have a voice in reclassification decisions. Unions insist that employees be properly compensated for working temporarily in jobs at higher-rated classifications, and they are concerned about the relationship between position classification and pay structure.

Reformers recommend that states dramatically reduce the number of narrow position classes and (raising a red flag of warning to unions) grant managers greater discretion in allocating jobs to classes through broad-banding of positions. Among collective bargaining states, Illinois reduced the number of job titles from 1,700 to around 1,000, New Jersey cut some 1,000 titles (keeping a formidable 8,000 on the books), and New York managed to eliminate some 2,000 job titles (retaining another 4,220). Several other bargaining states are actively working on classification reform (Hays 2001). Unions have been able to derail classification reform in Ohio, Connecticut, California, and Vermont. In some cases, such as New York, classification reform and broad-banding can be brought about through administrative fiat. In others, such reform falls within the scope of bargaining and must be negotiated with the unions.

Compensation

Despite the vociferous criticism of scholars (Kellough and Lu 1993; Perry 1995), a major premise of civil service reform is that states must become more performance-oriented, and that some type of pay-for-performance, or merit pay, system is needed to provide the incentives for higher employee performance. Nonbargaining states such as South Carolina (see chapter 8 in this book by Hays, Byrd, and

Wilkins), Georgia, Oklahoma, and Wyoming are using bonuses, skill-based pay, competency-based pay, and other individual pay incentives to spur employees into higher productivity. Unions are strongly opposed to merit pay schemes, considering them to be rife with management abuse and the playing of favorites (Garen 1999). They want to set pay and benefit levels at the bargaining table and take management discretion out of the compensation determination process. Across-the-board pay increases and step increases are preferred to any form of merit increase.

Union opposition notwithstanding, a large majority of states have adopted some type of pay-for-performance plan (California, Nebraska, and Rhode Island are among the exceptions). In those states in which collective bargaining rights are in place, unions have insisted on having a voice in structuring the terms of any pay-for-performance plan.

Retention

Civil service systems are popularly ridiculed by everyone from politicians to talk show hosts for allegedly protecting incompetent, lazy, or badly behaving workers. This widespread belief, although exaggerated, is a product of the traditional civil service goal of protecting public employees from political pressures and dismissals. Procedures are in place for disciplining and dismissing employees and if applied properly they can be effective (Hays 1995). Too often, however, managers forsake their responsibilities to engage in appropriate record keeping and correctly administer progressive disciplinary procedures. For their part, unions are bound by their contract and the principle of exclusive representation to defend aggressively any member of the bargaining unit who experiences discipline, dismissal, or any other adverse action.

Procedural safeguards against dismissal tend to be elaborate and time-consuming even in traditional civil service systems (with the exception of firing probationary employees). Through negotiated or statutory grievance procedures, unions and grievance arbitrators add further complexity to the process and place a heavier burden on the employer to establish just cause for taking adverse action against a member of the bargaining unit. Discharge appeals can drag on for several years, and even minor disciplinary cases can take a year to resolve. Unions are sometimes criticized for staunchly defending, to the bitter end, seemingly hopeless cases (see Kearney 2001, 205).

During reductions in force, employees' procedural protections are minimized. Nonetheless, union contracts can influence decisions on which workers are to be laid off, what the "bumping" priority will be, and policies and procedures for reemployment. The union position is that workers should be laid off in reverse seniority. Using negotiated bumping rights, an employee laid off from one work unit or agency may displace a more junior worker in a different work unit as long as the senior employee is qualified for the job. Thus, reductions in force create considerable uncertainty and disruption. Similarly, the right of qualified, laid-off workers to be offered preference for any new openings lengthens the hiring process. Wisconsin has simplified and streamlined the rehiring process through a computerized Lay-off Referral Service for affected employees (Beil and Litscher 1998, 7–8). In other jurisdictions, in some instances, unions have sought alternatives to layoffs, including work sharing, pay cuts, furloughs, rotating layoffs, and voluntary days off without pay.

Many state employees in Georgia and Florida have essentially lost their job security by being shifted into "at will" status through far-reaching statutory reforms. Among other significant (some have called them "radical") provisions, Georgia's Act 816 of 1996 placed all employees hired after the law's effective date into an unclassified status, effectively removing them from civil service protection. The intent was to accelerate the pace of adverse actions against underperforming or misbehaving workers (Nigro and Kellough 2000, 42). It has been projected that more than three-quarters of all Georgia state employees will be in unclassified positions by 2006 (Condrey 2002). With the absence of collective bargaining rights and strong state employee organizations, little stood in the path of a governor and legislature intent on dismantling the traditional civil service system (West 2002, 81).

Florida's controversial "Service First" legislation reduced the "for cause" standard for suspension or dismissal for most categories of employees to a less rigorous "reasonable cause" standard, and prohibited appeals of employee layoffs or transfers. Service First also immediately removed more than 16,000 positions from the career civil service and effectively made them at-will by eliminating the right to appeal suspensions or dismissals (West 2002, 87). Bumping rights were also terminated for most state employees. Florida's civil service reform met much stronger resistance than Georgia's because of the opposition of AFSCME and its labor allies in a collective bargaining state (West 2002, 85–86). Reformers ultimately prevailed, however, presenting a sobering intimation of what could befall state employees and their unions elsewhere.

Privatization

A major tenet of the contemporary reinventing government movement is that, where feasible, government functions should be outsourced to private and nonprofit providers. In theory, the vast majority of state human resource management functions could be handled by firms or nonprofits. This notion has penetrated civil service reform in some jurisdictions through the contracting out of everything from public assistance job training and placement services to highway rest stop operations. In nonbargaining states, the decision to privatize is treated as a management right related to efficient management of the workplace and therefore fully within management's sphere of authority.

Because outsourcing often means elimination of state employee jobs and the creation of new, nonunion jobs in the private or nonprofit sector, unions can usually be counted on to fervidly resist it and insist that any such decisions have personnel implications and therefore belong at the bargaining table. With the exceptions of New Hampshire and New Jersey, labor relations boards and the courts have supported the union position and held that outsourcing decisions with personnel impacts should be a mandatory bargaining topic (Kearney 2001, 210). On occasion, the certain prospect of strident union opposition has killed a privatization initiative soon after it was vetted. Even if union opposition is overcome, subsequent court challenges are decided in management's favor, and outsourcing becomes a reality, the unions will conscientiously expose and publicize every misstep or oversight in an attempt to demonstrate that privatization is a failure.

In cases where some sort of privatization appears to be inevitable, unions may compromise at the bargaining table. Most importantly, unions demand that no present members of the bargaining unit lose their jobs. They may also ask that management seriously consider union cost-saving ideas that might obviate the need for outsourcing (Elam 1997). Any jobs shifted out of state employment are likely to be filled at lower pay and benefits, but unions want displaced members of the bargaining unit to receive first hiring priority.

The case of Florida notwithstanding, civil service reform is highly problematic when public employee unions are allied against it. In bargaining states in which the need for significant reform is patently obvious, labor-management collaboration may be the most appropriate and productive road.

Toward Labor-Management Partnerships for Civil Service Reform

In government, unlike business, managers and bargaining unit members share important interests. All state employees benefit from safe highways, secure prisons, efficient processing of drivers' licenses and auto registration, and the other services that state government provides on a daily basis. Similarly, the glow of positive public opinion can eventually result in the willingness of taxpayers and elected officials to fund public services and, possibly, lead to improved pay and benefits. Civil service reform poses threats to both unions and management, but collaboration can result in win-win outcomes, when modestly defined as agreements that both parties can live with. Such an outcome satisfies the interests of each party and facilitates implementation of the terms of the agreement.

In many collective bargaining states, labor-management cooperation requires the parties to set aside decades of nasty fighting and bad blood. It presumes a new, much less adversarial model for conducting labor-management interactions at the negotiating table and elsewhere. From a practical perspective, cooperation depends to a great extent on the gap between union and management expectations. When there is a chasm separating the perceived interests and objectives of labor and management, the inertia of adversarial relations prevails. Also critically important for successful labor-management cooperation are a foundation of trust and mutual respect among the participants, a genuine commitment by all key parties to make the program work over the long haul, and an expectation that win-win outcomes will be attained. When these conditions do not obtain, participative endeavors are unlikely to succeed (Kearney 2001, 340–341).

Whether the vehicle entails labor-management committees, interest-based negotiations, quality of work-life committees, participative decision making (Kearney and Hays 1994), gain sharing, productivity bargaining, performance improvement committees, or similar designs, the goal is to set aside differences and rationally discuss, analyze, and resolve problems arising in the work place (Kearney 2003). The core feature of all these techniques is participative decision making, in which employee voices and views are seriously considered in agency decision making. Participative decision-making routines have been widely adopted in the private sector, with an estimated 50 percent of large firms using them in some form (Osterman 1994; Delaney 1996). The scholarly literature identifies important advantages that accrue to organizations and individuals practicing collaborative techniques. Among them are positive effects on individual and organizational productivity, job satisfaction, personal growth and development, and enhanced willingness to change (Kearney and Hays 1994). There is also evidence that cooperation may have a positive effect on work attendance, accident rates (Schwochau et al. 1997, 381), and commitment to the organization (Verma and McKersie 1987), and help to reduce the number of grievances and unfair labor practice charges.

Experience with labor-management participation is slowly beginning to accumulate in the public sector. In New York, labor-management committees (LMCs) helped develop employee assistance and day-care programs, producing savings in health-care expenses and increased employee morale and attendance rates. In Massachusetts, LMCs were established throughout state government to consider career ladders, performance appraisal approaches, childcare, and health and safety issues (Kearney 2001, 340).

The recognized leader in fostering labor-management partnerships is Wisconsin. Collaborative problem solving and win-win negotiations in the Badger State are bolstered by comprehensive training programs and the systematic nurturing of a nonadversarial culture. These trail-blazing initiatives have been underway since 1991, yielding much more cooperative labor-management negotiations through "consensus bargaining" along with specific outcomes including an alternative grievance process that has recorded new health and safety initiatives and a significant reduction in the number of grievances filed. Under the Working Together project, labor-management committees have actively reviewed and offered recommendations on a variety of pressing issues (see Beil and Litscher 1998; Lavigna 2002) and identified "best practices" in union-management cooperation in state government (see Lavigna and Fox, chapter 12 in this book). Taken together, these participative programs are estimated to have saved taxpayers more than $1 million and helped to improve employee efficiency and morale (Lavigna, 2002, 2).

Conclusion

Civil service reform is tough, uphill work. If substantial change is involved, gubernatorial leadership and legislative action are usually required. A lengthy and perhaps emotional fight with state employees and their supporters is typically part of the price that must be paid. Often, elected officials and top political appointees judge the price of reform to be too dear. That is the principal reason that it is so rare, even in nonbargaining states.

In states in which workers have won bargaining rights, the stakes are even higher. If unions are not at least reluctant partners in the dance to change the civil service, they will act as intransigent enemies. Their weapons include litigation, pressure politics, electoral activities, working to the rule, and picketing; in some jurisdictions, they might even walk off the job in protest. Any meaningful reinvention of the civil service under conditions of strong union opposition is likely to remain an unfulfilled dream.

As this chapter has attempted to make clear, reform of the civil service is not easy, but it is certainly not outside the realm of possibility in bargaining states. Recruitment and selection procedures have been streamlined, position classification plans have been simplified, pay and benefit changes have been attained, the rehiring of laid-off workers has been expedited, and functions and positions have been privatized. Some collective bargaining states, including Delaware, Illinois, Iowa, Maryland, Michigan, Ohio, Pennsylvania, Washington, and Wisconsin, have been rated highly on the quality of human resource management (Table 4.1). As noted above, Florida even managed to move some 16,000 positions from civil service protection into at-will status.

Wisconsin and other states have demonstrated that inviting unions as partners on the civil service reform dance floor is an idea that can have positive outcomes. If state government is to truly be reinvented, unions must be productively involved. When they are ignored or underestimated, the dance of reform may be over before the music even begins.

Notes

1. Meet and confer is a process in which the employer formally retains final authority to make decisions concerning wages, benefits, and terms and con-

ditions of employment. In practice, meet and confer and collective bargaining are difficult to distinguish.

2. Housed at the Maxwell School at Syracuse University, the Government Performance Project ranked the states on five human resource management criteria: strategic workforce analysis; obtaining a skilled workforce; maintaining a skilled workforce; motivating effective performance; and structuring the workforce.

References

AFL-CIO (1997). *Public Employees Bargain for Excellence: A Compendium of State Labor Relations Laws,* Public Employee Department: 3–4.

Beil, Martin, and Litscher, Jon E. (1998). "Consensus Bargaining in Wisconsin State Government: A New Approach to Labor Negotiation." *Public Personnel Management* 27 (1), 39–50.

Belmon, D., Heywood, J.S., and Lund, J. (1997). "Public Sector Earnings and the Extent of Unionization." *Industrial and Labor Relations Review* 50 (4), 610.

Condrey, Steven E. (2002). "Reinventing State Civil Service Systems: The Georgia Experience." *Review of Public Personnel Administration* 22 (2), 114–124.

Delaney, John T. (1996). "Workplace Compensation: Current Problems, New Techniques." *Journal of Labor Research* 9 (Summer), 45–61.

Elam, L.B. (1997). "Reinventing the Government Privatization-Style: Avoiding the Legal Pitfalls of Replacing Civil Servants with Contract Providers." *Public Personnel Management* 26 (1), 15–34.

Garen, J. (1999). "Unions, Incentive Systems, and Job Design." *Journal of Labor Research* 20 (4), 589–603.

Gossett, Charles W. (2002). "Civil Service Reform: The Case of Georgia." *Review of Public Personnel Administration* 22 (2), 94–113.

Hays, Steven W. (2001). "Changing Roles and Duties Within Government's Human Resources Profession: Contemporary Models and Challenges." PP. 205–224 in Liou, K.T., ed., *Handbook of Public Management Practice and Reform.* New York: Marcel Dekker.

Hays, Steven W. (1995). "Employee Discipline and Removal: Coping with Job Security." In Hays, S.B. and Kearney, R.C., eds., *Public Personnel Administration: Problems and Prospects,* 145–161. Englewood Cliffs, NJ: Prentice Hall.

Kearney, Richard C. (2001). *Labor Relations in the Public Sector,* 3rd ed. New York: Marcel Dekker.

Kearney, Richard C. (2003). "Problems and Prospects for Public Employee Unions and Managers." In Hays, Steven W. and Kearney, Richard C., eds., *Public Personnel Administration Problems and Prospects,* 4th ed. Upper Saddle River, NJ: Prentice Hall, 319–333.

Kearney, Richard C., and Steven W. Hays (1994). "Labor-Management Relations and Participative Decision Making: Toward a New Paradigm." *Public Administration Review* 54 (1), 44–51.

Kearney, Richard C. (2003). "The Determinants of State Employee Compensation." *Review of Public Personnel Administration* 23(4), 305–322.

Kellough, J. Edward, and Lu, H. (1993). "The Paradox of Merit Pay in the Public Sector Persistence of a Problematic Procedure." *Review of Public Personnel Administration* 13 (2), 45–64.

Lavigna, Bob (2002). "Working Together with Labor." *ASPA Online Columns* www.aspanet.org June 6.

Nigro, Lloyd G., and Kellough, J. Edward (2000). "Civil Service Reform in Georgia." *Review of Public Personnel Administration* 20 (4), 41–54.

Osterman, P. (1994). "How Common is Workplace Transformation and Who Adopts It?" *Industrial and Labor Relations Review* 47, 173–191.

Perry, James L. (1995). "Compensation, Merit Pay, and Motivation." pp. 121–132 in Steven W. Hays and Richard C. Kearney, eds., *Public Personnel Administration: Problems and Prospects* 3rd ed. Englewood Cliffs, NJ: Prentice Hall.

Schwochau, Susan et al. (1997). "Employee Participation and Assessment of Support for Organizational Policy Change." *Journal of Labor Research* 18 (Summer): 379–401.

U.S. Bureau of Labor Statistics (2002). "Union Members Summary." www.bls.gov/news.release/union2.nr0.htm (May 21).

Verma, Anil, and McKersie, Robert B. (1987). "Employee Involvement: The Implication of Noninvolvement by Unions." *Industrial and Labor Relations Review* 40 (July): 556–568.

Walters, Jonathan (2000). "Work-Force Liberator." *Governing* (November): 29.

Walters, Jonathan (1998). "Untangling Albany." *Governing* (December): 18–22.

West, Jonathan P. (2002). "Georgia on the Mind of Radical Civil Service Reformers." *Review of Public Personnel Administration* 22 (2), 79–93.

CHAPTER 5

Public Employment Reforms and Constitutional Due Process

Stefanie A. Lindquist
Stephen E. Condrey

In recent years, state legislators and public administrators have exhibited a strong interest in personnel reforms aimed at increasing flexibility in human resource management. These reforms reflect a shift in emphasis from centralized control of personnel matters to decentralized discretion and managerial accountability (Coggburn 2000; Carnevale and Housel 2001). Proposed personnel reforms often involve: (a) the elimination of grievance procedures for terminated or demoted employees and the establishment of an at-will employment relationship, and (b) the decentralization of personnel decisions to allow managers in line agencies to exert greater authority over policy related to hiring, pay, and promotions. According to proponents, such personnel deregulation will increase governmental efficiency by allowing managers to remove unsatisfactory employees more easily, and by reducing managers' reliance on centralized bureaucracies in the process of hiring, promoting, compensating, and dismissing employees (see Maranto and Condrey 2001). In effect, advocates seek to promote efficiency by reducing procedural protections for employees and potential employees in the hiring and firing process.

These reforms do come with some costs, however, both for employee and employer. It has been argued that reform movements in public administration fluctuate between enhancing either rationality or responsiveness in agency decision making (West 1984). Administrative due process serves to structure bureaucratic discretion and enhance the rationality of decisions rendered by unelected agents by ensuring that those decisions are not arbitrary or discriminatory. At the same time, however, the judicialization of administrative process "militates against efficiency, economy [and] managerial effectiveness"

(Rosenbloom 1983, 517). As Rosenbloom points out, the legal approach to public administration, with its focus on procedural due process for individuals, emphasizes the protection of individual rights and liberties, at times even at substantial cost to the public fisc and to administrative efficiency (Rosenbloom 1983; see also Rosenbloom, Carroll and Carroll 2000, 128–132). Yet efficiency—though desirable—cannot be viewed as a moral value or an end in itself, since efficiency is relative: what is efficient with respect to one value dimension is inefficient with respect to another (see Rosenbloom et al., 128, quoting Dwight Waldo). Indeed, some inefficiency may be necessary in a constitutional democracy, where the discretion of unelected administrative agents must be constrained in order to preserve other values, such as individual rights or equitable government practices toward citizens. In this chapter, we consider the legal implications of recent calls for personnel reform in the public sector, with particular emphasis on concerns for employee due process rights under the federal constitution.

At-Will Employment Reforms: Eliminating Procedural Due Process for Public Employees

Many states follow the doctrine of at-will employment with respect to private sector employment, which provides that both employer and employee may terminate the employment relationship at-will, for good cause or no cause. In public sector employment, however, the at-will doctrine has been modified in most states because statutes or regulations provide public employees with certain procedural protections before employment may be terminated or otherwise adversely affected. In addition, the most fundamental protection for public employees stems from the United States Constitution; these constitutional protections apply to government but not private employment. According to constitutional law, where the employee can claim entitlement to a property right in his job, he may also claim the right to certain procedural protections, including notice and a hearing, when his employer seeks to terminate or otherwise adversely affect his employment.[1] Proposals for personnel reforms often rest on the claim that these constitutionally mandated protections create such a cumbersome and elaborate grievance process that managers cannot efficiently address employee disciplinary problems. As described below, however, because property interests arise under state law, in many circumstances governments have the ability to eliminate public employees' constitutional rights to due process simply by amending statutes or regulations that support employees' claims to property interests in their employment.

The Fifth and Fourteenth Amendments to the United States Constitution ensure that federal and state governments may not deprive persons "of life, liberty or property without due process of law." Because interpretation and application of the due process clause to particular situations is not self-evident, the task has fallen to the courts to establish the meaning of liberty, property, and due process in various contexts, including public employment. Courts faced with a procedural due process challenge must follow a two-step analysis. First, the court determines whether the individual possesses a protected property or liberty interest such that due process protections are applicable. If so, the court then determines the appropriate procedures—that is, the "process due"—required under the circumstances.

Creating Property Interests

State or local governmental employees may enjoy a property interest in their jobs if they have a reasonable expectation in continued employment based on existing rules and understandings that are grounded in state law.[2] Thus, property interests are not created by the Constitution, but rather depend on extra-constitutional rules and understandings that are enforceable under state law. To create a protected property interest, these extra-constitutional rules or understandings must constrain employers' discretion regarding adverse employment actions by, for example, delineating the conditions under which an employee may be demoted or terminated.[3] In effect, constitutionally protected property interests in a government job alter the traditional at-will employment relationship by placing clear substantive restrictions on the employer's treatment of the employee. Although the employer may still fire the employee if the conditions are met, it may not do so without providing the affected employee notice and some form of a hearing.[4]

Courts have recognized a variety of discretion-constraining rules or understandings that may give rise to a protected property interest in public employment (see McGuinness 1999). First, state statutes and regulations create property rights in public employment if they provide that an employee may only be demoted or terminated for specified reasons (malfeasance, nonfeasance, etc.) or "for just cause." In such circumstances, employees have a legitimate claim of entitlement to employment unless they engage in the prohibited conduct.

Employment contracts may similarly constrain the employer's discretion by identifying grounds for adverse employment actions. Employment contracts may be "express" written or oral agreements where the employee and employer clearly communicate their intentions to enter an agreement that is enforceable under state law. In addition, however, state law may also recognize the existence of employment contracts that are "implied-in-fact." Like express contracts, contracts that are implied-in-fact must reveal that the parties experienced a "meeting of the minds" with respect to the terms of the contract, and that both mutually assented to those terms. In the employment context, implied contracts may arise when a personnel policy manual, handbook, or other document provides that employees will be terminated only "for cause" or for some other specified reasons (Markowitz 1995; Munson 1997). Where such manuals or documents are communicated or distributed to employees, they create a legitimate expectation in continued employment under the specified conditions and thus give rise to a protected property interest. However, a property interest is not established by general statements that an employee will be judged based on some criteria unless those criteria place specific substantive restrictions on the employer's discretion.[5]

Employees may also claim that an employer's customs, practices, or *de facto* policies create an implied contract establishing that the employee may be terminated or demoted only for just cause.[6] As one court has held, "an employer's unilateral declarations, promises, or conduct regarding conditions of continued employment might in some circumstances create a 'legitimate claim of entitlement to job tenure.'"[7] But proving the existence of a property interest through an employer's custom or practice often poses a difficult evidentiary hurdle for the plaintiff. In *Board of Regents v. Roth* (1972), for example, the Supreme Court refused to find a property interest in a non-tenured professor's employment under a "custom or practice" argument, even though most professors hired by the defendant-university were in fact rehired each year.[8] At least one court has held that "[s]uch a common law of employment is established through rules or mutually explicit understandings, and not solely through the past practices of the employer."[9] Nor may such "mutual understandings" create an implied contract or property interest when they are contrary to state law.[10]

Eliminating Property Interests

Since property interests depend on laws, rules, policies, practices, and customs that are often within the government's control, public employers may unilaterally eliminate employees' property rights in their jobs and thereby impose an at-will employment relationship. This objective may be accomplished in a number of ways. First, the legislature or other governing body may modify employee classification systems by explicitly eliminating "good cause" requirements for demotion or termination, or by specifying that employees do not enjoy a property interest in their employment. For example, in 1996, the Georgia state legislature amended the state personnel law to provide that all employees hired after June 30, 1996, would fall within the "unclassified service," rather than the "classified service" (see Gossett 2002a; Nigro and Kellough, chapter 6 of this volume). Unlike unclassified employees, classified employees undergo a working test period, after which they become "permanent" employees who are subject to the rules and regulations of the State Personnel Board.[11] According to Personnel Board rules, permanent employees may be dismissed only if they are negligent, inefficient, unfit, insubordinate, or engage in other misconduct, thus creating a property interest in employment.[12] By eliminating classified status for all employees hired after June 30, 1996, therefore, the legislature explicitly repudiated property interests for state employees in Georgia who were not grandfathered under the statute.

To reinforce the message further, government employers may add disclaimers to employee handbooks or other documents to ensure that no misunderstanding arises with respect to employees' rights to their jobs. For example, an employee manual might specify that "Either party may terminate the employment relationship at will and without cause," or that "Nothing in this manual shall be construed to create an implied or express agreement of employment." As long as such a disclaimer is adequately communicated to the employee, courts are likely to hold them to be dispositive evidence that the employment relationship is at-will.[13]

Creating Property Rights "Inadvertently"

Plaintiffs may nevertheless argue that an employer has inadvertently created a property interest in government employment by establishing grievance procedures for disciplinary actions or by otherwise mandating policies with respect to employee discipline. Indeed, a government employer may intend to eliminate due process protections or incorporate at-will rhetoric in regulations or other documents, but find in court that it has failed to clean house sufficiently to eliminate the constitutional right to due process. In Georgia, for example, the Merit Systems Act provides that "permanent status employees may be dismissed from employment or otherwise adversely affected . . . only if such action is taken in accordance with the rules and regulations of the State Personnel Board," but further adds that *"[t]his article is not intended to create a property interest in the job . . . ."*[14] In the late 1980s, when the Georgia Department of Revenue attempted to argue that this statutory disclaimer eliminated due process protections even for a classified, permanent employee, the Eleventh Circuit disregarded the disclaimer in favor of the Personnel Board regulations requiring cause for dismissal.[15] Similarly, although an employer may add a provision to an employment manual specifying that it may unilaterally modify or amend the manual, the absence of a specific disclaimer concerning the creation of a contract may be perceived as manifesting the employer's intent to be bound by its provisions.[16] And where the disclaimer applies only to the specific document, and does not explicitly extend to all policy manuals or other handbooks that may otherwise establish a property right, a court may find that disclaimer insufficient to determine the nature of the employment relationship.[17]

On the other hand, courts are not likely to find that the employer has inadvertently created a property right in public employment merely because it provides for grievance procedures alone, unless it can be demonstrated that those procedural protections impose a *substantive restriction on managerial discretion.* "A governing body does not create a property interest in a benefit merely by providing a particular procedure for the removal of that benefit."[18] This is especially true where a disclaimer is incorporated into the procedures. For example, after eliminating due process protections for public employees, Georgia's governor issued an executive order mandating grievance procedures for unclassified employees, but which also specified that the procedures were not applicable to disciplinary actions and did not "alter the employment at-will relationship between the agency and its at-will employees."[19] Without some additional evidence that managers' discretion to make personnel decisions is substantively constrained under some other legally enforceable provision, these new procedures in Georgia are not likely to reestablish a property right for unclassified employees. As individual agencies craft their own personnel policies in Georgia following its decentralization of personnel management, however, line-agencies may create property rights if they impose substantive restrictions on administrators' authority to terminate or otherwise adversely affect employees' status within the agency.

Finally, it is worth noting that employees do not have constitutionally protected property interests in any particular *procedures themselves*, as opposed to a property interest in *continued employment*. Process is not "an end in itself," but rather a method for protecting a substantive interest, and there can be no constitutional interest in receiving the procedures provided under state law.[20] Thus, an employee may claim that the employer must follow its own grievance procedures,[21] but in the absence of a property interest, the employee cannot claim a violation of constitutional rights to any additional due process or for damages based on violation of her constitutional rights.

Because procedural rights hinge on provisions of state law, therefore, carefully crafted personnel reforms may eliminate such constitutional protections for state employees and streamline the disciplinary process. Eliminating property interests through personnel reforms may also reduce the incidence of litigation as well. Where property rights exist, an employee bringing a wrongful discharge suit may claim that the employer violated the employee's constitutional rights, potentially resulting in the award of attorney fees and costs against the defendant and providing an additional incentive to litigate. In theory, then, at-will employment expands managerial authority to discipline unsatisfactory public employees with less concern for legal ramifications, and thus substantially enlarges managerial discretion to make personnel decisions that are adverse to the employee.

Predictions concerning beneficial effects of managerial flexibility rest on several assumptions, however. First, they assume that procedural protections actually do impede effective management under the merit system. Second, they assume that the reforms will free managers to render personnel decisions more efficiently and remove unsatisfactory employees more easily. Third, they rest on the hope that managers will act reasonably with respect to employment decisions, and will not impose standards arbitrarily or in a discriminatory manner. Fourth, they assume that employees will respond favorably to the reforms by improving their performance. And finally, they discount as less weighty than efficiency those values that underlie procedural due process. We assess each of these assumptions in turn.

Assumptions Underlying At-Will Personnel Reforms

*Procedures Impede Discipline and Termination of
Unsatisfactory Employees*

At-will employment reforms are often promoted on grounds that cumbersome procedures create disincentives for managers to discipline substandard employees. Because managers must defend their employment decisions in the appeals process, due process protections require managers to document poor performance carefully. Furthermore, managers must spend time preparing for and participating in hearings, which may also deter supervisors from using disciplinary channels. And where it is difficult to replace employees quickly, managers may prefer to tolerate the unsatisfactory employee rather than an extended vacancy in a critical position (Cohen and Eimicke 1994).

Whether the procedures themselves impede discipline, or whether supervisors' perceptions regarding the difficulty of complying with those procedures impede discipline, is a critical practical distinction, however. Certainly, complying with procedures is more time-consuming than firing an employee outright, and may entail tolerance of that employee remaining on the job until the process is complete. In response to a survey of the federal bureaucracy, for example, supervisors recommended that the grievance process be simplified, that avenues for appeal be narrowed, and that time periods for performance improvement plans be shortened (OPM 1999, 25). Yet at least some of the reluctance to terminate or discipline unsatisfactory employees may stem from supervisors' negative perceptions of burdens associated with grievance procedures, which may be exacerbated by inadequate training in the use of those processes and a general desire to avoid conflict. According to one study of the New York City Civil Service, "interviews revealed fairly consistent sentiment that many managers, particularly low level managers, do not understand the system and have never been taught or encouraged to use it" (Cohen and Eimecke 1994, 20). Indeed, in her study of the appeals process under the Florida merit protection system, a former member of Florida's Public Employee Relations Commission (PERC), Sally Gertz, found that the appeals process was generally fast and effective. For cases involving a hearing on appeal in 1999, appeals were resolved in only 118 days on average, and only 7 percent of appeals resulted in reversal of the agency decision and 3 percent in mitigation.[22] Based on these statistics, Gertz concluded that "[i]f it is true that state supervisors do not discipline career service employees (an assumption that has not been supported by research), it seems unlikely that speed, cost, or outcomes of the appeal process are the reason" (2001, 133). But because her study focused only on disciplinary actions actually pursued by supervisors, Gertz further remarked that:

> Another reason supervisors may be inhibited from disciplining career service employees is misconception about the 'protectiveness' of the appeals system. Agency attorneys and personnel professionals who routinely interact with PERC should have an accurate understanding of the appeal process, and in particular the overwhelming likelihood that the agency will prevail if an appeal is filed, but that information may not be penetrating to first-line supervisors and managers. They may believe that civil service protections are so strong as to make employee discipline a futile endeavor in the first place. If so, the impact of civil service protections may not be fully revealed by looking only at the appeal process. Supervisors who hold this view may be taking disciplinary action in only the most egregious cases (2001, 134).

Thus, at least some of the concerns related to due process protections and employee discipline could be remedied through increased training for supervisors and managers. In its 1999 study of poor performers in the federal government, for example, the U.S. Office of Personnel Management learned that while most supervisors had received some training in improving employee performance and in disciplinary procedures, many noted that the training "was too abstract" and "did not provide the step-by-step tools needed to monitor and counsel employees on their performance, make appropriate documentation, and effect the proper formal personnel actions" (1999, 8). In addition, some of the concerns may stem from supervisors' perceptions that upper-level management is not supportive of their efforts at employee discipline (OPM 1999, 32). And in Georgia, much of the inefficiencies related to merit protections stemmed from the "control mentality" of staff in the central personnel agency, rather than from the procedures themselves (Condrey 2002).

These studies and observations suggest that, while procedures no doubt lengthen the employee discipline process to some extent, at least some of the negative perceptions of grievance processes stem from supervisors' misunderstandings about the nature and results of that process, and upper management's lack of support for disciplinary action. Reformers who are ready to condemn due process protections must be careful, then, to distinguish among the reasons that such protections impede effective management. The problem may rest as much with managers' perceptions and training as with the procedures themselves.

At-Will Employment Will Enable Managers to Remove Poor Performers More Easily

Another assumption underlying at-will employment reforms is that elimination of due process protections will, in fact, streamline the disciplinary process. As noted above, there can be no doubt that procedures add an additional hurdle for managers and supervisors. Evidence exists to support this conclusion. In his evaluation of the Georgia's Department of Human Resources (DHR) following merits reforms in that state, Lasseter (2002) noted that, as the percentage of unclassified employees increased in that agency, so too did the number of terminations. As an agency, DHR was clearly "quicker to terminate an employee . . . than before reform" (2002, 128). Nevertheless, other impediments exist that may render chimerical the notion that employees can be terminated quickly and painlessly (for the employer) following at-will reforms. For example, supervisors may be constrained by norms within the organization that make firing more difficult; even after Georgia's reforms, Lasseter reported that DHR's terminations changed minimally from .9 percent of the workforce in 1994 (prereform) to 1.6 percent in 2000 (postreform)(2002, 128). As Lasseter suggests, this small increase may be due to DHR's continuing effort to implement its personnel policies fairly and because such fairness norms constrain decision makers regardless of the lack of legal protections. Moreover, after personnel reforms are enacted agencies may adopt their own grievance policies to enhance perceptions of fairness toward employees. In Georgia, the governor's 1999 executive order mandated such procedures following personnel reform, allowing unclassified employees to appeal a number of issues, including allegations of unlawful discrimination, sexual harassment, retaliation, unsafe working conditions, and "erroneous, arbitrary or capricious interpretation or application of personnel policies and procedures" (Section V). This latter provision appears to provide some recourse for unclassified employees claiming that they were disciplined unfairly.

Furthermore, eliminating property rights will not completely free states from the need to provide due process in some circumstances. Where an employee's termination or discipline is also accompanied by some public disclosure of negative information about his performance, Supreme Court precedent provides that the employee's liberty interests may have been infringed.[23] According to the Court, employees enjoy a liberty interest in their reputations and in the opportunity to obtain future employment; when government employers infringe that liberty interest by stigmatizing an employee in connection with disciplinary action, the affected employee enjoys a right to a name-clearing hearing prior to the adverse decision (Shearer 1992). In addition, common-law defamation actions offer additional legal recourse for disgruntled employees. And employees continue to enjoy the opportunity to sue under federal and state anti-discrimination statutes, although recourse under some statutes (particularly under the federal Americans with Disabilities Act, Age Discrimination in Employment Act, and Fair Labor Standards Act) has been limited by recent U.S. Supreme Court decisions expanding state immunity under the Eleventh Amendment (see Kuykendall and Lindquist 2001). Where state employees claim they have been dismissed for purposes of patronage, they may seek relief for violation of their First Amendment rights.[24] And state and federal whistleblower protection statutes also provide recourse to employees for improper terminations in retaliation for exposure of wrongdoing and for employees' exercise of free speech rights (Lindquist and Wasby 2002).

Even in the private sector, employers are limited in their ability to fire unsatisfactory employees by a network of state and federal laws protecting employees from wrongful discharge. For example, limitations on the at-will employment doctrine imposed through judicial precedent or legislation provides recourse for terminated employees where the firing violates public policy, an implied contract, or the doctrine of good faith and fair dealing (Markowitz 1995; see also OPM 1999, 28–29). Nevertheless, survey research of public and private employers clearly demonstrates that public managers perceive far more significant constraints on their discretion to discipline than do their private counterparts (Rainey and Bozeman 2000; Bozeman and Bretschneider 1994), a perception linked to formalization of personnel rules in the public sector. But as noted above, at least some of this difference could be based on misapprehensions and shortcomings in employee training, rather than from the actual burdensomeness of the procedures themselves.

Under At-Will Employment, Managers Will Act Equitably Toward Employees

Originally, reforms that centralized personnel decision-making processes and imposed due process protections were intended in part to ensure that employees were treated equally and fairly across all agencies. Centralization would produce standardized personnel practices and thereby ensure equity toward all (Kettl, Ingraham, Sanders and Homer 1996; Durant and West 2001). Decentralization and deregulation thus have the potential to disrupt these principles. How serious is this potential problem? By championing decentralization and deregulation of personnel decisions, reformers must assume that these concerns are less worrisome than other "pathologies" (inefficiency, delay, etc.) associated with existing merit protections.

On this issue, existing research regarding variation in human resource management practices across agencies is not encouraging, although the evidence is mixed. For example, research on decisions by the federal Merits Systems Protection Board (MSPB) has demonstrated that agencies varied significantly in terms of the extent to which their personnel decisions were upheld by the MSPB (West and Durant 2000; Durant and West 2001). Although the MSPB upheld the large majority of agency personnel decisions, disposition trends differed substantially across individual agencies. These findings suggest that, at least in the federal sector, agencies vary in their treatment of employees even in the face of standardized and centralized personnel rules. Herculean logic is not required to conclude that in the absence of such standardization, variation in employee treatment is likely to increase. As West and Durant note: "our analysis indicates that it may at times be fanciful to rely exclusively or predominantly on agency managers to strike the right balance between protecting their employees' rights and wielding their managerial prerogatives to accomplish agency missions" (2000, 119).

Concerns about equitable treatment have arisen in Georgia following the reforms there. Anecdotal evidence indicates that at least some employees view the reforms as leading to "cronyism" (Condrey 2002, 121). Unclassified employees in Georgia agencies may perceive that they are treated more harshly for minor infractions than are classified employees (Gossett 2002b). And according to one observer in Florida, decentralization of the personnel system in that state has led to more "bureaucratic patronage than merit-based" personnel practices in some instances (Wechsler 1994). On the other hand, in his assessment of personnel reforms in Georgia, Florida, and Texas,

Walters (2002) did not find much evidence that patronage practices had increased, but did observe that issues of pay equity have or are likely to arise following decentralization.

At-Will Employment Will Encourage Better Employee Performance

Advocates of personnel reform also assume that elimination of due process protections will help promote higher-quality employee performance. This assumption rests on the further premise that at-will employees realize they are more vulnerable to adverse personnel actions than their classified counterparts and thus are more likely to conform their behavior to managerial expectations.

The empirical evidence regarding these underlying assumptions does not necessarily provide clear grounds for concluding that a connection exists between due process and performance. In several studies performed following Georgia's personnel reforms, the attitudes of unclassified employees were compared with those of classified employees. Based on an extensive survey of Georgia employees in the classified and unclassified service conducted in 2000, Kellough and Nigro (2001; 2002) found that unclassified employees had significantly more positive views of at-will employment reforms than did classified employees. Perhaps not surprisingly, unclassified employees were also more likely to agree that the reforms had caused state employees to be more "responsive to the goals and priorities of agency administrators" (2001, 11). And unclassified employees were also more likely to agree that the civil service reforms made the state workforce "more productive and responsive to the public" (2001, Table 5). Yet on both these survey items, the *majority* of respondents—whether classified or unclassified—disagreed that the reforms had improved employee responsiveness to managerial prerogatives or to the public interest.

In his study of the Georgia Department of Juvenile Justice (DJJ), Gossett (2000b) found little significant difference between the attitudes or perceptions of classified and unclassified employees following the reforms. Both classified and unclassified employees exhibited loyalty and commitment to the agency, were about equally likely to seek employment outside the agency in the future, and were about equally likely to agree that they would be removed or demoted for poor performance. Thus, if classified employees in the DJJ feel that they are insulated from adverse employment actions, they were not willing to indicate as much on a survey. Unclassified employees were significantly more likely to agree that unclassified employees "were treated more harshly than their classified counterparts when it comes to minor infractions," but as Gossett points out, this pattern of responses could be due to group identification and perceptions about the group's "tougher experiences" (2002b, 12). A study of the Georgia Department of Family and Child Services (DFCS) returned similarly discouraging results. According to a 1999 survey conducted within that agency, responses suggested "quite strongly" that many DFCS employees were not supportive of the merit system reforms, with more than 9 of 10 DFCS employees (91.3 percent) reporting that the reforms had not improved productivity in their offices (Hamilton, Facer, and Condrey 1999, 21).

Thus, empirical support for the assumption that elimination of due process protections will enhance employee performance is not uncontroverted. Of course, survey evidence reflecting the attitudes of the employees themselves is probably not the best indicator of the success of at-will reforms in terms of performance enhancement. Only systematic evaluation of employee performance before and after reforms, in combination with surveys of supervisors' attitudes, will shed brighter light on this important issue. But before reforms are undertaken in other states, Georgia's experience should be carefully evaluated on this dimension.

The Inherent Value to Procedural Due Process

The discussion above considered the legal implications of at-will employment reforms, and evaluated some of the underlying empirical premises to such reforms. But no such evaluation can be complete without careful consideration of the inherent value of due process protections in the first place. While an at-will employment regime may promote efficiency, it undermines other values that policy makers should not ignore (see Stone 1988).

First, hearing rights promote institutional legitimacy. Research on the appellate litigation process has demonstrated that litigants are often satisfied even with an adverse outcome, simply because they emerge from the process feeling as if they have been treated fairly and have been able to share their side of the story (Barclay 1999). This finding mirrors that of psychologists who study procedural justice (see, e.g., Tyler 1988; Lind and Tyler 1988; Thibaut and Walker 1975), whose studies indicate that procedural fairness "is a potent force for citizens' satisfaction with the performance of institutions, for support for institutions, for compliance with laws and judgments, for perceptions of legitimacy, and for acceptance of the outcomes of decisions, even when such acceptance does not appear to be in the short-run self-interest of the citizen" (Chevigny 1989, 1217). The concept of procedural justice has also been explored in the context of public organizations and employee rights (Rainey 1997). Thus, institutional legitimacy may often rest in large part on citizens' perceptions regarding whether that institution makes decisions in accordance with principles of procedural justice. While in the private sector these considerations may not trump the bottom line, they cannot be underestimated in the public sector, where institutional legitimacy is the coin of the realm.

Second, hearing rights promote employees' dignitary interests and job satisfaction. At-will employment means that an employee can be dismissed without explanation and without an opportunity to respond to charges—even if those charges are unsubstantiated. Hearing rights thus provide employees with the opportunity to maintain their dignity in the face of a potentially humiliating disciplinary action. Such protections no doubt enhance employee job satisfaction and may therefore lead to reduced attrition rates. In a recent study of the Georgia Department of Family and Children Services, almost two-thirds of survey respondents indicated that they would not be comfortable in an unclassified position. Additionally, more than four of ten employees indicated that they would be more likely to leave their jobs at DFCS if they lost merit system protections (Hamilton et al. 1999, 21). Clearly, job security—in the form of procedural protections—is meaningful to many state employees. In terms of job satisfaction, job security ranks close to financial compensation as an important factor for DFCS. In Table 5.1 below, job security ranks second only to salary considerations in terms of employee perception of job satisfaction. And state merit system protections, while initially ranked fairly low in the original employment decision, became increasingly important for employees over time, with 87.4 percent indicating it as an important factor by 2000. While it is not appropriate to generalize from a study of one agency to all state employees, these findings are suggestive.[25]

Third, it should not be forgotten that employment decisions in the public sector are made on behalf of and in the name of the polity. For that reason, accurate and just decision making is not simply a matter of peripheral interest when compared to the bottom line of cost savings or efficiency. Managers and supervisors within administrative agencies are not subject to electoral constraints on their discretionary behavior as a means to ensure ethical, just, fair,

Table 5.1
DFCS Employee Perceptions of the Relative Importance of Job Satisfaction Factors

Rank-Order (2000)	Job Satisfaction Factors	% Reporting Original Employment Decision	"Important" for retention 1999	"Important" for retention 2000	Percent Change
1	Salary considerations	88.3	94.9	99.0	4.1
2	Job security	93.9	94.5	98.4	3.9
3	Fringe benefits	93.4	96.0	98.3	2.3
4	Opportunity to help less fortunate	94.0	93.8	97.7	3.9
5	Challenging work responsibilities	90.7	91.6	94.8	3.2
6	Desirable working hours	91.0	91.8	94.2	2.4
7	Desire to serve the public	88.8	88.9	93.8	4.9
8	Opportunity for public service	85.6	86.1	88.7	2.6
9	State merit system protections	77.8	82.0	87.4	5.4
10	Commitment to welfare reform	64.6	81.0	84.8	3.8
11	Having an impact on public affairs	73.3	77.8	80.6	2.8

Source: Hamilton, Facer and Condrey 1999, Table 5.

consistent, or principled decision making. Instead, administrative discretion must be constrained by other means—and institutional processes provide one form of insurance against arbitrary official action. To be sure, the empirical evidence suggests that most personnel decisions made by managers are upheld through institutional processes where they exist. Two studies mentioned above, of Florida (Gertz 2001) and of the federal government (West and Durant 2000), indicated that for the years studied, personnel decisions were reversed or mitigated on appeal in less than 10 percent of all cases in the state context, and in about 20 percent of all cases in the federal context. But these figures reveal that in a nonminimal percentage of cases, the personnel decisions were somehow faulty according to the adjudictator(s). When policy makers remove procedural protections for public employees, therefore, they are manifesting a tolerance for inaccurate, biased or otherwise improper discipline in what may be a significant percentage of cases. And these inaccurate decisions are made in the name of the citizenry, not simply in the name of profit.

Notes

The authors would like to thank Jason Fleury of the Carl Vinson Institute of Government for his helpful research assistance.

1. Due process protections also arise in the administrative context where a person's liberty interests are affected.

2. *Cleveland Board of Education v. Loudermill*, 470 U.S. 532 (1985).

3. *Wallace v. Robinson*, 940 F.2d 243, 247 (7th Cir.1991) (en banc), *cert. denied*, 503 U.S. 961 (1992) ("Due process comes into play when substantive rules limit the reasons that support action."). Thus, for example, even if a university's policies identify "teaching, research and service" as the three criteria on which to evaluate faculty for tenure and promotion, such broad guidelines fail to constrain discretion sufficiently to give rise to a property interest under the due process clause. *Colburn v. Trustees of Indiana Univ.*, 973 F.2d 581 (7th Cir. 1992).

4. *See Cleveland v. Loudermill, supra* note 2.

5. *See, e.g., Colburn v. Trustees of Indiana Univ.*, 973 F.2d 581 (7th Cir. 1992); *Hullen v. Yates*, 322 F.3d 1229 (10th Cir. 2003); *Bennett v. Watters*, 260 F.3d 925 (8th Cir. 2001).

6. *Perry v. Sinderman*, 408 U.S. 593 (1972).

7. *Correa-Martinez v. Arrillaga-Belendez*, 903 F.2d 49, 55 (1st Cir.1990) (quoting *Perry v. Sindermann*, 408 U.S. 593, 602 [1972]).

8. *See also Bollow v. Federal Reserve Bank of San Francisco*, 650 F.2d 1093 (9th Cir. 1981)(no property interest created where plaintiff demonstrated that bank had never terminated someone like plaintiff).

9. *Hermes v. Hein*, 742 F.2d 350, 355 (7th Cir. 1984)(citations omitted).

10. *See, e.g., Warren v. Crawford*, 927 F.2d 559 (11th Cir. 1991); *City of Buchanan v. Pope*, 476 S.E.2d 53 (Ga.App. 1996).

11. Ga.Code 45–20-2, 45–20-6 (2001)(emphasis added).

12. State Personnel Board Rule #15 (Par. 15.204 "Dismissal").

13. *See, e.g., Warren v. City of Junction City*, 176 F.Supp.2d 1118 (D.Kan. 2001).

14. Ga.Code. 45–20-8(a)-(b) (2001)(emphasis added).

15. *Brown v. Georgia Department of Revenue*, 881 F.2d 1018 (11th Cir. 1989).

16. *See, e.g., Golem v. Village of Put-in-Bay*, 222 F.Supp.2d 924 (N.D.Ohio 2002).

17. *DeShazer v. Cook County*, 142 Lab. Cas. P 59,094 (N.D.Ill. 2000).

18. *Sanchez v. City of Santa Ana*, 915 F.2d 424, 428 (9th Cir. 1990); *see also Brown v. City of Los Angeles*, 102 Cal.App.4th 155 (2002); *Burns v. County of Jackson*, 197 F.Supp.2d 1278 (D.Kan. 2002).

19. Executive Order, Employee Grievance Procedure (Unclassified Service) (August 20, 1999), available at http://www.gms.state.ga.us/pdf/misc/grvpolicy.pdf.

20. *Mandel v. Allen*, 889 F. Supp. 857 (E.D.Va. 1995).

21. For example, the employee may bring suit for writ of mandamus or injunction to force the agency to comply with its own grievance procedures, or may sue for breach of contract where the procedures are part of the employment contract. *See Hensley v. West Virginia Dept of Health and*

Human Services, 508 S.E.2d 616 (W.Va. 1998); *Bunting v. City of Columbia*, 639 F.2d 1090 (4th Cir. 1981).
   22. *See also* West and Durant 2000, (showing reversal rates between 13.1 and 29.2 percent, depending on the agency).
   23. *E.g. Board of Regents v. Roth*, 408 U.S. 564 (1985).
   24. *Rutan v. Republican Party of Illinois*, 497 U.S. 62 (1990).
   25. Future research could evaluate whether, for example, public sector employees remain on the job longer than their private sector counterparts.

References

Barclay, Scott (1999). *An Appealing Act: Why People Appeal in Civil Cases*. Chicago: Northwestern University Press.
Bozeman, Barry, and S. Bretschneider (1994). "The 'Publicness Puzzle' in Organization theory: A Test of Alternative Explanations of Differences Between Public and Private Organizations." *Journal of Public Administration Research and Theory* 4 (2):197–223.
Carnevale, David G., and Steven W. Housel (2001). "Human Resource Management Reform in the States: Entrepreneurialism and Incremental Change," in Stephen E. Condrey and Robert Maranto, eds. *Radical Reform of the Civil Service*. New York: Lexington Books.
Chevigny, Paul G. (1989). "Review of *The Social Psychology of Procedural Justice*," by E. Allan Lind and Tom R. Tyler. *New York University Law Review* 64:1211–1223.
Cohen, Steven, and William Eimicke (1994). "The Overregulated Civil Service: The Case of New York City." *Review of Public Personnel Administration* 14 (2):10–27.
Condrey, Stephen E. (2002). "Reinventing State Civil Service Systems." *Review of Public Personnel Administration* 22 (2):114–132.
Durant, Robert, and William F. West (2001). "Merit Protection, Federal Agencies, and the New Personnel Management: Explaining Cross-Agency Variation in MSPB Appeals Decisions, FY 1988–1997." *Administration and Society* 32 (6):627–667.
Gertz, Sally (2001). "Florida Civil Service Appeals Process: How Protective Is It?" *Justice System Journal* 22 (2):117–35.
Gossett, Charles W. (2002a). "Civil Service Reform: The Case of Georgia." *Review of Public Personnel Administration* 22 (2):94–113.
Gossett, Charles W. (2002b). "The Changing Face of Georgia's Merit System: Results from an Employee Attitude Survey in the Georgia Department of Juvenile Justice." Typescript.
Hamilton, Jack, Rex L. Facer II, and Stephen E. Condrey (1999). *Organizational Assessment for the Division of Family and Children*. Athens, GA: Carl Vinson Institute of Government.

Kellough, J. Edward, and Lloyd G. Nigro (2002). "Pay for Performance in Georgia State Government: Employee Perspectives on GeorgiaGain After 5 Years." *Review of Public Personnel Administration* 22 (2):146–166.

Kellough, J. Edward, and Lloyd G. Nigro (2001). "Classified vs. Unclassified State Employees in Georgia: A Difference that Makes a Difference?" Paper presented at the annual meeting of the American Political Science Association, Boston, MA.

Kettl, Donald F., Patricia W. Ingraham, Ronald P. Sanders, and Constance Horner (1996). *Civil Service Reform: Building a Government that Works.* Washington, DC: Brookings Institute.

Kuykendall, Christine L., and Stefanie A. Lindquist (2001). "*Board of Trustees of the University of Alabama v. Garrett*: Implications for Public Personnel Management." *Review of Public Personnel Administration* 21 (1):65–69.

Lind, W. Allan, and Tom R. Tyler (1988). *The Social Psychology of Procedural Justice.* New York: Plenum Press.

Lindquist, Stefanie A., and Stephen L. Wasby (2002). "Defining Free Speech Protections for Public Employees." *Review of Public Personnel Administration* 22 (1):63–66.

Maranto, Robert, and Stephen E. Condrey (2001). "Why Radical Reform? The Rise of Government by Business." In Stephen E. Condrey and Robert Maranto, eds. *Radical Reform of the Civil Service.* New York: Lexington Books.

Markowitz, Deborah L. (1995). "The Demise of At-Will Employment and the Public Employee Conundrum." *The Urban Lawyer* 27 (2):303–331.

McGuinness, J. Michael (1999). "Procedural Due Process Rights of Public Employees: Basic Rules and Rationale for a Return to Rule-Oriented Process." *New England Law Review* 33:931–965.

Munson, Gregory M. (1997). "A Straitjacket for Employment At-Will: Recognizing Breach of implied Contract Actions for Wrongful Demotion." *Vanderbilt Law Review* 50:1577–1617.

Rainey, Hal (1997). "The 'How Much Process is Due?' Debate: Legal and Managerial Perspectives," in Phillip J. Cooper and Chester A. Newland, eds. *Handbook of Public Law and Administration* San Francisco: Jossey-Bass.

Rainey, Hal, and Barry Boseman (2000). "Comparing Public and Private Organizations: Empirical Research and the Power of the A Priori." *Journal of Public Administration Theory and Research* 10 (2):447–469.

Rosenbloom, David H., James D. Carroll, Jonathan D. Carroll (2000). *Constitutional Competence for Public Managers: Cases and Commentary.* Itasca, IL: F.E. Peacock.

Rosenbloom, David H. (1983). "Public Administrative Theory and the Separation of Powers," in Shafritz and Hyde, *Classics of Public Administration.* Pacific Grove, CA: Brooks/Cole.

Shearer, Robert A. (1992). "Due Process Liability in Personnel Record: Preserving Employee Liberty Interests." *Public Personnel Management* 21 (4):523–532.

Stone, Deborah A. (1988). *Policy Paradox and Political Reason.* New York: Scott Foresman and Co.

Tyler, Tom R. (1988). "What is Procedural Justice? Criteria Used by Citizens to Assess the Fairness of Legal Procedures." *Law and Society Review* 22:103–132.

United States Office of Personnel Management, Office of Merit Systems Oversight and Effectiveness (1999). "Poor Performers in Government: A Quest for the True Story."

Walters, Jonathan (2002). *Life After Civil Service Reform: The Texas, Georgia, and Florida Experiences.* IBM Endowment for The Business of Government: Human Capital Series.

Walters, Jonathan (1997). "Who Needs Civil Service" *Governing* (August). 10 (11):17–21.

Wechsler, Barton (1994). "Reinventing Florida's Civil Service System." *Review of Public Personnel Administration* 14 (2):64–76.

West, William F. (1984). "Structuring Administrative Discretion: The Pursuit of Rationality and Responsiveness." *American Journal of Political Science* 28:340–360.

West, William F. and Robert F. Durant (2000). "Merit, Management and Neutral Competence: Lessons from the U.S. Merit Systems Protection Board." *Public Administration Review* 60 (2):111–122.

PART TWO

The Experiences of Selected States

CHAPTER 6

Civil Service Reform in Georgia:
A View from the Trenches

Lloyd G. Nigro
J. Edward Kellough

In the United States, civil service reform has been a popular response to complaints about the performance of government and its administrative agencies. Whether well-founded or not, the list of complaints is long and very familiar: inefficiency, inflexibility, ineffectiveness, and a lack of responsiveness to executive leadership and to the public. The list of endorsed reforms is equally well-known: decentralization, deregulation, debureaucratization, customer service, worker empowerment, managing for performance, privatization, and merit pay (Barzelay 1992; Gore 1993; Hays 1996; Kearney and Hays 1998; Kettl, et al. 1996; National Commission on the Public Service 1989; Osborne and Gaebler 1992; Osborne and Plastrik 1997; National Commission on the State and Local Public Service 1993; Savas 2000; Thompson 1994; Thompson and Radin 1997).

During the 1990s the state of Georgia embraced the reform agenda and significantly altered its civil service law and human resources management (HRM) systems. The transformation of state personnel and human resources management policies involved two distinct events. The first event to take place was the development and implementation of a new performance management system called GeorgiaGain. Placed into operation during 1995 and 1996, Georgia-Gain was designed to increase employee motivation and productivity by providing the state's supervisors with the state-of-the-art performance management tools considered necessary to achieve high levels of effectiveness and efficiency. GeorgiaGain was intended to be a comprehensive refurbishing and modernizing of the state's human resources policies and practices. A key part was a pay-for-performance system, and variable pay increases are now used to differentially

117

reward levels of performance. A new performance appraisal process tied to job-related performance standards also was put into place. Written performance goals, expectations, and performance plans are required. New, accurate job descriptions were developed and information systems to support constant updating of descriptions were installed. In support of the new approach, a substantial reduction in the number of pay grades was achieved and competitive mid-points and entry-level salaries were set for each grade in order to make it possible for the state to compete effectively in the labor market. As the implementation of GeorgiaGain progressed, substantial efforts were made to offer appropriate training to all supervisors in the operation of the new system.

The second major event took place in early 1996 with passage of Act 816 by the Georgia legislature. This was a civil service reform law intended to achieve higher levels of bureaucratic responsiveness to executive leadership (the governor and state agency heads) and to raise civil servants' productivity by removing cumbersome merit system procedures and creating an "at-will" employment relationship between the state and all employees selected after July 1, 1996. Everybody hired into state civil service positions since that date is in the "unclassified" service, meaning that they have no property interest in their jobs and that as a result they do not enjoy certain merit system protections. Employees hired into current positions prior to July 1, 1996, retain typical merit system safeguards including relative security of tenure and are considered part of the state's "classified" service. Needless to say, the proportion of the state workforce in unclassified positions has been growing steadily.

Along lines suggested by influential reform groups, such as the Winter Commission and the federal National Performance Review (NPR), the Georgia legislation also emphasized decentralization and deregulation of human resources management by giving state agencies wide discretion and flexibility in managing their personnel systems (National Commission on the State and Local Public Service 1993, 25, 34). Among other things, it was hoped that this reform would encourage agencies to implement streamlined recruiting and hiring processes tailored to their specific needs and circumstances, to allow agencies to expedite previously cumbersome adverse actions and appeals procedures, and to permit agencies to establish personnel policies that supported timely and effective responses to executive leadership and policy priorities. The decentralizing thrust of Act 816 was especially clear in its provisions regarding agencies' responsibilities, which are: (1) defining job classes that are unique to the agency and setting qualifications and pay ranges for these classes; (2) allocating all agency positions to defined job classes; (3) recruiting and screening applicants for job vacancies; and (4) developing policies needed to ensure compliance with all applicable employment-related state and federal laws (State of Georgia 1996, 685–686).

Act 816 was also intended "to establish in the state a system of personnel administration which will attract, select, and retain the best employees based on merit, free from coercive political influence, with incentives in the form of equal opportunities for all which will provide technically competent and loyal personnel to render impartial service to the public, and at all times to render such service according to the dictates of ethics and morality; and which will climinate unnecessary and inefficient employees" (684). Although these goals were enthusiastically endorsed by then-Governor Zell Miller and enacted into law very quickly by the state legislature, no systematic effort to assess their consequences had been undertaken prior to 2000. As Barrett and Greene (1999) said in a special edition of *Governing Magazine*:

> While other states have been reforming their civil service laws, Georgia went to the edge: It eliminated the civil service code entirely for state employees hired after July 1, 1996 . . . Georgia deserves great credit for having the guts to embark on a reform of these dimensions; further praise, however, will have to await conclusive evidence about the result. (39)

The 2000 Survey

This chapter reports on the findings of a survey of State of Georgia employees conducted during the first quarter of 2000. The purpose of the survey was to obtain an accurate picture of the attitudes, feelings, and perceptions of all state employees regarding the key elements of GeorgiaGain and Act 816. The perceptions or viewpoints of state employees, of course, were not expected to yield all of the data necessary to achieve a complete evaluation of either reform, or to provide a foundation upon which future human resources policies of the state should necessarily be determined. Quantitative indicators or "hard measures" of system outputs and outcomes, such as program-level-performance, organizational productivity, and responsiveness to executive leadership are required as well. But employees' perceptions, nonetheless, are considered relevant because it is the employees who must deal with material consequences of GeorgiaGain and Act 816 on a daily basis. It is reasonable to expect that the long-term success of these reforms will depend to a significant extent on state employees' confidence in them and on their willingness to support them in practice, and a survey seemed to be one appropriate way of getting at these attitudes and sentiments.

This research assumed that Georgia's employees would form beliefs and take actions based on how satisfied they were with their jobs, as well as how they felt about state agencies as places to work and to pursue careers. Research suggests, for example, that employees who feel that performance appraisal systems are not operating fairly or predictably are not likely to be motivated by pay-for-performance mechanisms that link individual pay to measures of individual performance. Likewise, workers who believe they are disadvantaged by a personnel system that is driven by "politics" and favoritism are more likely to be alienated, less than fully productive, and at best grudgingly responsive to agency leadership. Indeed, such perceptions could lead to a pervasive lack of trust in management and growing employee cynicism. Under such circumstances, it would be difficult to achieve and sustain the high levels of individual and organizational performance sought by the framers of GeorgiaGain and Act 816. By 2000, therefore, it was important to determine how state employees and their supervisors saw these reforms and how satisfied they were with their affects on the operating levels of state agencies.

The survey instrument was specifically designed to solicit employee perceptions of aspects of the operation and implementation of GeorgiaGain and Act 816. In order to formulate items for the survey, we consulted with the staff of the State Merit System, reviewed available documents and commentaries on the specific reforms under study, and reviewed the published research on civil service reform in state governments (e.g., Ban 1998; Brudney et al. 1999; deLeon and Denhardt 2000; Ingraham 1995; Hays 1997; Kearney and Hays 1998; Perry, et al. 1994; Wechsler 1994). An important step in this effort to accurately reflect State of Georgia employees' concerns regarding GeorgiaGain and Act 816 in the survey was a set of four preliminary focus-group discussions. Two were held with nonsupervisors and two with supervisors. Seven to eight state employees attended each session. Participants were selected to participate by their agencies and the resulting groups, in terms of characteristics such as race, gender, age, employing agency, and geographic location of work site constituted a reasonable, although far from perfect, cross-section of the state workforce. We drafted the questions needed to guide the focus group discussions and these were reviewed by Georgia State Merit System staff. The resulting discussion items and sequences of questions were administered by a professional facilitator under contract to the Georgia State Merit System from the Applied Research Center (ARC) of Georgia State University in Atlanta. While the information collected from the focus groups could not be generalized to the entire state workforce, it was used to help confirm that certain issues were significant to employees and to identify new issues and concerns deserving further inquiry through the more systematic survey (Krueger and Casey 2000; Krueger 1998; Morgan 1988).

Following analysis of the written transcripts of the focus group discussions, an initial draft of the survey instrument was developed. It was provided to the State Merit System for expert review by top staff members to assure that technical language and details of the descriptions of aspects of the personnel process addressed in the survey were correct. Following this review a final version of the instrument was created and forwarded to the ARC, which executed the survey and generated the data files used in this analysis.

The survey employed a stratified random sampling methodology. Simple random samples of 2,542 nonsupervisory personnel and 452 supervisory personnel were drawn from data files maintained by the State Merit System. Each of these samples comprised approximately 5 percent of the respective populations. The subsamples were combined to produce a total sample of 2,994 employees. As the procedures described below suggest, an effort was made to make sure that the response rate obtained would allow high confidence in the validity of the findings.

During the last week of April 2000, a postcard was mailed to all sample members at their home addresses. This postcard provided a brief explanation of the research project and its purpose, notified the recipient that they had been randomly selected for participation in the study, and asked that they help in the research effort by completing and returning the survey promptly. One week after the notification postcard, the surveys were mailed. The mailing included an introductory cover letter from the Commissioner of the State Merit System, a copy of the survey instrument, a postage-paid return envelope, and a postage-paid postcard with a unique respondent identification number. Respondents were instructed to return the completed survey and the postcard to the ARC separately. Receipt of the returned postcard by the ARC would indicate that the employee had returned the survey, but obviously there would be no way of knowing which completed survey came from which respondent and in this way respondent anonymity was protected (Dillman 1978). Those who returned their respondent postcards were subsequently removed from the list used for follow-up mailings. About one week after the first mailing, reminder postcards were sent to all sample members. One week later, a second copy of the survey, a postage-paid return envelope, and a respondent postcard were sent to those who had not yet responded. In a final effort to obtain the best possible response rate, a third mailing was sent to everybody who had not responded.

An overall response rate of 65.06 percent was achieved (1,948 useable completed surveys out of 2,994 in the original sample). For supervisors, the return rate was 78.76 percent or 356 of 452. For non-supervisory line personnel, the return was 62.63 percent (1,592 out of 2,542). For a survey of this type, this return rate is exceptionally high, allowing in turn a high level of confidence in the findings. In terms of factors or characteristics such as agency, supervisory status, race, sex, and age, those who responded to the survey were representative of the original random sample of state employees provided by the State Merit System. Based on the return rate and representativeness of that return, we are able to conclude that the attitudes and perceptions of state employees reported here accurately reflect those of the state workforce at large, subject to a statistical margin of error of ± 1.10 percentage points.

Findings

Survey results are broken down into four general areas: (1) the characteristics of the respondents; (2) the respondents' job satisfaction, their attitudes about working for their agencies, and their feelings about employment with the State of Georgia; (3) how state employees perceive several dimensions of the GeorgiaGain system and its implementation and (4) respondents' perceptions about the implementation and impact of Civil Service Reform (Act 816).

As noted above, the random sampling methodology yielded a population of respondents that was representative of the state workforce at large in areas such as gender, race-ethnicity, age, education, time worked for the state, and time in current position. Slightly more than 39 percent of the respondents were male and about 61 percent were female. Sixty-three percent of nonsupervisors were women, but respondents from the state's supervisory ranks were almost equally divided between men and women. With regard to race and ethnicity, close to 63 percent (62.6%) of the respondents classified themselves as white, while almost 40 percent (33.6%) reported they were African-American. The balance (3.8%) were Asian, Hispanic, Multiracial, and Native American. More than 61 percent of the nonsupervisors were white and about 35 percent were African-American, with 4.1 percent falling into the other categories. Among supervisors, these percentages were found to be significantly different: 67.8 percent were white and 29.6 were African-American. The other categories comprised 2.6 percent of supervisory personnel who responded to the survey. Most of the responding state employees (84%) were between 31 and 60 years of age. Predictably, supervisors tended to be somewhat older as a group. Nearly half of the respondents did not have a college degree, and about one-third (37%) had at least a four-year college degree. For supervisors, these figures were different, with 53 percent having a four-year college degree or a higher level of education. About one-third of non-supervisors (33.4%) fell into this category.

Reflecting the provisions of Act 816 mandating hires only into the unclassified service and some four years after implementation, about 40 percent of the respondents held unclassified positions. For supervisors, this figure was roughly 32 percent, and for nonsupervisors it was 41 percent. For all respondents, close to 10 percent were unsure as to whether their positions were in the classified or unclassified service. Close to 27 percent of the respondents had worked for the state four or fewer years. Over 37 percent had 15 years or more service, while a roughly equal percentage (39%) had between 5 and 14 years of service. Supervisors, not unexpectedly, tended to have worked longer for the state than nonsupervisors. With regard to tenure in current position, fully 48.1 percent had four or fewer years of service with the state. Those in the 5 to 14 years of service category represented 36.2 percent, while 15.6 percent had 15 or more years in position. Finally, roughly proportional representation of state agencies was achieved. Accordingly, the largest percentages of respondents came from the state's largest agencies, most notably, corrections (21.9%) and human resources (27.4%). The State Department of Transportation contributed 6.6 percent, while community health added 4.8 percent. The balance of the responses were distributed across other smaller state agencies.

Previous research on pay-for-performance systems in the public sector has revealed that employee job satisfaction, confidence and trust in agency management, and feelings about working for the government concerned are important factors associated with the degree to which these systems are accepted by employees and the supervisors who must implement them. In this regard, a stated goal of the GeorgiaGain initiative was to create working conditions that would improve state employees' confidence in the fairness and equity of the human resources management (HRM) system and its administration across all state agencies and on all levels of responsibility. Accordingly, the survey probed state employees' satisfaction with their jobs and their feelings about working for the state and for their particular agencies. Responses to those items are presented in Table 6.1.

Most of the respondents reported having positive feelings about their jobs, their agencies, and working for the State of Georgia. For example, 90.5 percent agreed to at least some extent, and 32.3 percent agreed strongly, with the statement "I like my job." Likewise, over 70 percent saw their agencies as good places to work. Job satisfaction has been found to be related to turnover and absenteeism rates in many studies, and about 75 percent of these respondents indicated that they had *no* intention of leaving state employment during the coming year, and almost two-thirds responded that they would recommend employment with the state to family members and friends. Despite these encouraging findings, however, there were several areas where the pattern of responses suggested potential or emerging problems for management. More than two-thirds reported experiencing "a lot of turnover" in their work groups. Also, they were almost evenly split on the question of whether or not they trusted their agencies to treat them fairly. Even more problematic was the finding that 65 percent *did not* agree with the statement that they are appreciated as valuable assets by senior agency management. Less surprising was the finding that a vast majority of the respondents (over 80%) were not satisfied with their pay. Only 30 percent thought that morale in their work units was relatively high. In most of these areas, there were no meaningful differences found between supervisors and nonsupervisors.

Two of the satisfaction-related items in the current survey replicated questions from the *1993 GaGain Employee Opinion Survey* conducted for the Georgia State Merit System by William M. Mercer Inc. On both items, a negative trend was found. In 1993, 94 percent agreed with the statement "I like my job," but by 2000, that percentage was down to 90.5. Likewise, in 1993, 17 percent indicated their intent to leave state employment within the coming year; that percentage had risen to 25.5 in 2000.

Table 6.1
Employee Job Satisfaction
(percent agreeing with the survey item)

Survey Item	Nonsupervisory Employees	Supervisory Employees	All Employees
1. I like my job.	90.3	92.0*	90.6
2. There is a lot of turnover (retirements, resignations, terminations, etc.) in my work group.	68.5	70.1	68.9
3. Because of dissatisfaction with my job or with State government, I am likely to leave Georgia State government within the next twelve months to take another job.	25.7	24.4*	25.4
4. I would recommend employment with the State of Georgia to family members and friends.	63.1	57.3	62.1
	63.1	57.3	62.1
5. My agency is a good place to work.	71.6	71.0	71.0
6. I do not trust my agency to treat me fairly.	52.9	54.9	53.3
7. State employees are appreciated as valuable assets by senior agency management.	34.1	38.5	35.0
8. I am doing work that is worthwhile.	92.3	96.0***	93.0
9. I am not satisfied with my pay.	83.1	79.8*	82.5
10. Morale is high in my work unit.	30.4	29.6	30.2

*p < .05
***p < .001
Note: Significance levels in Tables 6.1 and 6.2 refer to a two-tailed test of the difference of means between disaggregated responses of supervisors and nonsupervisors. Disaggregated responses included those who strongly disagreed, disagreed, slightly disagreed, slightly agreed, agreed, and strongly agreed. For ease of presentation in this and subsequent tables, the responses from those who slightly agreed, agreed, and strongly agreed were aggregated into a single "Agreed" category.

With one exception, no significant statistical associations were found between demographic and other characteristics of the respondents and the job satisfaction items. The exception was a predictable negative relationship between age and intent to leave or turnover within the coming year. As a rule, previous studies have revealed that older employees in all sectors of the economy are less likely to express an intent to leave their jobs (to turnover) than are younger employees, so this finding was neither anomalous nor unexpected.

Although these data did not suggest that there were serious and pressing problems with regard to job satisfaction among state employees, the trend suggested by the comparison with the 1993 data may be grounds for concern, especially since GeorgiaGain was intended to provide a stronger foundation for job satisfaction and confidence in agency HRM. Annual surveys of job satisfaction by agency human resources offices or by a central HRM services unit, which the Merit System has in large measure become under Act 816, might be very helpful in tracking and assessing GeorgiaGain's affects.

Do Employees Have Trust and Confidence in the Fairness of the State's HR System under GeorgiaGain?

Creating an effective and credible performance evaluation process, one seen by employees as fair in its administration and equitable in its outcomes, was an important objective of GeorgiaGain reforms. It was also hoped that the new process would measurably improve confidence in supervisors' ability to discriminate among levels of performance and, therefore, to allocate rewards accordingly. GeorgiaGain replaced the old traditional system with a new, objectives-focused, performance appraisal process. Emphasis was placed on developing and applying consistent, clearly defined performance standards to all state jobs. The system was also designed to encourage effective two-way communications between supervisors and subordinates about job-related goals and expectations. A related objective was to develop and maintain accurate and up-to-date position descriptions and standards that would support a performance management approach to human resources management. In the general scheme of things, GeorgiaGain's central goal was to greatly enhance supervisors' capacity to manage performance and, thereby, to raise productivity and responsiveness to citizen-customers throughout the state workforce. A key element of the strategy for achieving that goal was to build trust and confidence in the system throughout the state workforce.

The survey revealed that state workers had serious reservations about the purposes of GeorgiaGain and its day-to-day administration by agency administrators and supervisors. Table 6.2 summarizes these and other findings, but several deserve underscoring at this point. Most state employees apparently do not believe GeorgiaGain's promise to identify and reward high performers. Close to 85 percent of the respondents expressed the belief that management had imposed quotas or limits on the number of performance ratings above "met expectations" (the equivalent of a satisfactory rating) available to state employees. This was not a point of view restricted to non-supervisory personnel. In fact, a larger percentage of supervisors believed that quotas had been imposed. Such beliefs, of course, are not unique to the State of Georgia, studies of the federal experiment with merit pay, for example, identified budget-driven allocations (rationing) of performance ratings as a major reason for employee suspicion and cynicism about pay-for-performance.

Problems were found on other trust-related issues as well. More than three-quarters of the respondents agreed with the suggestion that "office politics had more to do with performance ratings than actual performance on the job." More than half of those responding expressed the belief that their performances, while rated as "exceeded" or "far exceeded" by their immediate supervisors had been changed to "met expectations" by higher management due to "budgetary constraints." Only about half of the respondents saw their most recent performance ratings as accurately reflecting their performances, and about the same proportion believed that performance appraisals were conducted fairly in their work units.

As the findings shown in Table 6.2 reveal, state workers also were less than confident in the operation of the new performance appraisal system. More than one-third of the respondents *disagreed* with the proposition that performance appraisal discussions with supervisors were helpful in improving performance, and a similar percentage did to some degree *not understand* how their supervisors evaluated their performance. Less than 60 percent believed that their supervisors were able to discriminate accurately between different levels of job performance, and barely more than half agreed with the statement that their supervisor's evaluation provided feedback that often helped them improve their job performance. It is also noteworthy that two-thirds of the respondents believed there were too many rating levels under GeorgiaGain. On the positive side, 80 percent of the respondents believed that the performance standards set forth in position descriptions accurately reflected job content, and close to 90 percent indicated that they understood what was expected of them on the job.

A comparison between the current survey's results and those of the 1993 Mercer survey revealed the same problematic trend that was found in the job satisfaction and intent to turnover areas. Responses to an item stating "On my job I know what is expected of me," showed a decline from 95 percent agreeing in 1993 to 86.8

Table 6.2 Employee Perceptions of GeorgiaGain (percent agreeing with the survey item)

Survey Item	Nonsupervisory Employees	Supervisory Employees	All Employees
1. The performance standards for my job are related to what I do.	77.8	76.5	77.6
2. On my job I know what is expected of me.	87.1	85.2	86.8
3. My supervisor is able to accurately determine different levels of employee performance.	56.4	55.4	56.2
4. Performance appraisal discussions are useful in helping me improve my performance.	66.0	58.4***	64.6
5. I understand how my supervisor evaluates my performance.	62.8	60.7	62.6
6. There are too many performance rating categories under GeorgiaGain.	65.8	65.8	65.8
7. My supervisor's evaluation provides feedback that often helps me improve my job performance.	53.4	52.6	53.2
8. My job description provides the information needed to establish clear standards and expectations used to evaluate my performance.	63.1	57.5	62.1
9. I believe my supervisor rated my performance as "exceeded" or "far exceeded" expectations, but that rating was changed to "met expectations" by higher management due to budgetary constraints.	55.0	55.7	55.2
10. Office politics has more to do with performance ratings than actual performance on the job.	76.7	68.8***	75.2
11. Performance ratings of better than "met expectations" are "rotated among employees who deserve meaningful pay raises.	32.1	45.6***	34.7
12. I believe that management has imposed "quotas" or limits on the number of performance ratings above "met expectations."	84.0	88.7*	84.9
13. My most recent performance rating accurately reflected my performance.	50.3	53.4	50.8
14. Performance appraisals in my work unit are conducted fairly.	49.6	53.4*	50.4
15. My supervisor really doesn't know enough about what I am doing to evaluate my performance accurately.	43.5	44.2	43.7
16. The pay-for-performance system set up by GeorgiaGain is a good way to motivate employees.	31.6	22.8***	30.0
17. There has been too much stress on money as an incentive and not enough on other sources of information.	52.6	54.2	52.9

18. My pay is based on how well I do my job.	21.3	23.3	21.6
19. Pay raises in my work unit often are not really related to performance.	28.2	33.0	29.0
20. Favoritism is a problem for the pay-for-performance program in my agency.	68.6	65.4	68.0
21. Performance appraisals are very helpful in determining my training and development needs.	49.8	46.4*	49.1
22. It is possible to identify employee weaknesses and related training needs during the performance development process.	63.5	65.9	63.9
23. There is a lot of effective teaching, training, and coaching of subordinates by my supervisor.	35.2	36.2	35.4
24. The state offers me enough training to grow and develop.	45.3	54.8*	47.0
25. Adequate resources and opportunities for career development are available to state employees.	37.8	39.6	38.1
26. State money has not been made available to reward good performers with good pay increases.	90.4	92.1	90.7
27. Pay-for-performance was promised and delivered under GeorgiaGain.	29.6	22.5*	28.2
28. GeorgiaGain has not been completely implemented.	68.3	67.6	68.2
29. Management's commitment to fully implementing GeorgiaGain has declined steadily over the past five years.	70.2	74.4**	71.0
30. Promised market adjustments to pay have taken place.	22.2	17.4**	21.3
31. The pay I receive is not competitive with what private employers are offering.	87.9	87.6	87.8
32. It is hard to recruit qualified applicants.	83.2	92.3***	84.9
33. The benefits available to state employees are competitive with those offered in the private sector.	57.1	60.3	57.7
34. GeorgiaGain is really a way of getting more work out of state employees without having to provide any real extra benefits.	74.1	69.2	73.2
35. The real purpose of GeorgiaGain is to control the state's payroll costs.	82.9	77.8	81.9

*p < .05
**p < .01
***p < .001

Table 6.3
A Comparison of Responses from the 1993 and 2000 Surveys

Item	Percent Agreeing in 1993	Percent Agreeing in 2000
1. I like my job.	94.0	90.5
2. Because of dissatisfaction with my job or with state government, I am likely to leave state government within the next 12 months for another job.	17.0	25.5
3. On my job, I know what is expected of me.	95.0	86.8
4. Performance appraisal discussions are useful in helping me improve my performance.	77.0	64.6
5. I understand how my supervisor evaluates my performance.	73.0	62.6
6. My job description provides the information needed to establish clear standards and expectations used to evaluate my performance.	78.0	62.2
7. Performance appraisals in my work unit are conducted fairly.	64.0	50.3
8. The state offers me enough training to grow and develop.	60.0	47.0
9. My work unit has very high performance expectations for employees.	88.0	77.1

percent agreeing in 2000. Between 1993 and 2000, the proportion of state employees agreeing with the statement that "Performance appraisals are conducted fairly" declined from 64 to 50 percent, a startling fourteen point decline. Overall, as the data shown in Table 6.3 show, on all of the comparison items, the decline in confidence in the performance evaluation system being used by the state was noteworthy.

Do State Employees Think Pay-for-Performance is Working?

A primary objective of GeorgiaGain was to equitably compensate superior performers and thereby to reliably encourage them to sustain high levels of performance. At the same time, by limiting or denying pay increases for poor performers, it was hoped that the system would also supply a useful mechanism by which to motivate poor performers to improve their performance or to leave state employment. The survey suggested, however, that state employees are very skeptical about pay-for-performances's effectiveness in these terms.

One of the most striking findings was that more than 70 percent of the respondents disagreed to at least some extent with the idea that, "the pay-for-performance system set up by GeorgiaGain is a good way to motivate state employees." More than a third strongly disagreed. Impressively, more than three out of every four of the supervisors questioned the motivational potential of pay-for-performance. Supervisors, of course, were in a position to observe employee effort and performance on a daily basis. A large majority of nonsupervisory employees also disagreed with the idea that pay-for-performance was a good way to motivate state workers.

Much the same result was obtained in response to the statement, "My pay is based on how well I do my job," where more than 78 percent disagreed and virtually no difference between supervisors and nonsupervisors was found. An often cited concern about pay-for-performance is its heavy reliance on monetary incentives, and a majority of the respondents to this survey agreed that, "There has been too much stress on money as an incentive and not enough on other sources of motivation." A substantial majority (68%) also agreed with a statement to the effect that favoritism had undermined pay-for-performance in their agencies. A similar item appeared in the 1993 Mercer survey in advance of the implementation of the pay-for-performance system and, at that time, 77 percent of the respondents anticipated that favoritism would be a problem.

Do State Employees Believe Pay Increases under GeorgiaGain Have Been Meaningful?

The answer to this question was a resounding "no." On all levels of government in the United States, merit pay or pay-for-performance systems have been chronically underfunded by legislative bodies. Georgia has been no exception and this situation is reflected in the responses to two items in the survey. First, more than 90 percent agreed with the following statement: "State money has not been made available to reward good performers with good pay increases." In 1993, when a similar question was asked on the Mercer survey, 87 percent indicated that they *did not trust* that state money would be made available to reward good performers with good pay increases. It appeared that most of the respondents in 2000 thought this prediction had been accurate, with only 28 percent willing to agree that, "Pay for performance was promised and delivered under Georgia Gain." The findings were a bit more positive in one important area, the overall connection between different levels of performance and relative pay outcomes. Less than 30 percent agreed with the statement, "Pay raises in my work unit are not really related to performance."

Have GeorgiaGain's Promises Concerning Training and Development Been Realized?

A key part of the GeorgiaGain package was a commitment to establishing a firm linkage between the results of the performance evaluation process and opportunities for needed training and development. Here, the survey results indicated that state employees were about evenly split on the question of whether the performance appraisal process and the resulting ratings were in practice very helpful in determining training and development needs, with about 49 percent saying that they were useful. There was a similar division on the question of whether employee training needs were clearly identified in the performance development plans called for under GeorgiaGain. Actual practice notwithstanding, a substantial majority (64%) agreed that, "It is possible to identify employee weaknesses and related training needs during the performance appraisal process." Many of the respondents believed that the training and development resources needed to support GeorgiaGain's developmental goals had not materialized. Along these lines, less than half of the respondents thought that the state offered them enough training to "grow and develop," although supervisors were somewhat more likely to believe that it did. Only about 35 percent thought that their supervisors had provided "a lot" of effective teaching, training, and coaching, and less than 40 percent agreed that adequate resources and opportunities for career development were available to state employees. Supervisors and nonsupervisors did not differ significantly in their responses.

Has GeorgiaGain Improved the State's Competitive Position in the Labor Market?

GeorgiaGain's new classification and pay grade structure, combined with regular market adjustments, were intended to make it possible for the state to attract, hire, and retain highly qualified employees in a competitive labor market. The need to keep state employee pay and benefits competitive with those in the private sector market was also stressed by supporters of the reform agenda. The 2000 survey, nonetheless, indicated that workers saw little if any real improvement in the state's competitive position.

Despite the implementation of GeorgiaGain, nearly 85 percent of all respondents indicated that it was difficult to recruit qualified applicants. When only responses for supervisory personnel were considered, the proportion in agreement with this point of view climbed to more than 92 percent. A fair interpretation of this finding was difficult because it was not known what such responses would have been like in the years prior to the implementation of GeorgiaGain, but it was hard to imagine that in those years recruitment could have been perceived as substantially more difficult, so it is most likely that GeorgiaGain has not made the task of attracting and retaining qualified employees for state agencies significantly easier. Turnover appeared to be a statewide problem, since approximately 69 percent of the respondents indicated that there was "a lot" of turnover in their work groups. A related and critical component of the GeorgiaGain reform was a commitment to regular market adjustments to keep state pay and benefits in line with prevailing rates for comparable jobs and levels of responsibility. In 2000, state employees believed that the promised market adjustments simply had been taken off the table. On the question of pay comparability with the private sector, a large proportion of the respondents agreed with the statement, "The pay I receive is not competitive with what private employers are offering." In addition, few agreed that, "Promised market adjustments to pay have taken place." In addition, more than 57 percent thought that the benefits available to state employees were *not* competitive with those offered in the private sector. Supervisors and non-supervisors tended to be in general agreement on these questions.

How Did State Employees Interpret the Motives of Those Backing GeorgiaGain?

If the findings of the survey are to be believed, many members of the state's workforce are quite cynical about the motives of the designers of GeorgiaGain, seeing it as a way of getting more productivity without having to provide any real increases in pay and benefits. Seventy-three percent of the respondents agreed with a statement to that effect. A closely related finding was that nearly 82 percent believed that the real purpose of GeorgiaGain was to control the state's payroll costs. Likewise, roughly two-thirds (68.2%) believed that the reforms had not been fully implemented and that management's commitment to full implementation had declined steadily.

In general terms, therefore, the survey revealed that State of Georgia employees had very serious doubts about GeorgiaGain and the degree to which it had or was even in the process of achieving its central goals and objectives. Like many such reforms elsewhere, pay-for-performance, while attractive in theory, was not seen as being implemented fairly and consistently or funded by the state legislature at the levels necessary to make it work effectively as a part of the reform's performance management strategy. Other key components were also given low grades, as summarized in Table 6.1.

Act 816's Impact on Agency Personnel Practices in General

With regard to questions concerning Act 816, its implementation, and its impact, state employees were largely unimpressed with its effects on agency personnel management, recruitment, and the like. There were, however, significant and interesting differences of opinion across categories of employees on a variety of specific questions and issues. Table 6.4 displays these findings.

The survey inquired as to whether respondents believed their agencies had been able to establish effective human resource programs under Act 816. The law gave agencies extensive control over agency-unique job classes, including the authority to establish associated qualifications, assign classes to pay ranges, and determine performance standards. As can be seen in Table 6.4, only slightly more than 36 percent of all respondents agreed that this authority was exercised effectively. Sixty-four percent of those responding disagreed with the statement that their agencies had effective human resources programs under the new law. Similarly, about 70 percent agreed that there had been "little if any real change" in the human resources practices of their agencies since enactment of Act 816, and more than 56 percent *did not* see their agencies as having "made good use" of the discretion over human resources matters given them by Act 816. Interestingly, unclassified employees were significantly more supportive of the law than were classified employees on each of these issues. It appears, however, that supervisors and nonsupervisors were approximately equally pessimistic with regard to these matters. It is also interesting to observe that most employees (63.5%) did not believe that the provisions and purposes of Act 816 had been clearly communicated to state workers, with close to 60 percent of supervisors sharing this perception.

Impact on Recruitment and Hiring

As noted earlier, one of the primary stated objectives of Act 816 was to make it easier for state agencies to recruit and hire qualified people in a timely manner. The law was designed to improve the effectiveness of agency recruiting and hiring processes through extensive delegation and decentralization of examination and selection procedures and other human resources policy and management authority to the agency level. With regard to the legislation's impact in this area, the survey revealed considerable pessimism among state employees. For example, as shown in Table 6.4, only 38.4 percent of all employees agreed with the idea that the Act had resulted in their agencies being able to hire highly qualified people in a timely manner, which means that almost 62 percent disagreed. It is worth noting, however, that unclassified employees were significantly more likely to see success of the law with respect to this goal than were classified employees. What is perhaps even more striking is that supervisors, who presumably would be well positioned to assess the selection process, were significantly less sanguine about the reform on this issue than were nonsupervisory employees.

Impact on Agency Ability to Terminate Low Performers

Act 816 was also intended to improve the effectiveness and efficiency of agency human resources management by mandating that all new hires be placed into the unclassified service. As was noted earlier, this change was intended to establish an "at-will" employment system for the state. Personnel processes were also to be streamlined so that expedited adverse actions and appeals and the timely dismissal of poor performers could be accomplished. In regard to this set of related goals and objectives, about 75 percent of those responding agreed that the Act had made it easier to fire state employees, although nonsupervisors were much more likely to agree that this objective had been achieved than were supervisors.

In contrast, respondents were almost equally divided on the question of whether the Act had made it possible to terminate low performers without major procedural delays. This last finding is interesting, of course, because "procedural delays" were a prime justification for the reform. The respondents emphatically (78.3%) rejected the idea that unclassified state employees "tend to work harder than classified employees," and an overwhelming majority (75.5%) disagreed with the proposition that it was easier to supervise workers occupying unclassified positions than those in classified positions.

The pattern of responses to survey items dealing with job security, however, did indicate that Act 816 has had an impact on how state employees view this aspect of their employment relationship

Table 6.4
Employee Perceptions of the Implementation and Impact of the Georgia Civil Service Reform Legislation
(percent agreeing with each statement)

	Supervisors	Nonsupervisors	Classified	Unclassified	All
1. The provisions and purposes of the civil service reform law have been clearly communicated to state employees like me.	40.1	35.6	36.3	39.5	36.5
2. The civil service reform law has made the state workforce more productive and responsive to the public.	25.3	24.6	21.9	26.8*	24.6
3. The civil service reform law has made it easier to fire employees.	64.0	76.9***	75.4	76.9	74.5
4. There has been little if any real change in the human resources practices of my agency since the civil service reform law was enacted.	71.2	67.7	70.3	64.1*	68.4
5. I believe my agency has made good use of the greater discretion it has under the civil service reform law.	45.6	43.5	39.2	50.2***	43.9
6. Under authority provided by the civil service reform law my agency can hire highly qualified people in a timely manner.	33.4	39.6***	34.6	44.1***	38.4
7. Under the civil service reform law my agency has established an effective human resources program.	34.3	36.4	30.5	43.0***	36.1
8. It has been possible to terminate low performers without major procedural delays in my agency.	39.2	49.6***	46.8	50.1	47.6

(cont.) Table 6.4

9. Classified state employees really don't have any more job security in my agency than unclassified employees.	53.4	55.9	62.4	39.5***	55.4
10. Unclassified state employees tend to work harder than classified employees.	18.4	22.6	9.8	44.1***	21.7
11. Because of the civil service reform law, I believe that now there is no job security in state employment.	64.2	70.4*	70.0	71.2	69.2
12. Leaving a classified position for an unclassified position is a very risky step.	73.2	80.7**	85.1	68.9***	79.2
13. The civil service reform law causes state employees to be more responsive to the goals and priorities of agency administrators.	36.4	42.9*	38.5	44.4*	41.6
14. Supervising workers in unclassified positions is easier than supervising workers in classified positions.	19.8	25.6*	20.0	34.6***	24.5

*p < .05
**P < .01
***p < .001

Note: Significance levels refer to a two-tailed test of the difference of means between disaggregated responses of supervisors and nonsupervisors and between disaggregated responses of classified and unclassified employees.

with the state. Almost 70 percent agreed that Act 816 had created conditions under which "there is now no job security in state employment," and nearly 80 percent expressed the belief that, "leaving a classified position for an unclassified position is a very risky step." It should be noted, however, that supervisors were less likely to agree with these statements than were nonsupervisors, and that classified employees were much more likely to agree that leaving a classified position is risky than were unclassified employees. It is also noteworthy that a majority of the respondents (about 55%) agreed with the idea that classified employees in their agencies did not have any more job security than those in the unclassified service, although classified employees are substantially more likely to agree with that statement than were unclassified employees.

Impact on Bureaucratic Responsiveness

The survey also inquired into the matter of whether employees believe that the Georgia civil service reform has had the effect of making state employees more responsive to the public or to executive leadership. Act 816 was intended to enhance bureaucratic responsiveness to executive leadership by empowering agency heads flexibly to align human resources policies and practices with the policies and program mandates of the state's elected officials. Responses to survey items dealing with productivity and responsiveness under Act 816 reveal that state employees are at best dubious about the legislation's impacts in these areas. As the data in Table 6.4 reveal, more than 75 percent disagreed with the idea that Act 816 had resulted in a state workforce that is now more productive and responsive to the public, and only slightly more than 42 percent saw any improvement in state employees' responsiveness to goals and priorities of state administrators that was attributable to Act 816. Again, unclassified employees were more likely to see the law as effective in this manner than were classified employees.

Impact on Employee Statutory Protections and Constitutional Rights

A key component of Act 816 was to change the role of the Georgia State Merit System from that of a central personnel agency and regulator to an organization that provides needed human resources services, expertise, and technical assistance to state agencies largely at their request. In light of the Georgia State Merit System's changed role, responsibility for assuring the protection of constitutional and

Table 6.5

Employee Perceptions of Discrimination and Political Manipulation Following Implementation of the Georgia Civil Service Reform Law

(percent responding "yes" to each statement)

In the past three years (1997, 1998, and 1999) do you believe any of the following events happened to you personally?

	Supervisors	Non-supervisors	Classified	Unclassified	All
I was denied a job, a promotion, or a job reward because of my race, religion, sex, age, national origin, or disability.	13.8	15.1	15.7	15.9	15.2
I was solicited by someone in authority to make a campaign contribution.	3.4	3.8	3.8	3.8	3.8
I was asked to resign a position or transfer to another position on account of my political beliefs or political connections.	2.0	1.5	1.3	2.6*	1.6
I did not get a job, promotion, or job reward I was qualified for because of my political beliefs or the political connections of others.	11.4	9.3	10.7	9.1	9.7

*p < .063

Note: Significance level refers to a two-tailed test of the difference of means between disaggregated responses of classified and unclassified employees.

statutory rights and protections of state employees is a major responsibility of agency management and human resources offices.

The responses to survey items dealing with constitutional and
statutory protections afforded state employees by the state and federal governments suggest that to date no major problems have developed on the agency level. As shown in Table 6.5, most state employees
did not see themselves as exposed to partisan political coercion on the
job or perceive the personnel practices of their agencies to be meaningfully influenced by partisan political motives. Approximately 4
percent of all employees reported that they had been solicited to make
campaign contributions, and 1.6 percent reported that they had been
asked to resign a position or transfer to another position because of
their political beliefs or political connections. On this last point, however, it is interesting to note that unclassified employees were significantly more likely to report such political pressure than were
classified employees. Somewhat larger numbers of employees (9.7%),
however, did agree that they were at some time denied a job, a promotion, or a job reward because of their political beliefs of connections.

In general, similar results were found regarding perceptions of
discrimination, although more concern may be justified in this area,
since more than 15 percent of all respondents expressed the belief that
they had experienced some form of discrimination based on race, religion, sex, age, national origin, or disability during the three years
immediately preceding the survey. The fact that any employee believes
that he or she has been the victim of discrimination should be taken
seriously, and 15 percent is not an insignificant proportion of the
state's workforce. The pattern of responses on this issue are consistent

Table 6.6
Relationship Between Race/Ethnicity and Perceptions
of Discrimination

I was denied a job, a promotion, or a job reward because of my race, religion, sex,
age, national origin, or disability.

	White	Minority	Total
Yes	122	158	280
	10.6%	23.0%	15.3%
No	1,025	528	1,553
	89.4%	77.0%	84.7%
	1,147	686	1,833
	100.0%	100.0%	100.0%

between classified and unclassified employees and supervisors and nonsupervisors. However, as shown in Table 6.6, and as might be expected, minority employees are significantly more likely to believe they have experienced discrimination than are nonminority employees. While 15.3 percent of all employees perceived discrimination, and only 10.6 percent of white employees believed that they were denied job rewards or promotions because of discrimination, fully 23 percent of the minority respondents believed they had been victimized.

Conclusion

Particularly in regard to GeorgiaGain, the survey's findings were not encouraging, although not entirely unexpected, given the anecdotal evidence of widespread dissatisfaction existing before the survey was done. Across the board, state employees were highly critical of the way GeorgiaGain has operated, and many were suspicious of the motives of those who advocated for these reforms. Internal and external pay equities were a sore point for state workers, many of whom were convinced that GeorgiaGain had not delivered on its promises in these key areas. In response, the state legislature authorized a set of changes that allowed payment of one-time bonuses or "Performance Plus" additions to annual increases, and Governor Barnes recommended in 2001 a set of pay increases based on: (1) moving all state employees now paid less than the target for their pay grade to the target rate; (2) providing a 3.5 percent increase for those who "meet expectations, including those with salaries exceeding the maximum annual salary for their pay grade; (3) making an additional one-time lump sum payment of 2 percent for everybody who "exceeds expectations"; and (4) increasing the state's pay grade minimums and maximums by 4 percent (Georgia Merit System 2001; General Assembly of Georgia 2001, 1–7). In subsequent years, however, a sharp economic downturn within the state resulted in no pay raises for state employees until January of 2005. During that time, Georgia's pay-for-performance system was effectively placed on "hold."

The survey's findings about Act 816 produced a far less clearly defined picture, but the overall impression was of a system having had little of the desired impact on agency performance beyond redefining workers' understanding of the level of job security offered by state employment. Fears that the state's agencies would resort to wholesale patronage and at best loosely enforce federal and state anti-discrimination laws had not been confirmed, which must be considered a reassuring finding. In general, however, state employees' perceptions of Act 816's impact did not suggest that major changes along the desired lines had taken place. It is in this area that an analysis of existing multiyear data on state personnel actions might provide a much clearer picture of Act 816's impact on agency personnel practices.

If anything, the findings of the present survey were cause for some concern about Act 816's long-term consequences for human resources policy and management in Georgia. Widespread employee cynicism may be looming on the horizon. With the exception of beliefs about job security, where "at-will" expectations (or fears) appear to be taking hold, the Act's effects appear largely to be marginal at best in the eyes of the state's workforce. For the most part, the workforce is not convinced that the Act has done much to improve human resources practices or performance at the agency level. This is particularly true for those occupying classified positions, and unclassified employees tend to be somewhat more optimistic in some areas, such as agency uses of discretion and streamlining of recruitment and hiring. Clearly, the jury is still out. Keeping close tabs on trends in employee perceptions of these areas over the next two or three years should provide the information needed to reach some firm conclusions about the likelihood that Act 816 will achieve its authors' purposes in whole or in part.

Note

This chapter is drawn in part from work we previously published in the *Review of Public Personnel Administration* and used with permission of Sage Publications. See, Nigro and Kellough (2000) and Kellough and Nigro (2002).

References

Ban, Carolyn (1998). "The Changing Role of the Personnel Office," in Stephen E. Condrey, ed., *Handbook of Human Resource Management in Government*. San Francisco: Jossey-Bass: 19–34.

Barrett, Katherine, and Richard Greene (1999). "Grading the States" A Management Report Card." *Governing* 12 (February): 17–90.

Barzelay, Michael (1992). *Breaking Through Bureaucracy*. Berkeley: University of California Press.

Brudney, Jeffrey L., F. Ted Hebert, and Deil S. Wright (1999). "Reinventing Government in the American States: Measuring and Explaining

Administrative Reform." *Public Administration Review* 59 (January/February): 19–30.

deLeon, Linda, and Robert B. Denhardt (2000). "The Political Theory of Reinvention." *Public Administration Review* 60 (March/April): 89–97.

Dillman, D.A. (1978). *Mail and Telephone Surveys: The Total Design Method.* New York: John Wiley and Sons.

General Assembly of Georgia (2001). *152679 Working Draft 6.* (January 24) Atlanta, GA.

Georgia Merit System (2001). *Memorandum: Governor's Recommendations for Salary Increases and Merit System Legislation.* (January 24) Atlanta, GA: Office of the Commissioner.

Gore, Albert (1993). *Creating a Government That Works Better and Costs Less: Report of the National Performance Review.* Washington DC: Government Printing Office.

Hays, Steven W. (1996). "The 'State of the Discipline' in Public Personnel Administration." *Public Administration Quarterly* 20 (Fall): 285–304.

Hays, Steven W. (1997). "Reinventing the Personnel Function: Lessons Learned from a Hope-Filled Beginning in One State." *American Review of Public Administration* 27 (December): 324–342.

Hays, Steven W., and Richard C. Kearney (1997). "Riding the Crest of a Wave: The National Performance Review and Public Management Reform." *International Journal of Public Administration* 20 (January): 11–40.

Howard, Phillip (1994). *The Death of Common Sense: How Law is Suffocating America.* New York: Random House.

Ingraham, Patricia W. (1995). *The Foundation of Merit: Public Service in the American Bureaucracy.* Baltimore, MD: Johns Hopkins Press.

Ingraham, Patricia W., and Carolyn Ban (1984). *Legislating Bureaucratic Change: The Civil Service Reform Act of 1978.* Albany: State University of New York Press.

Kearney, Richard C., and Steven W. Hays (1998). "Reinventing Government, The New Public Management and Civil Service Systems." *Review of Public Personnel Administration.* 18 (Fall): 38–54.

Kellough, J. Edward (1999). "Reinventing Public Personnel Management: Ethical Implications for Managers and Public Personnel Systems." *Public Personnel Management.* 28 (Winter): 655–671.

Kellough, J. Edward and Lloyd G. Nigro (2002). "Pay for Performance in Georgia State Government: Employee Perspectives on GeorgiaGain after 5 Years." *Review of Public Personnel Administration* 22 (Summer): 146–166.

Kettle, Donald F., Patricia W. Ingraham, Ronald P. Sanders, and Constance Horner (1996). *Civil Service Reform: Building a Government that Works.* Washington, DC: Brookings Institution Press.

Krueger, Richard A. (1998). *The Focus Group Kit, Vol. 1: The Focus Group Guidebook.* Thousand Oaks, CA: Sage Publications.

Krueger, Richard A., and Mary Ann Casey (2000). *Focus Groups: A Practical Guide for Applied Research*. Thousand Oaks, CA: Sage Publications.

Morgan, David L. (1988). *Focus Groups as Qualitative Research*. Newbury Park, CA: Sage Publications.

National Commission on the Public Service (1993). *Hard Truths/Tough Choices: An Agenda for State and Local Reform*. Albany: Nelson A. Rockefeller Institute of Government.

Nigro, Lloyd G. and J. Edward Kellough (2000). "Civil Service Reform in Georgia: Going to the Edge?" *Review of Public Personnel Administration* 20 (Fall): 41–54.

Osbourne, David, and P. Plastrik (1997). *Banishing Bureaucracy*. Reading, MA: Addison-Wesley.

Osborne, David, and Ted Gaebler. (1992) *Reinventing Government: How the Entrepreneurial Spirit is Transforming the Public Sector*. Reading, MA: Addison-Wesley.

O'Sullivan, Elizabethann, and Gary R. Rassel (1999). *Research Methods for Public Administration*, 3rd ed. New York: Longman.

Perry, James L. (1991). "Linking Pay to Performance: The Controversy Continues," in Carolyn Ban and Norma M. Riccucci, eds., *Public Personnel Management: Current Concerns, Future Challenges*. New York: Longman.

Perry, James L., Lois R. Wise, and Margo Martin (1994). "Breaking the Civil Service Mold." *Review of Public Personnel Administration* 14 (Spring): 40–54.

Savas, E.S. (2000). *Privatization and Public-Private Partnerships*. New York: Chatham House.

State of Georgia (1996). "Public Officers and Employees' Personnel Administration; Veterans; Unclassified Service Defined to Include All Positions filled by New Hires; Classified Service Employees to Remain in Classified Service on Certain Conditions." No. 816 (Senate Bill 635). *General Acts and Resolutions*, Vol. 1: 684–691.

State of Georgia (1996a). "Remarks by Governor Zell Miller." *State of the State Address*. Atlanta, GA: Office of the Governor.

State of Georgia (1996b). *Executive Order*. A-11–0007-1996. Atlanta, GA (May 3).

Thompson, Frank J. (1994). "The Winter Commission." *Review of Public Personnel Administration* 14 (Spring): 5–10.

Thompson, Frank J., and Beryl A. Radin (1997). "Reinventing Public Personnel Management: The Winter and Gore Initiatives," in Carolyn Ban and Norma M. Riccucci, eds., *Public Personnel Management: Current Concerns, Future Challenges*. White Plains, NY: Longman.

Thompson, James R., and Patricia W. Ingraham (1996). "The Reinvention Game." *Public Administration Review*. 56 (May/June): 291–298.

Wechsler, Barton (1994). "Reinventing Florida's Civil Service System." *Review of Public Personnel Administration* 14 (Spring): 64–76.

CHAPTER 7

Florida's *Service First*:
Radical Reform in the Sunshine State

James S. Bowman
Jonathan P. West
Sally C. Gertz

During the past twenty years, Florida has become a "mega-state," challenging California as a trendsetter in popular culture and public policy. This status is based on population growth of nearly 25 percent in the 1990s and corresponding political clout on the national stage. Evidence that Florida is "hot" is seen in news stories capturing national attention: the Elian Gonzalez case, shark attacks, the Gianni Versace murder, court battles over Ted Williams' frozen remains, women biting dogs, hurricanes, Dale Earnhardt's death, terrorists attending flight schools, O.J. Simpson's latest troubles, and the 2000 presidential election recount. It is the home of cocaine cowboys, the Redneck Riviera, refugee rafters, massive prison populations and meager education budgets, citrus canker, the nation's senior citizens, Disney devotees, universities dedicated to sports, lenient bankruptcy laws, rock bottom indicators of public health and social well-being, Latin American-style income distribution, no state income tax, and condo commandos. It is entirely apropos that the Salvador Dali museum is located in the Sunshine State as "Floridians have come to expect the surreal," according to the *New York Times* (Paterniti 2002, 31).

Indeed, Florida occupied center stage for 36 days during the 2000 presidential election and remained in the spotlight as two controversial contenders vied for the governorship in 2002: incumbent Jeb Bush and former Clinton cabinet officer Janet Reno. One of the

145

issues in the race was the nature of the state employment. Bush, proud of his "Service First" civil service reform, believes that it will enhance productivity; the law, according to Reno and candidate Bill McBride (who upset her in the Democratic primary), should be repealed. For all the controversy in Florida culture and politics, the strange aspect of this debate is this: the state personnel system, consisting of 124,000 people, is one of the most productive in the country based on the number of workers compared to population.

Reform is here, there, and everywhere as shown in this volume. It is, however, seldom as radical as Florida's initiative, which dismantles civil service safeguards for public workers. Deeply conservative (if not politically reactionary), the state is clearly capable of dramatic change. Some five years after neighboring Georgia eliminated job tenure for all new state employees in 1996 (West 2002; Condrey and Maranto 2001; Nigro and Kellough, this volume), Florida business and taxpayer interests aligned to redefine the state's civil service. Governor Bush signed Service First into law on May 14, 2001; it became effective July 1 of that year.

Civil service reform in Florida is not a new idea as some dozen relevant studies have been done in the last several decades. Most recently, the Democratic Chiles-MacKay administration (1993–1999), guided by the philosophy of "reinventing government," sponsored legislation to promote total quality management, create a flexible employee reward system, reduce the number of classifications, improve training and development, streamline organizational processes, and decentralize decision making.[1] It did not, however, question the need for a merit-based civil service system, which appeared to be guaranteed by the state constitution. Service First posed such a challenge by abolishing merit system defenses for a large group of current employees. It is as radical in its thrust, if not its reach, as the reforms in Georgia (indeed, because it eliminated vested property rights of current employees, Florida's reforms in some ways are even more bold than Georgia's).

Given the state's trendsetter status, it is important to understand why this initiative was undertaken, the nature of the changes introduced, and the prospects for the future. This analysis will emphasize the most striking aspect of the reform: the removal of civil service job protections in state government and the institution of employment at-will, a private sector philosophy that gives an employer the unquestioned right to terminate an employee "at-will" at any time without due process for any or no reason not contrary to law (Muhl 2001).

Background

This section traces antecedents to Service First and its passage into law. The legislation sprang from long-standing "bash the bureaucrat," "run government like a business," and "government is the problem, not the solution" attitudes common in the state and national political culture.

The foundation for a merit-based civil service was established in 1883 on the federal level to eliminate the graft and corruption of that century's patronage-based, carnival-like, scandal-ridden spoils system. Reformers believed government should be operated in a business-like manner; a merit system, therefore, was needed to block tawdry, capricious political influences in the appointment and removal of employees. Public administration could be responsible and efficient only if civil servants were selected on the basis of qualifications and insulated from partisan intrigue by career service tenure. Most states and many localities eventually established their own centralized merit systems to reduce corruption and stabilize the workforce, thereby enhancing productivity. The moral and economic virtue of shielding public employees from predatory partisan pressures was self-evident for generations of Americans; it was seldom necessary to explain, much less defend, the merit system.

Florida's statewide career service system, one of the last to be established in the nation, was created in 1967, although a civil service provision had been added to the state constitution in 1955 requiring that state agencies subject to federal grant-in-aid guidelines to be brought under a merit system. As found in contemporary law (Florida Statutes, section 110), the civil service has been in place since 1979. The system emanated from complaints that frequent employee turnover damaged banking, real estate, and retail interests: loans and big-ticket sales could not be prudently made to unemployed people or a workforce subject to widespread job losses after every election. In the wake of the federal 1978 Civil Service Reform Act that established the Senior Executive Service, the Florida legislature created the Senior Management Service in 1980 for top political appointees and the Selected Professional Service (later called the Selected Exempt Service) in 1985 for agency bureau chiefs. Both of these personnel categories were placed outside the permanent public service, thereby truncating the career ladder for most civil servants.

An early indication of Jeb Bush's interest in the state employment system occurred when he was Florida Secretary of Commerce in the Republican administration of Governor Bob Martinez (1987–

1991). He sent a memorandum to all agency heads advocating the elimination of job tenure for state workers as a way to save money and improve service. Beyond general antipathy toward government, the origin of his view is not known. Some knowledgeable observers have speculated that Bush, as a former real estate developer, may have been frustrated by public officials in the course of doing business.

The memorandum may not have had a direct impact, but two related developments occurred between this time and when he assumed the governorship. When the state lottery was created in 1987, the agency was placed outside of the civil service system as a business-style sales enterprise. And in 1995, the Department of Commerce was privatized with the result that all employees lost their positions. These events, in retrospect, demonstrated the vulnerability of the principle of job security in state government: services could be provided without public servants (by steering contracts to vendors who would also donate campaign funds) and employment rights of those employees not privatized could be eroded (in the name of discouraging governmental interference with private enterprise). Further, employees of the judicial and legislative branches of government, as well as those of the governor's office, provided on-going examples of at-will employment: when "serious" work had to been accomplished quickly, reliably, and with unquestioned loyalty, staff could be hired and terminated as necessary. Downsizing and outsourcing continued during the administration of Democratic Governor Lawton Chiles (1993–1999), but there was no encroachment on the job property rights of state employees (which guarantee due process in cases of adverse personnel actions).

Jeb Bush was elected by a wide margin in 1998, promising CEO-like efficiency and no-nonsense management.[2] It would be the first time since post-Civil-War Reconstruction that Florida had both a governor and a legislature controlled by the Republican party. To make their mark, the government bureaucracy was a convenient target to attack in this right-to-work state. Consistent with the massive cutbacks in the private sector, Bush announced that state government staffing would be reduced by 25 percent in five years and directed agency heads to produce budgets reflecting that goal. Yet this was primarily a "state capital" concern as policy issues of greater interest statewide (such as education, crime, tax cuts, the environment, and affirmative action) were the focus of the governor's first two years in office. He believed, however, that his initiatives would be jeopardized if the state's employment system was not changed. By the end of his second legislative session, then, Bush was ready to turn attention inward to the mechanics of government.

In late 2000 the Florida Council of One Hundred, a group with close ties to the governor's office, published *Modernizing Florida's Civil Service System: Moving from Protection to Performance.* Representing corporate executives, this organization contended that the state's largest employer—state government—was long overdue for organizational transformation. Specifically, it believed that "providing 'permanent'. . . employment . . . is detrimental to all—to state government, the public being served, and ultimately the individual employee" (Florida Council 2000, 7); accordingly, it recommended an at-will employment system for the state.[3]

To address possible legal concerns, the report included a written opinion; it argued that although the constitution provides job property rights for tenured employees, when government abolishes positions it has created, then due process requirements may be satisfied by the legislative process (Karl 2000; Florida House of Representatives 2001, 32). The tone of the document (especially its emphasis on firing public servants) and the absence of any factual basis for the report (e.g., showing that poor performance results when employees are protected from arbitrary management decisions), may have misled some to dismiss it as just another ideological attack on government that could be debunked with accurate information. If so, this proved to be a serious miscalculation.

Contending that the merit system had changed from protecting the public to protecting employees without regard for performance,[4] Service First was announced in the governor's March 2001 state of the state address.[5] In line with the Council's report, it was assumed that there was no reason that state workers should be treated any differently from employees in nonunionized private companies.

Indeed Bush later argued, in an interesting twist of logic, that since partisanship, cronyism, nepotism, and favoritism could corrupt the existing career service system, job safeguards designed to prevent such problems should be abolished (Cotterell 2001c). Bush appointee, Department of Management Services Secretary Cynthia Henderson (2001) stated that one of the biggest frustrations with state employees was the "we be's"—"we be here when you came, and we be here when you gone." There could be no doubt the administration believed that the only way to make state workers responsive was to make them subject to the at-will doctrine. Relatively noncontroversial—a popular governor telling voters that government had to be modernized to improve services—the plan also could be an attractive reelection issue the following year.

The measure (modeled after the Council's report) was rushed through the House of Representatives very early in the session on party-line committee and floor votes. This process produced charges of stacked committees, one-sided hearings, and limitations on amendments and floor debates. One critical legislator claimed that, "We are all tired of injecting politics into public service, but this is simply politics over policy, politics over principle, and politics over people" (quoted in Cotterell 2001b, 4B).

The Senate mitigated some of the most extreme aspects of the bill (e.g., deletion of a "for cause" adverse personnel action standard for career staff) and passed it, largely along party lines. Its key provision moved more than 16,000 career employees—in supervisory, managerial, and confidential (i.e., any nonmanagerial professionals involved in budgetary and personnel matters as well as anyone else who assists a manager in such activities) positions—into Selected Exempt Service; in this capacity they serve at the pleasure of the department head and have no appeal rights in adverse personnel actions. Unions that had endorsed Bush in the last election (Police Benevolent Association, International Union of Police Associations, Florida Nurses Association) were able to exempt their members from coverage. They argued that their members needed job protections when making public safety and medical decisions, and without them there would be considerable difficulty in recruiting and retaining quality personnel. Other unions (e.g., the American Federation of State, County, and Municipal Employees), whose members had critical regulatory responsibilities, but had not supported the governor in 1998, were unsuccessful in making that argument.

The editorial pages of the state's largest newspapers were divided on Service First. The *Miami Herald* was supportive, running two editorials summarizing past efforts to modify the civil service, reviewing the claims of backers and opponents of reform, and pointing out "half-truths" and scare tactics used by unions challenging the bill ("Civil Service Reform for State Workers" 2001; "Sounding a False Alarm" 2001b). The *Jacksonville Times-Union* also backed the Bush initiative ("State Government: Improving Service" 2001).

The *Tampa Tribune, Palm Beach Post, St. Petersburg Times,* and *Daytona Beach News-Journal*, however, were opposed. Reform was seen as irrational and impractical and part of a larger Bush strategy of "overreaching for power" and seeking privatization and cost-saving while failing to recognize the difference between business and government. These dailies did support pay based on performance, bonuses, and improved benefits, but argued that the plan was either a ploy (to break public employee unions, victimize state employees, and leave supervisors free to fire employees "any time, for any reason"), or a poorly conceived initiative hastily pushed through the policy process without diligent deliberation. Service First was identified as one of the "trust-us-we're-the-government" bills, passed by the conservative Republican legislature not known for its faith in government ("Civil-Service 'Reform' Just a Grab for Power" 2001; "Bush Civil Service Plan Victimizes State Workers" 2001; "Legislature 2001" 2001; Dyckman 2001; "Governor's Efficiency Expert Resigns" 2001; Troxler 2001). Other large papers—the *Orlando Sentinel*, *South Florida Sun-Sentinel*, *Sarasota Herald-Tribune*, and *Fort Meyers News-Press*—did not take an editorial position.

The only independent expert to examine Service First prior to passage was a labor mediator "Special Master," mandated by law to give the legislature nonpartisan advice when collective bargaining negotiations break down. His report concluded that, "There was no factual evidence brought forward to show that the (existing) system was broken or dysfunctional" (Special Master Report 2001, 58). He opined that Service First would become "Service Worst" because the elimination of job protections while simultaneously seeking the most qualified staff "is not logical and will not work" (2001, 74). The legislature rejected the Special Master's recommendations and decided to never again be troubled with them: a provision in the Service First legislation abolished the Special Master's role in resolving impasses between the state and its employees.

Some state officials were also dubious about the reform. One Department of Agriculture and Consumer Services manager commented, "Service First gives you a better chance to get rid of the one or two percent of marginal performers—but you can't protect the other 98 percent" (David Heil, personnel communication, February 15, 2002). A Department of Transportation contract inspector told the state capitol newspaper that, "I have been involved in the private sector that Jeb (Bush) so wants to emulate, and if someone proposed a complete overhaul of an existing system without showing any facts or figures to back them up, like the governor is doing, they would earn a quick ticket to 'downsizing'" (quoted in Cotterell 2001a, 2E). The employee, while experiencing no direct retaliation for his views, is concerned about the doubling of workloads caused by cutbacks and policies permitting contractors to inspect their own projects (Roger Turbaugh, personal communication, June 18, 2002).

The governor's "efficiency czar," Ruth Sykes, resigned in protest the day the bill was signed into law. She argued that she was unable to "slow down the headlong rush to privatize, computerize, and downsize" state jobs, a reckless process that lacked analysis or justification. As someone appointed to help Bush achieve his goals, she was especially concerned about Service First and its expansion of the employment-at-will doctrine to careerists. "I was 'at-will'. . . and you can't voice your opinion or be critical" in such an environment (Cotterell 2001c, 2A).

Even before passage of the final bill, high profile, questionable terminations and appointments began. "Just when the Bush Administration should be bending over backwards to dispel worries about cronyism," one editorial page observed, "(these actions) appear to lend credence to that concern" ("DMS Hiring Smacks of Tone Deafness" 2001, 11; see also, "Nepotism? If It Walks Like a Duck . . ." 2001). In summary, Service First, as an effort to deregulate and limit the size of government, built upon contemporary federal and state trends (Condrey and Maranto 2001; Coggburn 2001). It stemmed from business interests, who some claimed were uncomfortable with having to compete with a large government employer that offered benefits and job security. The governor's program, however, was called into question by its scanty background research, legislative maneuvering, as well as related events during and at the end of the legislative session. Nevertheless, traditional civil service job protections of middle managers were eliminated.

Service First Reforms and Success Indicators

This section examines key provisions of Service First: employee rights; recruitment and selection; compensation and classification; performance evaluation; education, training, and development; and organizational changes. This is followed by a discussion of metrics under development to gauge the performance of reform.

Employee Rights

The most contentious part of the reform was the movement of a substantial number of Career Service (CS) personnel to Selected Exempt Service (SES). In an attempt to achieve greater accountability for managers, supervisors, and confidential employees, the new law shifted 16,300 such employees from Career Service into the

Selected Exempt Service (the preexisting cap on both SES and SMS positions was lifted). Those transferred became at-will personnel as no cause is required for suspensions, demotions, or dismissals; adverse actions are unlawful only if they violate civil rights laws (the state is immune from many such suits) or other employment laws (e.g., whistleblower statutes), and individuals must access the courts for redress.

For those remaining in Career Service, Service First instituted changes in appeal rights and processes, layoff "bumping" rights, and the probationary period. An employee who is suspended, demoted, dismissed or has his/her pay reduced may still appeal to the agency head, appeal the agency decision to the Public Employee Relations Commission (PERC), and appeal the Commission's ruling to the District Courts of Appeal. The Commission is under newly established constraints in processing cases: it must decide cases within shortened time limits, it may not consider information from prior cases or other sets of facts, and it cannot reduce the severity of an agency's disciplinary action. In addition, the Commission can no longer award a prevailing employee attorney fees—a policy likely to discourage appeals.

Furthermore, Career Service personnel who are laid off or transferred can no longer appeal these actions to PERC (such appeals have traditionally been small in number and seldom successful) as the agency head has final say on all grievances not related to dismissal, suspension, demotion, or reduced pay. New rules also do not allow for retention based on seniority. The practice of bumping (a laid-off senior employee can bump a junior employee from his position) is prohibited. Furthermore, the term "layoff" is broadened to include privatizing or outsourcing of career staff. In addition, when career service staff move to another agency, they lose job tenure and are placed on one-year probation (when they are promoted into the SES, their preexisting protections are also eliminated). As a result of these changes, long-term Career Service workers have reason to question their job security.

In short, the reforms may enhance organizational efficiency (by allowing the state to dismiss or lay off staff more quickly), but it remains to be seen whether such gains offset the corresponding forfeiture of employee protections. There will no longer be a thorough and thoughtful review of a range of legitimate grievances.[6] The greatest loss was felt by those whose appeal rights were eliminated; the eradication of seniority rights in layoffs was also a significant deprivation. Although the above personnel policy changes represent a diminution of state employee rights, reformers suggest that corresponding benefits (e.g., free health insurance) make them desirable from an employee as well as an organizational perspective (see compensation and benefits section). Critics are less sanguine since SES employees in the past received better pay to make up for the loss of job security; those transferred into the SES received only free insurance (since the cost was not foreseen, this put a strain on the insurance trust fund).

Recruitment and Selection

The needs of organizations and individuals are well served by an efficient, simple recruitment and selection process. When hiring time lags result in loss of talent as candidates pursue other job opportunities, both the state and the applicant lose out. This had been a problem in prereform Florida, where it took 60 days on average to hire a career service employee with a minimum hiring time of 45 days. Service First streamlines the hiring process and enhances agency head discretion.

By reducing recruitment time and complexity, reformers believe administrative costs can be decreased and productivity increased. For instance, prior to Service First considerable documentation was compiled on job candidates: eligibility determination, applicant demographic profiles, documentation of interviews, and candidate ratings based on each selection tool used. Now, the only documentation mandated is a written rationale demonstrating that the recommended person is qualified and satisfies job requirements; minimum qualifications are no longer required. This eliminates the voluminous paperwork previously compiled on all eligible individuals; application material is needed only for the final candidate.

Completion of a single document is intended to reduce hiring time to a few days after a brief period of advertising. While candidates must meet minimum qualifications, rules that selection procedures be based on adequate job analysis and valid/objective criteria have been dropped. In addition, vendors may now assist recruitment. Finally, the reform extends the Career Service probationary period from six months to one year.

Compensation / Classification

The streamlining theme is also reprised in compensation and classification. The law curtails the need to reclassify employees (due to "broad-banding")[7] and promises managerial flexibility to reward employees (by offering additional salary inducements and bonuses). There is no provision that compensation be market-based, but "competitive pay differentials" and "critical market pay" may be available. The Department of Management Services (DMS) developed a new classification and compensation system, reducing 32,343 job classes (positions with similar kinds of work were grouped into classes) to 145 broad-banded classification levels (jobs in the same occupational group are assigned to a broad level). As might be expected, this process was not without difficulties (Figure 7.1). Indeed, broad-banding tends to increase payroll costs, diminish promotion opportunities, and expose agencies to federal Equal Pay Act of 1963 violations unless policies exist detailing the method of pay progression within the band.

Employees were previously eligible for the Meritorious Awards Program if their ideas resulted in increased productivity or revenues or decreased costs (award amounts were capped and token funds for employee recognition were provided). The Savings Sharing Plan (a gain-sharing initiative) replaced this program and authorizes

Figure 7.1 Broad-Banding Under Service First

> "Broadbanding won't raise or lower anybody's pay. Their jobs will be moved, laterally, into corresponding rungs of the new organizational ladder. But in the spirit of Service First, it will make it easier for agencies to 'adjust' salaries when they need to. The idea is to make it possible for people to move up without moving out. . .
>
> One department personnel director said pay grades 18 through 22 were, for instance, collapsed into one band. . . (S)o the new range was $26,977 to $55,184. . . But employees are worried that broadbanding will let a favored few soar up the pay scale. Experience with bonuses has not exactly convinced everyone that merit is measured, much less rewarded.
>
> Many state workers are concerned that broadbanding will mean the newly hired will languish even lower than before. They figure the state wants to hire them cheap, keep them three to five years and give out performance bonuses instead of performance pay raises" (Cotterell, 2002: 1B).
>
> Such speculation aside, the banding process "is turning into a disaster," according to a university observer. "For example, a lot of the work was done by people not knowledgeable in the various areas of work by just collapsing previous KSAs (knowledge, skill, and ability categories) into broadbands. . . Some examples would be humorous if they were not so stupid. To be in a computer network band, you have to have firearms proficiency and programmers have to know stenography" (anonymous personal communication, June 15, 2002).

awards to CS and SES employees and work units when improvements reduce or eliminate expenditures. While there is no cap, the Legislative Budget Commission must approve all awards and monetary compensation. The Commission also receives budget amendment submissions from agency heads, which can result in an agency retaining at least 20 percent of salary monies saved due to elimination of positions. The state awards recognition program was eliminated as was the purchase of lunch for honorees at the annual Davis Productivity Award banquet (the actual awards, which go up to $2,000 and represented $500 million in savings during 2001, are privately funded).

The legislation authorizes a bonus program as well, a provision envisioned by the governor as a substitute for salary raises. Peer input must account for at least 40 percent in determining awards (agency plans outlining eligibility criteria vary widely in definition of peer group, confidentiality, and participation rules). No more than 35 percent of a department's staff can receive bonuses unless this cap is waived by the Office of Policy and Budget (OPB). The 2001 and 2002 legislature appropriated a small fraction of the bonus monies requested by the governor to make the program viable (historically, lawmakers have questioned why employees should be given extra funds for doing what they are supposed to do). The statute does not provide minimum or maximum annual bonus amounts; agencies' guidelines range from $250 to $5,000. One department limits the program to 15 percent of employees due to limited resources. Another provided 18 percent of its staff with $500 bonuses.

Cash payouts of unused annual leave (maximum 24 hours) are authorized for Career Service employees on an annual basis conditioned on available funds (the payout reduces an individual's terminal annual leave payment). Eligibility requires that individuals have an available leave balance remaining of no fewer than 24 hours. Finally, the Department of Management Services is authorized to implement a tax-sheltered plan and regulations for depositing leave payments of employees separated from state government (an employee who is over 55 with 10 or more years of service must roll over his/her leave payouts into a tax-sheltered account).

Broad-banding, increased managerial discretion, gainsharing, performance bonuses, and cash leave payments potentially benefit both individuals and organizations. There is little evidence that the resulting programs were informed by past experience or existing literature documenting common problems that are often encountered (Kellough and Lu 1993; Gabris 1998; Berman et al. 2001). Purported benefits hinge on employee trust that administrative discretion will be exercised wisely, that resources will be adequate, and that rewards will be allocated fairly.

Performance Evaluation

The appraisal program was renamed the "Public Employee Performance Evaluation System" and provides a basis for bonuses. Service First policy for Career Service staff stipulates that employees must be evaluated at least annually (the governor prefers semiannual reviews and some agencies have followed suit), must be provided with a written copy of the appraisal, and they may receive an action plan indicating performance expectations.

The focus is shifted from promotions and dismissals to knowledge of weak and strong points in performance, training needs, and bonuses. Appraisals must be linked to job descriptions. If an employee falls short of performance standards, the agency head can exercise discretion in taking appropriate action. Once again, the design and implementation of these systems appear to overlook well-documented problems usually experienced by such programs (see, e.g., Berman et al. 2001).

Education, Training, and Development

Service First originally replaced tuition waivers for work-related classes with vouchers so that fees to learning institutions (community colleges, public technical centers, public universities) would be paid in full. Approval for participation was based on criteria allowing a downsized employee to take a course that might qualify him/her for another position. Since the program was little utilized (one class is unlikely to qualify someone for a new job), the 2002 legislature reinstated the fee waiver system. The new legislation provides for a professional development program for those in the Senior Management Service (SMS). It includes skill-building to enhance team leadership, strategic planning, employee-organization relationships, and individual-group performance improvement. Consideration is given to such topics as motivation, pay incentives, performance measurement, program planning, reengineering, and productivity improvement. Basic supervisory training was eliminated.

Organizational Changes

Service First organizational changes, summarized here, have less to do with changes affecting individual employees and more to do with altering existing institutional structures and processes. First, the PERC is transferred to the Department of Management Service from the Department of Labor and Employment Security (which has been privatized). It retains its collective bargaining jurisdiction and role in handling unfair labor practice charges; however, Service First alters the way PERC processes appeals of personnel actions by career service employees, responds to veterans preference requests, and deals with collective bargaining impasses.

Second, collective bargaining impasse resolution timelines are shortened to no more than ten days prior to the legislative session. The legislature must be notified of unresolved impasses within five days of their occurrence with each party specifying the issues in contention. A joint select committee is then appointed and recommends a resolution of all issues within specific time limits. Finally, the legislature acts on the recommended resolution (the mediator or special master, as noted, is no longer part of the impasse resolution process); its action is binding on the parties.[8]

Third, to assist with implementation of Service First, a four-person Career Service Advisory Group was to be formed to advise the Governor's Office and DMS on issues related to the new law. The group, which was not established, was to be composed of human resource officials from Florida companies appointed by the governor, the senate president, and the speaker of the house. DMS, however, consulted with leading corporations in the state as needed.

Success Indicators

How will policy makers know if Service First is performing as planned? An effort will be needed to document and evaluate changes in performance and productivity of employees and work units resulting from the program. First, Bush Administration legal and human resource management representatives suggest that both subjective and objective data can be collected (personal communications with Kathleen Anders, January 14, 2002; Michael Mattimore, September 14, 2001; Fran Brooks, May 2, 2002). They allude to a belief that at-will employees will be more engaged and will take more pride in their work than before; accordingly, managers will report that staff is better able to do their jobs.

Second, as part of its oversight function, the legislature may commission an initial audit of Service First in the near future, although in 2003 the governor recommended downsizing and consolidation of audit agencies. The governor's office, third, is creating measures that may include cost of services, customer satisfaction, productivity, and turnover data. Other metrics may include time savings in recruitment, results from the new probationary period, the volume of SES terminations, grievance process outcomes, employee views of performance appraisal system, and numbers of Savings Sharing recommendations. Overall, Florida Taxwatch (2000), the business-sponsored "watchdog" organization, has put forth these principles to evaluate Service First: managerial accountability for results, development of a workplace culture for employee growth, competitive compensation, career advancement tied to performance measures, ability of managers to reward meritorious performance, and a flexible defined contribution benefit system. Clearly there will be a transition period before Service First can be fully assessed.

To summarize this section, while some SES employees may welcome promised benefit and award provisions, they have lost job security, employee rights, and protection from political interference. It is not clear at this time that Floridians will derive higher quality, lower cost, or more accountable services as a result of this reform.

Service First as Public Policy

Florida's reforms are an attempt to apply a business model to government. Instead of emphasizing the positive aspects of this strategy (e.g., competitive pay), lawmakers eliminated a positive aspect of government employment (i.e., job security) and instituted the private sector at-will employment concept common in nonunionized companies. The lead researcher for the Council of One Hundred indicated that the Council membership, Taxwatch, and Department of Management Services reportedly all understood that Service First would fail without adequate compensation (Keith Baker, personal communication, March 1, 2002; also see Florida Taxwatch 2000). Yet no strategy was developed to address the state's historic practice of not only paying below market but also failing to provide full cost-of-living adjustments (in effect, routinely approving annual pay cuts).

Government has traditionally justified public-private salary differentials on the grounds of employee job security—which Service First abolished for some 16,300 personnel.[9] State service is now defined for these middle managers as just another job in one's "port-folio"; it is no longer a career, much less a calling. Yet government needs dedicated career public servants to help ensure that children are educated, foster care is provided, taxes are collected, public health is protected, elections are conducted, businesses compete fairly, environmental quality is secured, and so on—unglamorous, but vital tasks that the profit-making sector cannot or will not per-form. As the terrorist events of 9/11/01 so poignantly demonstrated, "(P)ublic service is not . . . essentially an economic transaction; it requires a principled culture of professional responsibility and spe-cialized expertise that merits trusted exercise of the awesome authority of constitutional democracy" (Newland 2002, 645). When the *raison d'etre* of public service disappears,[10] according to Special Master Mark Sherman (personal communication, October 23, 2001), little remains to keep civil servants from fleeing to higher paying opportunities in business.

If a documented need for change was absent and the reform adopted emphasizes the negative part of the corporate model, then how is it that Service First was enacted into law? Beginning with Ponce de Leon's quest for the Fountain of Youth, Florida always has been fertile soil for myths such as the unquestioned assumption of reformers that the private sector is inherently superior to govern-ment (Rainey 2003). Secondly, Service First reflects a deeply held tenet of the political right: since government is a necessary evil, most public employees are a subtraction from the commonweal. Third, one party controlled the government and therefore had the power to act. Next, due to recently enacted term limits, more than one-third of legislators were vulnerable, freshmen lawmakers, inexperienced in lawmaking, with little legislative institutional knowledge or policy background in state government. Finally, Service First, because of its very boldness, developed a momentum of its own that neither rational argument nor political opposition could stop. Pandering to imagined public obsessions with feel-good law and cheap legislative victories can be intoxicating. "This too is part of the democratic republic," in the words of one legislative staffer who requested anonymity.

The program was prompted by the belief that private sector employment practices (Florida Taxwatch 2000: Florida Council of One Hundred 2000), not fraudulent accounting practices and illegal insider trading, nurtured the ballyhooed New Economy of the 1990s. Abolishing civil service job tenure was seen as key to making gov-ernment more business-like, thereby ameliorating the stultifying effects of public employment. Yet laissez-faire, fire-at-will personnel policies have little to do with positive economic performance (Werhane 1999), charges about the difficulty of terminating career employees are not borne out by the facts (Gertz 2001; see also, Kaufman 2002), and corporations are moving away from employment at-will (Martucci and Place 2000). The attempt to use this employment doctrine in government, virtually unknown in the developed world outside of some American businesses, is best described as a solution in search of a problem.

As such, radical reforms like Service First are exhibits of the degraded state of political debate—that is, how problems are approached and just what constitutes a public policy problem. The reform ideology of today has less to do with its actual validity than the harsh realities of American commerce and raw political clout. That power is aimed at the civil service as a diversion from, and substitute for, real social and economic issues such as campaign finance reform, education, health care, or tax reform (Bowman 2002). In a classic example of the "wrong problem" problem, reformers would have citizens believe that problems confronting government are administrative in character. Root causes of problems in the state system are political, not administrative: arbitrary employee cuts, highly paid appointees with few duties, relentless political pressures to hire unqualified workers, poor pay and benefits for career employees. By claiming to increase public confidence in government by removing civil service protections, reformers actually risk the opposite by inviting patronage, graft, and corruption.[11] An aggressively ahistorical, "see-no-evil" approach, Service First is ill-informed reform.

Future of Service First

Insofar as such things can be readily documented, it is interesting that apparently there has not been widespread abuse to date.[12] This may not be surprising considering the embarrassment caused by early cases and lawsuits. There is also a practical difficulty of quickly hiring large numbers of people in a downsizing era. Added to this is the problem of recruiting businesspeople willing to work for state salaries, to say nothing of dealing with government ethics laws. Finally, the capable performance of most civil servants and enduring public service values no doubt are important factors. For all these reasons, some "cronies" and term-limited legislators (soon-to-be consultants and lobbyists) may be more interested in government contracts and political campaign consultancies than old-style bureaucratic job patronage.

An important issue, however, is what happens in coming years as privatization continues, institutional memories fade, and public service values dissipate. Indeed, even under the merit system,

> (P)ublic servants are demoralized when they see appoint-ments made mainly for political reasons . . . (and) the gov-ernment's workforce is debased . . . as (p)atronage insidiously attacks the best government employees (when) they see the mission obscured by political considerations. . . Cynicism, resentment, and resignation are the sure results." (New York Commission on Government Integrity, quoted in Freedman 1994, 182)

With a plan like Service First—which dramatically increases the number of personnel subject to political appointment, interference and/or replacement—these consequences are all but predictable, especially in the aftermath of elections. Indeed at one agency, 65 employees were summarily terminated and immediately escorted from the premises; the department secretary indicated that he had no problem with the forced resignations: "I think that we handled it well" (Lauer 2002, 1). The very capacity of government to protect its own integrity was further placed at risk by two recent events: the governor's second inaugural speech pledging to "make these (state office) buildings around us empty of workers" (Twiddy 2003, 1) and the targeting for elimination or drastic reduction of two key auditing agencies designed to protect against corruption and waste (Lauer 2003, 1).

Will Service First itself be expanded beyond supervisory, mana-gerial, and confidential employees?[13] There are quite different pre-dictions from knowledgeable sources inside and outside of state government. One view held by a diverse group—the governor's labor relations attorney, a union negotiator, an agency personnel chief, a taxpayer organization representative, and an agency senior man-ager—is that Bush got much of what he wanted and the policy focus has shifted elsewhere (personal communications, respectively, with Michael Mattimore, September 14, 2001; Stephen Kreisberg, January 10, 2002; Fran Brooks, May 10, 2002; Keith Baker, March 1, 2002; William Ellis, December 13, 2001).

While there may be piecemeal reforms in the offing, the overall system is currently operative and the issue is simply not important enough to warrant the expenditure of political capital necessary to spread the program throughout the civil service. Indeed, the privatization of the state's entire personnel function by the 2002 legislature facilitates patronage hiring without enlarging Service First. That is, the new private contract employees administering the hiring process, who lack job security and a public service ethos, are not as likely as career civil servants to vigorously enforce merit-based employment standards in the face of political pressure. Too, this reform is expected to take one-half of the time needed to hire an applicant (partly because of the deletion of documentation requirements demonstrating why competing candidates were not selected). Taken together, these developments may interact in ways to significantly damage what remains of the career service.

Responses from another disparate collection of interviewees—a prominent senior Tallahassee attorney and former long-time legislator, the state government columnist, and a university state employee trainer—suggest a different view on the future of Service. The reelection of Mr. Bush presents an opportunity to fulfill the Council of One Hundred's goal to make all state employees at-will (personal communications, respectively, with Mallory Horne, September 19, 2001; Bill Cotterell, September 16, 2001; Howard Rassmussen, February 19, 2002). The political attractiveness of reducing job rights is illustrated by two recent developments. In 2000 all state purchasing agents were made personally responsible for increasing minority procurement awards as part of the governor's One Florida initiative that superceded the state affirmative action program. And in 2002 a blue ribbon panel convened to investigate the Rilya Wilson foster childcare scandal, recommended, as part of a special legislative session, that all 23,000 Department of Children and Families employees be stripped of career service covenants.[14] In short, Service First is part of a larger strategy to limit government; if the executive branch cannot literally be cut 25 percent in a rapidly growing state, then its services can be privatized and its protections for remaining employees circumscribed.[15]

Conclusion

The old oracle said, "All things have two handles: beware of the wrong one." The difficulty, of course, is deciding which is which. The civil service reform debate in Florida and elsewhere is over how government can best meet the challenges of the new millennium.

Reformers hold that government today should not be encumbered by dated merit systems and advocate the employment-at-will doctrine. Critics fear that destroying the merit system reinvents the corrupt spoils system of the 19th century—the last time government used at-will employment.

There is reason to believe, based on historical experience, that political appointees will use their short-term jobs to position themselves for corporate opportunities when they leave public service. "There is a significant difference, " writes Charles Gossett, "between grooming one's self for a position in a . . . merit-based career system and getting ready to move" on (2002, 103). He further observes:

> (O)ne can anticipate that as the state's elected executive branch offices change hands, there will be pressure not only to make changes in policy-making positions . . . but to reward supporters with jobs at lower levels. The ability to resist requests . . . , assuming the elected official was inclined to resist such pressure, will be more difficult inasmuch as he or she lacks the ability to refer to the 'rules' that prevent an unqualified or less qualified supporter from being appointed or promoted. (2002, 105)

A tradition, nonetheless, might develop wherein the election cycle does not significantly affect the workforce. Also, patronage appointments may be self-limiting since incompetent workers may reflect badly on those who selected them. This scenario, however, needlessly exposes the public service to political favoritism, retaliation, intimidation, and corruption while ignoring political advantages of rewarding campaign workers, friends, and relatives with government sinecures. The impending baby boom retirement exodus from public service, plus the lack of a statutory limitation on the number of selected exempt positions, suggests that there will be no shortage of opportunities in the near future.[16] An apt reform strategy would be preventive in nature; instead, by permitting ample room for mischief, Service First is at best an after-the-fact corrective, one predicated on scandal. Such a premeritocratic approach—masquerading as modern management—is an execrable policy for government whose purpose is to champion and protect the public, not partisan, interest.

Like the reformers of yesteryear, those of today believed that government should be run like a business. The difference is that merit system advocates sought to do so by keeping the spoilsmen out, while Service First supporters—with rampant arrogance, simplistic nostrums, and disdain for public service—invite them in. The program, as a result, contains the seeds of its own destruction. Some day reformers will be held accountable for any corruption that their changes spawn.

Notes

The authors are grateful to Russell L. Williams, Henry Thompson, Sandy deLopez, and an anonymous state manager for their comments on a draft of this chapter.

1. It was subsequently judged a failure due to conflicting objectives, loss of gubernatorial interest, stakeholder resistance, inadequate training, administrative restructuring, and limited resources (Weschler 1993, 1994; Chackerian and Mavima 2001).

2. These promises apparently stemmed from an ideology based on a romanticized image of the business model—an image inconsistent with the governor's own business ventures, surging corporate crime, commercial bankruptcies, and corrupt government contractors. The stereotype would lead Bush to use inexpensive self-service Wal-Mart stores and the expensive Disney World entertainment park as models for state government.

3. Staffed by Florida Taxwatch, the researchers visited Georgia but were unable to examine evaluations of that state's 1996 reform because of a pressing deadline (for a scholarly version, see Kellough and Nigro 2002). The 32-page report (including appendices) was prepared by an Atlanta consulting firm. One long-time national observer of state government described the effort as "comical" and a local newspaper letter to the editor called it "sophomoric." The Council did not meet to discuss or approve the document.

4. Like Georgia (Gossett 2002), and in the absence of systematic studies, such claims were substantiated with undocumented anecdotes (Bowman 2002). In addition, the governor's office later solicited some 7,000 state employee e-mails, most of which dealt with technical questions about the proposal.

5. Source materials include: Senate Bill 466, Summary of Service First as passed by the Florida Legislature, Career Service and Selected Exempt Service Comparison, Effect of Changes Due to Senate Bill 466, Governor Bush Unveils "Service First," Service First Initiative, Senate Staff Analysis and Economic Impact Statement, and other documents (see http://www.myflorida.com/myflorida/servicefirst/documents/change_effect.doc).

6. American Federation of State, County, and Municipal Employees has requested hearings for a number of new SES employees who have been discharged, claiming that they were unlawfully reclassified into the SES, and were terminated without just cause. These individuals variously assert that

they were terminated because of false allegations of sexual harassment, requesting leave under the Family Medical Leave Act, mistakes by the agency's human resource department, personal animosity by a supervisor, and retaliation for prevailing in a previous disciplinary hearing. Unless the union succeeds in proving that these employees were unlawfully reclassified, these grievances will likely never be heard. See Benny Chestnut v. Department of Corrections, Case No. 01-0604 (Fla. 1st Dist. Ct. App.); Lori Cooper v. Department of Children and Family Services, Case No. 1D02-2375 (Fla. 1st Dist. Ct. App.); Robert Reinshuttle v. Agency for Health Care Administration, Case No. 1D02-1505 (Fla. 1st Dist. Ct. App); Barbara Watson v. Department of Children and Family Services, Case No. 1D02-1751 (Fla. 1st Dist. Ct. App.); Judith Jolly v. Department of Children and Family Services, Case No. 1D02-3504 (Fla. 1st Dist. Ct. App.); Ernest Barkley v. Department of Children and Family Services, Case No. 1D02-3511 (Fla. 1st Dist. Ct. App.)

7. Broad-banding shrinks job classifications by replacing very specific occupational series with broad job titles. This enhances managerial discretion to move employees up, down, or across work assignments without going through complex reclassification or promotion processes. Professional groups like the National Academy of Public Administration (1991, 1995a, 1995b) have long supported broad-banding, and Florida is not alone among the states pursing this reform strategy (Naff 2003).

8. Clearly, the enthusiasm to run government like a business did not extend to providing public employees with the right to strike, a common right enjoyed by private sector workers.

9. Historically, low public service salaries also have been partially offset by benefit programs reputed to be superior to those found in the private domain. When governments are compared to large corporations, not small companies, the advantages of such programs all but disappear.

10. This appears to already be a problem in the federal government, as an increasing number of civilian employees at the Defense Department "come to work solely for the paycheck" according to a recent Brookings Institution study (Robb 2002).

11. Indeed, at the federal level a national survey concluded that the "public's disappointment with the qualifications and motivations of presidential appointees may factor into Americans' distrust of government" ("Survey: Government Jobs Falling Out of Favor" 2001, 2).

12. This is not the case in neighboring Georgia where substantial changes have occurred (Condrey 2002; Lasseter 2002). Ironically, those more comprehensive reforms were not met with court challenges (Kuykendall and Facer 2002), while those in Florida have been confronted, so far unsuccessfully, with lawsuits (cf., note 6 above).

13. The next several paragraphs are drawn from Bowman, et al. (2002).

14. The seductiveness of terminating civil service protections is also evident at the federal level as the new airport security screeners (more than 67,000) were specifically exempted from career service protections as well as

from the full protections from the Whistle Blower Protection Act. The proposed Department of Homeland Security (with an estimated 170,000 employees) has similar provisions. Ironically, the lack of free speech safeguards may make citizens even more vulnerable to terrorism.

15. A recent statewide survey of recently converted SESers (Bowman et al. 2002), in fact, reveals they believe that: "a goal of Service First is to downsize government," the at-will coverage will expand to the rest of the civil service, and reform "will make government less productive."

16. In the last generation, the number of high political appointees has dramatically increased in the federal government. This well-documented "thickening" of government has resulted in a top-heavy, cumbersome bureaucracy that actually interferes with the achievement of the President's agenda (Light 1995). Florida has followed a similar path, one substantially widened by the passage of Service First.

References

Berman, E., Bowman, J., West, J., and Van Wart, M. (2001). *Human resource management in public service*. Thousand Oaks, California: Sage.

Bowman, J. (2002). "Employment At Will in Florida Government: A Naked Formula to Corrupt the Public Service." *WorkingUSA* 6 (2): 90–102.

Bowman, J., Gertz, S., Gertz, M., and Williams, R. (2003). "Civil Service Reform in Florida: State Employee Attitudes One Year Later." *Review of Public Personnel Administration* 23(4): 286–304.

Bush civil service plan victimizes state workers. (2001, March 9). *The News-Journal Corp* (Daytona Beach), 4A.

Chackerian, R., and Mavima, P. (2001). "Comprehensive Administration Reform Implementation: Moving Beyond Single Issue Implementation Research." *Journal of Public Administration Research and Theory* 11 (3): 353–377.

"Civil Service Reform for State Workers" (2001, March 16). *Miami Herald*, 8B.

"Civil-Service 'Reform' Just a Grab for Power" (2001, May 1). *The Palm Beach Post*, 14A.

Coggburn, J. (2001). "Personnel Deregulation: Exploring Differences in the American States." *Journal of Public Administration Research and Theory* 11 (2): 223–244.

Condrey, S. (2002). "Reinventing State Civil Service Systems: The Case of Georgia." *Review of Public Personnel Administration* 22: 114–124.

Condrey, S., and Maranto, R. (2001). *Radical reform of the civil service*. NY: Lexington Books.

Cotterell, B. (2001a, February 7). "Bracing for Change." *Tallahassee Democrat*, 1–2E.

Cotterell, B. (2001b, March 20). "House Speeds State Worker Bill." *Tallahassee Democrat*, 4B.

Cotterell, B. (2001c, May 15). "State 'Efficiency Czar Resigns In Protest." *Tallahassee Democrat*, 1–2A.

Cotterell, B. (2002, June 24). "'Broadbanded' Pay Categories a Lateral Change." Tallahassee Democrat, 1B.

"DMS Hiring Smacks of Tone Deafness" (2001, May 31). *Tallahassee Democrat*, 8A.

Dyckman, M. (2001). "From Construction to Deconstruction." *St. Petersburg Times* April 3: 3D.

Florida Council of One Hundred (2000). *Modernizing Florida's civil service system: moving from protection to performance.* (November). Tampa: The Council.

Florida House of Representatives, Committee on Administration (2001). *Staff analysis*, Bill 369, February 26.

Florida Taxwatch (2000). "Briefing: modernizing Florida's civil service: A necessary beginning for meaningful change." Tallahassee: Florida Tax Watch.

Freedman, A. (1994). *Patronage.* Chicago: Nelson-Hall.

Gabris, G. (1998). "Merit Pay Mania." In S. Condrey, ed., Handbook of human resource management in government (627–657). San Francisco: Jossey-Bass.

Gertz, S. (2001). "Florida's Civil Service Appeal Process: How 'Protective' Is It?" *Justice System Journal* 22: 117–135.

Gossett, C. (2002). "Civil Service Reform: The Case of Georgia." *Review of Public Personnel Administration* 22 (2): 94–113.

"Governor's Efficiency Expert Resigns." (2001, May 26). *St. Petersburg Times*, 1B.

Henderson, C. (2001). Speech before the Florida Personnel Association, Tallahassee, February 22.

Karl, F. (2000). "Frederick B. Karl Opinion." In Florida Council of One Hundred, *Modernizing Florida's civil service system* (25–28). Tampa: The Council.

Kaufman, T. (2002). "Managers' Reluctance, Not Rules, Deter Firings." *Federal Times*, February 4.

Kellough, E., and Lu, H. (1993). "The Paradox of Merit Pay." *Review of Public Personnel Administration* 12: 45–63.

Kellough, E., and Nigro, L. (2002). "Pay for Performance in Georgia State Government: Employee Perspectives on GeorgiaGain After Five Years." *Review of Public Personnel Administration* 22: 146–166.

Kuykendall, C. and Facer, R. (2002). "Public Employment in Georgia State Agencies: The Elimination of the Merit System." *Review of Public Personnel Administration* 22: 133–145.

Lasseter, R. (2002). "Georgia's Merit System Reform 1996–2001: An Operating Agency's Perspective." *Review of Public Personnel Administration* 22: 125–132.

Lauer, N. (2002). "Agency Firings Rankle Workers." *Tallahassee Democrat*, December 11, 1–2.

Lauer, N. (2003). "Gov. Bush Wants to Kill Two Watchdog Agencies." *Tallahassee Democrat,* January 29, 1, 5A.
"Legislature 2001" (2001, March 4). *The Palm Beach Post,* C1.
Light, P. (1995). *The thickening of government.* Washington, DC: Brookings.
Martucci, M., and Place, J. (2000). "Employment Law at the Dawn of the New Millennium." *Employment Relations Today* 26, 109–117.
Muhl. C. (2001). "The Employment-At-Will Doctrine: Three Major Exceptions." *Monthly Labor Review* 124 (1): 3–12.
Naff, K.C. (2003). "Why Managers Hate Position Classification." In S.W. Hays and R.C. Kearney, eds. *Public personnel administration: problems and prospects,* 126–153. Upper Saddle River, NJ: Prentice Hall.
National Academy of Public Administration (1991). *Modernizing federal classification: An opportunity for excellence.* Washington, DC: NAPA.
National Academy of Public Administration (1995a). *Modernizing federal classification: operational broadbanding systems alternatives.* Washington, DC: NAPA.
National Academy of Public Administration (1995b). *Alternatives for federal agencies: summary report.* Washington, DC: NAPA.
"Nepotism? If It Walks Like A Duck . . ." (2001, May 4). *Tallahassee Democrat,*
Newland, C. (2002). "Fanatical Terrorism Versus Disciplines of Constitutional Democracy." *Public Administration Review* 61 (6): 643–650.
Paterniti, M. (2002, April 21). "America In Extremis: How Florida Became the New California." *New York Times Magazine,* 28–35, 66, 74, 82.
Rainey, H. (2003). "Facing Fundamental Challenges in Reforming Public Personnel Administration." In S.W. Hays and K.C. Kearney, eds. *Public personnel administration: problems and prospects.* 4th ed. 334–351. Upper Saddle River, NJ: Prentice Hall.
Robb, K. (2002, July 1). "Post-Sept. 11 Morale Rises at DOD, Sags Elsewhere." *Federal Times,* 1, 9.
"Sounding a false alarm" (2001, April 6). *Miami Herald,* 8B.
"State Government: Improving Service." *Jacksonville Times-Union* (February 3, 2001): www.jacksonville.com/tu-online/stories/020301opi_5300845.html (accessed on June 25, 2001).
Special Master Report. (2001). *In the matter of fact finding between the state of Florida and the American federation of state, county, and municipal employees council 79 Hearings and Special Master Recommendations,* March 12–14 (Tallahassee, FL).
"Survey: Government Jobs Falling Out of Favor" (2001, September 10). *Federal Times,* 2.
Troxler, H. (2001). "Democrats Resemble Whiners, Not Winners." *St. Petersburg Times* April 16, 1B.
Twiddy, D. (2003). "Governor Repeats Theme of Less Government." *Tallahassee Democrat,* January 8, 1–2A.
Wechsler, B. (1993). "Florida's Civil Service Reform." *Spectrum: The Journal of State Government* 66 (1): 45–51.
Wechsler, B. (1994). "Reinventing Florida's Civil Service System: The

Failure of Reform." *Review of Public Personnel Administration* 14 (2): 64–76.

Werhane, P. (1999). "Justice and Trust." *Journal of Business Ethics 21*: 237–249.

West, J. (2002). "Georgia on the Mind of Radical Civil Service Reformers." *Review of Public Personnel Administration* 21, 2: 79–93.

CHAPTER 8

South Carolina's Human Resource Management System: The Model for States with Decentralized Personnel Structures

Steven W. Hays
Chris Byrd
Samuel L. Wilkins

For a state that has seldom emerged as an icon in any area of public management, South Carolina's accomplishments in the field of Human Resource Management (HRM) appear at first glance to be stunning and dramatic. Beginning with the adoption of the State Government Accountability Act of 1993, in less than a decade the state's civil service system was transformed from a relatively archaic operation to one that is applauded by numerous external professional groups as a reinvention paragon.

The list of accolades bestowed on the revised HRM system is truly impressive. Perhaps the most celebrated examples are the two rankings by *Governing Magazine* in which South Carolina received the *highest* rating of all states in 1999 and 2001. In 1999 the Office of Human Resources (OHR) was the only state personnel agency to receive an A– (the highest score assigned during that evaluation cycle) (Barrett and Greene 1999, 77). At that time, the magazine reported that the state was engaged in "stem to stern" personnel management reform (*Governing* 1999, 24). Two years later, the State again finished as the "# 1" ranked HRM system among the fifty states (Barrett and Greene 2001, 34). South Carolina earned the only A ranking, and was (as our chapter title connotes) proclaimed the "model for states with a decentralized personnel structure" (Barrett and Greene 2001, 94). This recognition has been expanded and reinforced by several other professional groups. For example, the state won a Rooney Award for HRM innovations from the National Association of State Personnel Executives (NASPE) and the

171

International Personnel Management Association (IPMA) (1997). Two years later it received the IPMA Agency Award for Excellence in a Large Agency (1999). That same year, South Carolina was singled out for special praise by *Public HR* magazine. Meanwhile, many individual components of the state's reform agenda—such as alternative dispute resolution and the agency head evaluation process—received national attention from a variety of "good government" and "best practices" studies (Center for the Study of Social Policy 2002). The State's prominence as a hotbed of HR reform has led other states to seek advice and counsel from the S.C. OHR on such topics as broad-banding, HR partnering with client agencies, and the operation of decentralized employee incentive systems. States as diverse as Idaho, Florida, New York, New Jersey, Oklahoma, Virginia, and Wyoming have either emulated parts of the South Carolina HR agenda, or sought advice on how to do so.

The primary purposes of this chapter are to describe South Carolina's approach to HR reform, to delineate its many programmatic components, and to chronicle the factors that have made these initiatives possible. A secondary goal is to provide a status report on the reform process to date, and to assess the extent to which changes in HRM law and procedure have penetrated state agencies. Another important theme is to address whether or not the HR changes that have occurred in South Carolina are transportable to other jurisdictions that display different structural, legal, and/or labor-management characteristics. Finally, the ongoing process of HR reform is analyzed in the contemporary context of budget constraints, fiscal crises, and government downsizing. Both potential and actual shortcomings of the reform experience are addressed in the final section of the chapter.

Historical Antecedents

One of the more surprising aspects of the South Carolina HRM story is that no personnel "system" existed in any form prior to 1968. Up until that year, HRM was almost entirely left up to each individual agency. This meant that there was no standardized job terminology, salary schedule, or even a regularized set of vacation days. Each agency was responsible for its own HR practices, a fact that resulted in wild variations between and among public organizations in South Carolina. Some tried to adhere (more or less) to a semblance of a "merit system" through the use of selection exams and other niceties, while others essentially existed as the personal fiefdoms of whoever was in charge at a particular time. The only major exception to this extraordinarily decentralized approach to HR was, of course, the requirement that employees working in federally funded programs be managed through merit procedures, including competitive examinations, "for cause" discipline, and adherence to the general dictates of equal employment opportunity.

Due to the problems stemming from the absence of a coherent set of personnel policies—especially insofar as pay and EEO expectations were concerned—the State Personnel Division was established by the Budget and Control Board in order to create and administer a classification and compensation system in 1968. In addition to promoting "equal pay for equal work," the Personnel Division was charged with the responsibility of establishing operating procedures for classified employees. In so doing, the state "sought to devise a means for determining the relative worth of jobs, compensating individual employees accordingly, and ensuring that equity among positions in the classified service was developed and maintained" (Office of Human Resources 1995, 1). Ultimately, the Personnel Division created a complex array of job classifications, standardized employee benefits, established centralized record keeping, and implemented the basic elements of a traditional merit system. Interestingly enough, though, the formal merit system never applied to more than 11 of the 120-plus state agencies that once existed. Almost all of the agencies that fell under the merit system were those that were compelled to do so by federal law (i.e., large portions of their labor forces were employed in federal programs and paid through various forms of grants-in-aid). Only a tiny number of agencies—such as the Personnel Division—*voluntarily* became part of the centralized merit system. As such, South Carolina has never had comprehensive merit coverage, a fact that probably is very significant in furthering the current HRM reform movement. Without the bureaucratic obstacles attendant to an entrenched merit system (e.g., civil service commissions, heavy involvement by the state legislature in setting personnel policy, and volumes of highly bureaucratic procedures), there were fewer impediments to change than exist in states with long traditions of centralized merit operations.

Another indication of the recency of HR "reform" in the state is the fact that no standardized approach to resolving labor-management disputes existed before 1971. As a strong "right to work" state that does not recognize collective bargaining among civil servants, South Carolina has always been an inhospitable environment for labor unions. Indeed, fear of unionization was a (or perhaps *the*) primary contributor to passage of the State Employee Grievance Act in 1971. Stirred to action by an American Federation of State, County, and Municipal Employees (A.F.S.C.M.E.) effort to unionize disgruntled workers at the Medical University of South Carolina, the general assembly finally granted employees a legal right to challenge adverse actions. Even after creating grievance rights for its workers, however, the state restricted the definition of adverse action to include only the most obvious forms of employee complaints (demotions, terminations, involuntary reassignments, etc.). Unlike the federal government and many other states, employees could not (and cannot) grieve such matters as "terms of employment," salary, classification, and supervisory behavior. Obviously, the absence of any union presence in the South Carolina work environment, coupled with legal restrictions on the workers' ability to challenge supervisory decisions, simplified the process of introducing sweeping civil service reform. Without any organized opposition from labor unions, public employee input into the characteristics of the system reforms was somewhat limited.

By the early 1990s, South Carolina's personnel system contained a complex mixture of centralized and decentralized characteristics. The State Personnel Division—which had been renamed the Office of Human Resources (OHR)—supervised a salary and classification structure that contained nearly 2,500 job classes and 50 pay grades. Although most agencies were not part of the merit system, the OHR provided single point-of-entry recruitment for many of the labor-intensive job classifications. Civil service examinations were administered centrally, as was the authorization and approval of most reclassification requests and efforts to create new job titles or classes. And, as was true in most other locations, salary increases could only be granted according to cost-of-living adjustments and related appropriations from the general assembly. Performance-based salary enhancements were not technically part of the salary system. To reward and/or retain valued employees, managers were forced to either promote them to higher positions or to seek reclassifications on the grounds that their job duties had changed (leading to the age-old problem of "grade creep").

On the eve of administrative reform, the state's approach to HRM was generally regarded as being "unresponsive to contemporary needs" (Office of Human Resources 1995, 2). The litany of problems is so well-known and widespread that it requires little treatment here. A general consensus seemed to exist that centrally administered tests were inadequate predictors of job performance; agencies experienced excessive delays in filling vacancies; the salary structure was inflexible and contributed to attrition of the most valued workers; job classifications were confusing and unwieldy; and supervisors were unduly inhibited in the use of their employees' talents. Even though it was one of the most fragmentary and least centralized civil services in the country, South Carolina's approach to HRM exhibited most of the ailments that plague merit systems in far more traditional settings.

Catalysts and "Explanations" for HRM Reform

As was mentioned above, the HRM reform bandwagon began rolling more quickly with the passage of the State Government Accountability Act of 1993. To help place this piece of legislation in context, one can simply refer to the "reinvention" literature and its primary goals for modern public personnel systems. As articulated in the National Performance Review (NPR) programs at the federal level, government staffing activities were targeted for the following types of reforms during the early 1990s (U.S. General Accounting Office 1994):

- Empower line managers to make as many staffing decisions as feasible
- Abolish central job registers and application processes; decentralize hiring decisions to the operational level
- Eliminate procedural restrictions on the assignment, reassignment, transfer, and appointment of public workers
- Enhance the ability of public managers to reward and motivate their subordinates; emphasize flexibility in pay administration and classification systems, including the use of pay for performance strategies
- Strengthen the ability of public managers to purge their organizations of poor performers by reducing the number of steps needed to terminate workers; improve the operation of progressive discipline procedures by making supervisory decisions less susceptible to legal challenge.

The similarity between this list of reform goals and the content of the State Government Accountability Act is striking. Although the Act was passed without fanfare, it transformed the manner in which HRM is conducted in the state, and essentially makes South Carolina—for better or worse—a "poster child" for the reinvention agenda.

A complex stew of factors undoubtedly contributed to the state's willingness to embrace HRM reform. Some of the most critical factors relate to the changing nature of South Carolina's political culture and institutions during recent decades (see Hays and Whitney 1997). For its entire history (dating back to the Colonial Period), politics in the state were characterized by legislative domination and a weak executive branch. Recent political developments, however, have gradually altered the balance of power in state government. Like many states of the old confederacy, South Carolina's political establishment has become increasingly Republican in recent years. Republicans held the governor's mansion for more than a decade, and won control of the lower house of the general assembly during the 1992 general elections (subsequently, the upper house shifted to the Republicans when a Democratic Senator changed his party affiliation in 2001). As the state's political leadership became more economically conservative, the vocabulary of reinvention gained currency in legislative debates. Privatization, cost cutting, and enhanced efficiency became watchwords of political campaigns throughout both local and statewide elections. These sentiments ultimately found expression in a move toward the cabinet form of executive governance. After two centuries of highly fragmented, commission-based public administration, the state consolidated much executive power during the 1990s by placing a considerable number of agencies directly under the governor's control.

With these significant structural changes in place, the trend toward consolidated control and decentralization slowed with the election of a Democratic governor in 1998, but the seeds of reform—especially bureaucratic modernization—continued to bear fruit. The impact of the 2002 elections, in which the Republicans regained control of the governor's mansion and now dominate both the executive and legislative branches, have not yet been played out. As this chapter is being written, the new political regime is considering proposals that would remove career protections from additional classes of state workers, thereby transforming a significant percentage of the workforce into "at-will" employees. This action is symptomatic of what we are likely to experience in the near future—growing enthusiasm for even more decentralization and "flexibility" within the public workforce.

In the context of a fundamental reconfiguration of both the political and structural components of state government, reinvention appears to have emerged as a logical complement. During the early and mid-1990s—when the Republicans were ascendant and controlled the governor's mansion and one house of the general assembly—most of the state's politicians had an interest in consolidating power. Once the Republican governor's authority over additional state agencies was secure, he and his supporters obviously saw advantages in giving the newly appointed managers the requisite tools to implement their policies. Reinvention's emphasis on government efficiency and political accountability, and its fixation on executive accountability for public policy, dovetailed nicely with much of the emerging political agenda.

It is important to note, meanwhile, that HRM reform probably arose more from the political scenario described above than from any underlying dissatisfaction with the state's civil service system. Thanks to a long tradition of antiunion sentiment, coupled with a highly fragmented staffing system, the state's civil service was nowhere near as rule bound and restrictive as those that exist in many states (Argyle 1982). Although political patronage was (is) certainly present both before and after reform, easier access to patronage appointments was probably *not* a chief motive in the politicians' willingness to experiment with basic changes in the HRM system. Instead, the increased flexibility and efficiency offered by HRM decentralization and simplification seem to have propelled most facets of the reform program. A related catalyst may have been the recognition that, with a clear line of responsibility now running between the governor's office and many agencies that had heretofore been outside of his control, decentralization offered an effective management tool. Under a cabinet form of government, decentralized staffing functions posed less risk than before, and even promised to help the governor implement public policy initiatives within state agencies.

One final factor must be noted as a major contributor to the HRM changes that have occurred since 1993. It is probably safe to speculate that the parallels between the academic reinvention literature and the actual reforms introduced in South Carolina are no accident. At the time that the reform agenda was taking shape, the state's "chief bureaucrat" (the Executive Director of the Budget and Control Board) was a former professor of public administration who was an active researcher in the HRM field. Although his role in formulating the various proposals that ultimately led to the transformation of the state's personnel system is unclear, few observers would dispute that his fingerprints are evident throughout the administrative reform process. Another boon was the presence of supportive leaders in key positions within the Office of Human Resources (OHR). Rather than throwing obstacles in the path of reformers, the OHR was an eager participant. In so doing, the OHR successfully enlisted the cooperation of most agency and HR managers.

The Decentralized HRM System: The Specifics of Reform

The initial legislation that prompted revisions in the state personnel system focused primarily on relatively "easy" changes that did not require a tremendous amount of groundwork or high implementation costs. These include such initiatives as a pay-for-performance plan, group productivity incentives, increased flexibility in the utilization of human resources, and an expanded probationary period for new workers. Within just a few years, however, the OHR had sponsored much more ambitious reform programs that encompassed broad-banding, a complete reconfiguration in the way that human resource services are delivered, and a complementary array of support services to line agencies. The major components of this expansive reform agenda are detailed below. For the most part, the descriptions are fairly laconic because the underlying reform concepts are well-known within the HRM field. Where the South Carolina experience tends to differ significantly from developments in most other states, a more thorough explanation is offered. Later in the chapter, an effort is made to provide preliminary assessments of the impact that these many reforms have had upon line managers and the employees they supervise.

Performance-Based Salary Adjustments

The 1993 Act empowered agencies to develop procedures and evaluation standards to increase and decrease employees' salaries based on their performance. This represented the first systematic attempt by the state to implement a merit pay system applicable to all public employees. Previously, agencies commonly allocated "merit raises" in a (more or less) across-the-board manner, even when special monies were set aside for performance-based increases. Under the revised arrangement, managers are encouraged to use employee performance appraisals as the basis for salary adjustments to recognize exceptional performance. As long as the agency leaders approve the raises—a factor driven more by their own budget constraints than by any other factor—they are free to adjust salaries with a high level of flexibility and discretion.

The performance evaluation format, known as the Employee Performance Management System (EPMS), combines some of the best characteristics of behaviorally anchored rating scales, critical incidents, and management by objectives evaluation strategies. Designed "as a management tool to facilitate communication between supervisors and employees" (Carter 1999, 3), the EPMS both informs the employee of the nature of the work that is expected, and defines the manner in which the work should be performed. In 1996 the instrument was further refined through the addition of a "Toolbox" of options by which each agency can customize the evaluation instrument to fit its unique mission and organizational culture (Carter 1999, 3). Contained within this Toolbox are such options as team evaluations, 360-degree feedback, the linkage of EPMS results to staff development and training opportunities, and the use of a universal review date to systematize the evaluation process and aid in comparison of employee performance levels.

According to recommended procedures, managers are instructed to tailor each EPMS form to the individual employee's duties and responsibilities. Supervisors receive relevant training on how to identify appropriate job duties and objectives, and on how to construct observable measures of achievement. Moreover, the EPMS form provides managers with the opportunity (or obligation) to specify certain goals for the next review cycle that the employee might not ordinarily divine on his/her own initiative. For instance, a clerical employee might be told at the beginning of the annual review cycle that, by the end of the twelve-month period, he/she should have learned one or more new computer applications, purged files of a certain age, and/or undertaken other tasks that are viewed (hopefully) as worthwhile by both the manager and subordinate. Ultimately, employees are rated according to whether they "substantially exceeded requirements," "exceeded requirements," "met requirements," or "failed to meet requirements." With the exception of those who fail to meet requirements, all employees qualify for a merit increase, with those who exceed their performance standards typically qualifying for a larger increase (provided, of course, that sufficient funds are available for that purpose). A "failed to meet requirements" evaluation signals the supervisor and subordinate that remedial or punitive steps may be necessary. While supervisors are authorized to actually *decrease* an employee's salary as a result of the evaluation process, only six agencies in a 1997 survey reported that they considered such a strategy as "likely" (Hays and Whitney 1997, 332). Since that time, the number of salary reductions has been very low, while the number of "flexible pay actions" (merit increases) increased exponentially until budget problems lowered the agencies' ability to recognize superior employee performance through salary adjustments (a phenomenon that became severe during FY 2002–2003).

Group Productivity Incentives

This feature of the 1993 Act has probably exerted the least impact on HRM practice. The Act encouraged state agencies to establish productivity standards and to devise procedures to reward work *groups* for their efforts. However, no special provisions were made for funding this incentive program. Instead, agencies were allowed to share up to 25 percent of cost savings with the responsible work groups.

Four years after receiving approval to create such arrangements, only two agencies reported the existence of a group pay plan (which were administered at the department level), while a few other agencies were considering the idea. Perhaps the most successful example occurred at the Medical University of South Carolina, where employees involved in collecting overdue payments were permitted to share a portion of their increased collections. Little action has followed these embryonic steps, owing in large part to the many operational impediments to group-based pay adjustments. Listed among the reasons why group productivity incentives have not "caught on" are such factors as the difficulties involved in establishing meaningful performance standards, the investment in time and attention that would be required to implement such a system, the fact that many agency activities (e.g., corrections, regulation) are not conducive to collective output measures, and (of course) budgetary limitations. By 2003 the budget crisis was so severe that any savings attributable to productivity gains would almost certainly be absorbed rather than shared with employees, no matter how deserving they might be.

Employee Recognition

Encouraging agencies to make cash awards and to otherwise recognize deserving employees represents a classic example of "picking low-hanging fruit" in HRM reform. If we accept the notion that "it's the thought that counts," then the Accountability Act achieves high marks. Specifically, the legislation promotes the utilization of agency resources for plaques, meals, preferential parking, and other means of acknowledging the efforts of valued workers. Given the fact that many forms of recognition are inexpensive (or virtually cost-free), the popularity of such measures was immediate and extensive. Just two years after the Act took effect, more than 3,200 workers had received some form of recognition (Office of Human Resources 1995). Favored strategies included plaques, certificates, and cash awards. Use of such measures continued to expand over time, although the program's impact is thought to be minimized by statutory restrictions on the amount of cash awards ($50) (Hays and Whitney 1997, 335). By 2002 about half the agencies reported the "somewhat frequent" use of employee recognition programs.

Scheduling Innovations

The expanded use of flextime and other scheduling strategies represents another instance of picking low-hanging fruit. In an effort to make the state's labor policies more family-friendly, the Accountability Act enables agencies to implement flexible schedules and job-sharing arrangements without first obtaining centralized approval. Also, employees are permitted to work out of their homes when such arrangements are feasible. Within four years, more than 400 workers were telecommuting (or otherwise working out of their homes), and two-thirds of the line agencies had implemented formal flextime scheduling. About 20 percent of the agencies had established job-sharing policies, although that number grew significantly as budgetary pressures increased. By 2003 most state agencies offered a menu of scheduling options to at least a portion of their labor forces. For obvious reasons, there are many groups of workers whose responsibilities preclude a flextime schedule (correctional officers, public safety workers). However, in many agencies virtually the entire workforce is on some type of flexible schedule, including 30-hour workweeks and/or job-sharing arrangements that accommodate parents with young children.

Expanded Probationary Period

As has been noted elsewhere, reinvention of HRM introduces an element of "managerialism" into public organizations (Kettl 1994). Although cloaked in a veil of worker empowerment and increased flexibility (etc.), reinvention clearly introduces additional means of controlling civil servants. The South Carolina example includes several instances of this nature, with the most obvious being the expansion of employee probationary periods from six months to one year. The implicit purpose of this change is that with additional time to monitor the performance of newly appointed workers, there is a greater likelihood that problem employees will be culled prior to the acquisition of full career protections. Since probationary employees do not enjoy any procedural protections from removal—unless they allege discrimination, sexual harassment, or a small number of other causes of action—doubling the probationary period theoretically doubles managers' opportunities to detect and eliminate employees who are unable or unwilling to perform at an acceptable level.

Increased Supervisory Flexibility

In addition to the measures that have already been mentioned, the Accountability Act greatly expands supervisory latitude over important staffing decisions. Managers are now empowered to reassign, transfer, reclassify, and promote their subordinates, subject only to agency approval. In the case of promotions, the maximum allowable upgrade is one organizational level. Before these changes were implemented, reassignment and transfer decisions were restricted by agency procedures and by the threat of grievances (e.g., reassignments and transfers involving a move of 15 miles or more were grievable actions). Likewise, promotion and reclassification decisions ordinarily required lengthy clearance processes. Under the new procedures, supervisors enjoy almost as much discretion over HRM decisions as do their private sector counterparts (at least, those in nonunionized settings).

A related aspect of the decentralized HRM system is the elimination of centralized job registers, testing protocols, and other "single point of entry" strategies that often impede the flow of human resources into public agencies. In effect, recruitment and selection have been completely delegated to the operating agencies. They are thereby free to write their own position descriptions, advertise vacancies, screen applicants, and select successful candidates without ever having to consult with the central OHR. As is discussed below, the OHR's role in these activities is no longer that of supervision or management, but to provide support and/or technical assistance where necessary.

Classification and Pay Flexibility—Broad-Banding

Whenever the topic of "inflexible" public personnel systems is raised, the first thing that usually comes to mind is the way that public agencies have traditionally linked narrow job classifications to equally restrained pay grades. Restrictive job classifications that impede the ability of supervisors to assign and reassign workers have long represented one of the most intractable problems for public managers seeking to make their agencies and employees more responsive to supervisory authority. Likewise, the existence of tightly defined job categories and pay scales essentially negates the intended benefits of increased supervisory flexibility in worker assignments.

Due to the self-evident problems associated with the old classification scheme, the first item on the reformers' agenda after the implementation of the Accountability Act was the introduction of broad-banding (Office of Human Resources 1995b). As accomplished in South Carolina, broad-banding involved the consolidation of more than 2,500 job classifications into a much more manageable number, approximately 500. Similarly, the state's old pay system of 50 pay grades was collapsed into ten broad-bands with very large salary ranges. Under the revised format, employees are eligible to earn any amount of money that is permitted within the much broader bands that now are linked to their expanded job titles.

The revised classification and compensation system enables managers much greater flexibility at several important decision points. First, new hires can potentially be placed in jobs at salaries that might be substantially above the minimums that were once nearly mandatory. Thus, workers in such fields as information technology or nursing might be offered atypically high salaries because the usual compensation levels in government are not competitive with the private sector. Second, high-performing workers can be rewarded with substantial pay increases that are not restricted by artificial classification guidelines or narrow pay grades. Moreover, the consolidation of job titles and classes enables managers to assign and reassign workers to duties that may be more appropriate to their talents, interests, and/or wishes. Additionally, managers may be able to fashion counteroffers for critical personnel who are being courted by other employers. All of this flexibility relies upon the availability of adequate funds, of course, but the decisions concerning how an agency will use its salary money rests almost entirely *with* the agency and not with any external entity. If the agency leaders believe that a particular employee is sufficiently valuable, they are free to engineer a salary package that improves their retention efforts.

Agency involvement and participation constituted an important facet of the reform process leading to the implementation of broad-banding. HR managers and other supervisory employees were surveyed concerning their opinions about delegated pay authority, class consolidation, revised training and experience requirements, and pay equity considerations. In addition to written surveys, the managers were also given an opportunity to participate in focus groups that explored these issues in greater detail. Broad-banding received an overwhelming level of support from the respondent groups. For instance, 92 percent of all state agencies opposed retaining the former system of 2,500 job classifications and 50 pay grades. Increased pay flexibility was endorsed by 86 percent of the agencies, and decentralized salary authority was supported by 88 percent of the respondents. In-grade increases as a primary means of reward attracted support from 86 percent of all managers, as did the premise that greater numbers of jobs ought to be covered under one title specification (Office of Human Resources 1995, 43).

Building on this high level of top-level support, the rollout of broad-banding was preceded by intensive efforts to educate the workforce about the upcoming changes and how they would affect individual employees. The decision was made early in the transition process to communicate *through* the agency managers, and not from the central OHR. Thus, OHR disseminated its message by educating its managers first, and then using such vehicles as press releases in agency newsletters, the production of a video that explained the planned changes, and informational brochures that were widely distributed throughout state government. By the time the reform was formally introduced, it is safe to say that the vast majority of both managers and workers were at least reconciled to the advent of broad-banding.

The IBM Model of Human Resource Management Delivery

The move toward decentralization of most HRM decision making would not have been complete without significant organizational changes in the OHR. Consistent with the desire to "place decision-making at the appropriate level" and to "balance the interests of flexibility and accountability," the OHR underwent a rapid metamorphosis between 1995 and 2002. In effect, the state adopted what in the private sector is referred to as the "IBM Model" of HRM delivery. As noted, this approach turns almost all operational decisions over to line managers. Employees within OHR, meanwhile, were transitioned from specialists (e.g., classifiers, examiners) to generalists beginning with a pilot project and ultimately leading to the creation of an office titled Human Resource Consulting Services. As the name implies, the newly redefined job of OHR staff became that of generalist consultants who assist agency officials with their human resource management responsibilities. Their primary task is to provide problem-solving and technical assistance services to agency managers and internal personnel offices.

The preparatory phase that preceded the transition from specialists to generalists represents what is probably one of the most notable features of the South Carolina reform experience. Cross-training, job shadowing, and intensive training programs were employed to prepare members of the OHR staff to assume the role of HR consultants to client agencies. Because the new HR role resulted from the merger of two previously separate groups—compensation specialists and employee relations specialists—each worker had to acquire an entirely new set of competencies.

To accomplish this feat, training was offered in a wide range of topics. For example, the employee relations function was broken down into 15 major "proficiencies" and about 20 additional subject areas. The proficiencies span such topics as the reduction-in-force (RIF) policy, grievance processing, progressive discipline, the ADA, the FLSA, regulations concerning leave and transfers, and workers' compensation. Trainees were also expected to become familiar with diverse subjects like the Clean Indoor Air Act, the Hatch Act, alcoholism and its treatment, exit interview techniques, hazardous weather policies, ethics, back pay, *ad nauseam*. Those employees with backgrounds in employee relations, meanwhile, were confronted by an equally daunting array of proficiencies in pay and benefits administration. They were expected to demonstrate functional competency in the use of classification specifications, job audits, position descriptions, executive compensation, salary survey methodology, and the 25 different forms of "pay situations" that exist in South Carolina state government (e.g., supplemental pay, dual employment pay, geographical pay differential, in-band increases, shift differentials, overtime, trainee appointment pay, salary decreases, and the like).

These alterations exerted an immediate impact on the OHR's organizational chart. All references to the old specialties were eliminated, and three new offices emerged:

- Human Resource Consulting Services—Each consultant is assigned to work as a liaison between the OHR and one or more agencies. By constant attention and interaction with their client agencies, the consultants are able to acquire considerable expertise and familiarity with the issues and problems peculiar to their assigned organizations. Any topic might conceivably be fair game for consultative services, as exemplified by the list of training topics that is provided above.
- Human Resource Development Services—This office focuses on recruitment and workforce planning topics, as well as employee and organizational development. It conducts surveys of agency managers to assess long-term recruitment needs, engages in aggressive outreach efforts to attract high-need employees, and assesses client satisfaction with the quality and quantity of the employees who pursue public jobs. The office is also responsible for developing a Statewide Workforce Plan (a sophisticated long-term projection of staffing conditions and needs). In addition to a Certified Public Manager (CPM) Program (along with two additional professional certification programs), the state maintains a Career Center (centralized job bank and referral service), an office that recruits and places temporary employees (TEMPO), and many related services (e.g., career fairs, online job applications) to the public and to line agencies.
- Administration—Business management functions and a sophisticated information technology program are located in this small segment of the OHR.

Compared to the OHR of past years, the current one is a mere shadow of its former self. Having recently (1990) employed more than 100 workers, today's OHR has a staff of just over 40 full-time equivalent positions. The staff to employee ratio within South Carolina's OHR is the lowest in the nation at about 1 OHR worker for every 1,525 state employees (Traywick 2002). This transformation has been made possible by the virtual elimination of all control and oversight activities. Other than those that have already been mentioned (e.g., the Career Center), the only centralized functions that remain are grievance handling and the administration of the Agency Heads Salary

Commission. Under this latter program, the salaries of agency directors are set by a special committee consisting of legislators and gubernatorial appointees. Using evaluations that are conducted by the agency director's hiring authority, the Commission assesses the managers' performance and assigns pay increases accordingly. The process is regularized through the use of both objective measures and attitudinal feedback from the agency directors' staffs (including board and/or commission members in those agencies that have not yet been folded into the cabinet). This process is supplemented with a job analysis every four years (historically conducted by the Hay Group) that ascertains whether or not the existing salary levels are competitive and appropriate in the current labor market.

Grievance Handling and Alternative Dispute Resolution

Spurred by proposals emanating from within OHR, the general assembly significantly amended the State Employee Grievance Procedure Act in 1996. The legislation implemented a revised mediation process and created a separate mediation-arbitration track. These changes essentially produced a two-track grievance system. The most severe causes of action continue to be reviewed by a State Employee Grievance Committee in a highly formalized (adjudicatory) process, while lesser offenses are reviewed by a mediator-arbitrator. By diverting a substantial number of grievances to the mediator-arbitrator track, the state saves considerable time and money. Under the mediator-arbitrator option, formal rules of evidence do not apply. This leads to a much more expedient and informal hearing. Another facet of the OHR-led reforms in this area involves a concerted effort on the agency's part to encourage mediation of disputes before they rise to the level of formal grievances. OHR has presented widespread training in mediation skills to more than 150 individuals representing 46 state agencies. A related development has been the creation of a Statewide Mediators Pool to serve as neutral third parties for employment disputes. The pool is comprised of HR professionals from state agencies who must first undergo extensive preparation in the theory and practice of mediation and dispute resolution.

Overview and Summary of Reforms

In sum, South Carolina's public personnel system represents a blend of centralized accountability features that are complemented with an exceedingly decentralized form of service delivery. A measure of accountability is ensured by the state's continuing role as the administrator of the classification and pay plan that has been authorized by the Budget and Control Board. Agencies are not free to create new classes of jobs, or to exceed the minimal restrictions imposed by the pay bands. Otherwise, their personnel actions relating to job classes and salary determinations are relatively unfettered by state-level intervention. Similarly, the OHR provides an array of centralized services that are justified on the basis of their economies of scale. Manpower planning, proactive recruitment programs, the State Career Center, and related initiatives are probably best offered through a single-source provider. And, should any agency exceed its authority or otherwise violate an employee's right to due process and fair treatment, the grievance process is managed, maintained, and monitored by the central personnel office. Presumably, any agency that demonstrates a pattern of employee abuse will be detected through the passive police function that is performed through the grievance system. To date, no such problems have arisen.

Another feature that helps to tie this decentralized system together is the constant availability of HR consultants to assist agency managers with their personnel management needs. For those agencies that avail themselves of this resource, continuity in the application of various procedures is a likely byproduct. Since the consultants work essentially as a team, having experienced identical training and preparation, the services they deliver are probably as standardized as one can expect in a decentralized organizational form. The consultants' familiarity with the entire range of HR policies and procedures—not to mention relevant federal laws—provides some assurance (albeit not absolute by any means!) that agency HR offices are up-to-date and compliant with legal and procedural requirements. And, since the consultants follow a strategy of "continuous improvement," they are a potentially valuable resource to agencies seeking to upgrade and expand their range of HR services to their own employees. The saliency of this relationship is reflected in the fact that the OHR consultants often serve on recruitment committees for the HR directors in their client agencies, and they provide prompt "help desk" responses to agencies encountering problems with human resource issues.

Within this overall scheme, notably, the agencies are empowered to hire, fire, promote, transfer, reassign, and otherwise manage their employees without OHR interference. Provided that they play by the basic rules, their range of discretionary decision making is profound. The OHR essentially plays the role of technical assistant, consultant, teacher, and potential jack-of-all-trades HR resource, should the agencies choose to use it as such. The extent to which this idyllic relationship is realized is the next topic addressed.

Assessing the Impacts of HRM Reform

As is true in the case of most public management reforms, evaluation of progress is rarely conducted scientifically or systematically. Instead, analysis of impacts generally relies on *proxies* of performance. So called "hard data" is a rarity. In this regard, the South Carolina reform experience is no exception. Support for the changes that have occurred appears to be widespread, but it is largely anecdotal and/or attitudinal. The case *for* the state's approach to HRM reform is made in the following ways.

External Recognition

As was noted in the introduction to this chapter, the personnel system that has just been described is widely considered to be a—if not *the*—most successful approach to administering HR services in a decentralized setting. To repeat some of the plaudits that have been bestowed upon South Carolina's OHR, it has twice been recognized by *Governing Magazine* as the premier HRM system among the fifty states. This conclusion seems to be shared widely among HR professionals in other state capitals. No less than thirty states have sought advice and counsel from the state concerning various facets of its HRM reform program. In addition to merely asking for detailed descriptive information, many states have either sent representatives to South Carolina for on-site visits, or invited OHR employees to their locations for discussions. Among the most recent recipients of such technical assistance are the states of Florida, Oklahoma, Pennsylvania, Virginia, and Wyoming. Other forms of "face validity" occur in the many awards and positive recognition that the state has won from such groups as the International Personnel Managers Association, the National Association of State Personnel Executives, and the Annie E. Casey Foundation.

Measures of Managerial Satisfaction

The basic philosophy of OHR is grounded in the premise that its chief client group consists of the 74 public agencies in South Carolina state government. In striving to "create excellence in human resources," the Office "partners with [its] customers" (Thompson 2002, 1). Supporting this mission is "a vision to provide state government with the best human resource program, development, consultation, and delivery."

Having focused on agency management as its chief clients, the OHR assesses their opinions of its performance. The most recent survey of agency managers and HR professionals yielded a "customer satisfaction level of *92 percent*" (Office of Human Resources 2002, 3). All but 8 percent (about five agencies) expressed high levels of satisfaction with the OHR on numerous service dimensions. Based on the Malcolm Baldridge Award criteria, these include responsiveness, reliability, empathy, assurance, and "tangibles" (physical appearance of the people and facilities) (Merritt 2001). This level of customer satisfaction is not atypical, in that a similar rate (about 91%) was achieved during the preceding year. Notably, OHR attains high satisfaction scores despite undergoing a rapid attrition of employees between 1995 and the present. The agency's FTE count in 1995 was 74, and by 2003 had dropped to less than 40.

The erosion of OHR's staff has been primarily attributable to the ubiquitous budget exigencies faced by almost all state governments. Financial shortfalls have contributed to early buy-outs and other measures intended to trim costs. Yet, although OHR has probably endured one of the most pronounced cutbacks in staff, its ability to perform has not been crippled. In addition to high levels of customer satisfaction, the agency's own employees appear to be content with their job situations. A recent assessment of employee satisfaction revealed no pronounced areas of disgruntlement. Instead, the respondents provide positive feedback on 16 of 22 "keys to meaning at work" (Terez 2000). No less than 81 percent of the respondents expressed satisfaction with those 16 "keys," whereas the remaining six job factors attracted positive responses from between 60 and 80 percent of the employees. Thus, not a single job factor received negative feedback from more than 40 percent of the workforce.

This analysis of job satisfaction was based on Tom Terez's widely applied assessment tool that measures such qualities as acknowledgment, challenge, dialogue, direction, equality, fit, flexibility, informality, ownership, personal development, relationship-building, respect, service, support, and validation in one's work. Possible explanations for the ability of the OHR to maintain a satisfied and effective workforce under stressful workloads include a widely acclaimed organizational culture (it is known as being extremely open and supportive), and the fact that the nature of the work being performed has been reengineered. By moving to the consultant model of HR service delivery, almost all of the tedious and labor-intensive functions of traditional personnel operations have been eliminated, and the employees are thereby able to focus on the relatively "interesting" tasks (troubleshooting, problem-solving, and giving advice to line managers).

The Partnership Index

Another means of gauging OHR's performance is to examine its efforts to develop "partnerships" with agencies on important HRM programs and objectives. The goal of this exercise is to help state agencies refine and expand their internal HR systems by cooperating with OHR consultants and participating in OHR-sponsored initiatives.

OHR strives to partner with client agencies in six areas: Workforce Planning, Employee Relations, Compensation, Recruitment and Selection, Human Resources Development, and HRIS (HR information systems). The highest score has been achieved in Human Resources Development, where over 50 percent of all agencies have partnered in various ways (participating in training programs, contracting for customized training, etc.). HRIS and Compensation programs have also engendered considerable partnership activity (49% and 48%, respectively). The lowest amount of participation occurs in the Workforce Planning area (30%), followed by Recruitment and Selection (33%). The relatively low amount of interest in these last two programs might be explained in part by the fact that Planning is the most recent activity added to the OHR tool kit, and the topic also seems somewhat problematic during times of extreme budget scarcity (i.e., it is difficult to muster any interest in planning long-term hiring strategies when you are facing RIFs today). The paucity of partnerships in Recruitment and Selection may be a perverse measure of OHR's success at decentralizing staffing functions to line agencies. Having now been free to handle their own recruitment and selection processes for nearly a decade, many agencies probably have built their internal capacity to the point that they don't perceive much need for OHR's services. This is mere speculation, however, since the agencies have not been polled about their reasons for partnering or not partnering with OHR. The essential fact is that the amount of partnering continues to increase each year. This fact might be interpreted as a sign that OHR has achieved a degree of credibility among other public managers in state government.

If one wishes to look at the glass as half-empty, however, it can easily be argued that less than half of all agencies have chosen to partner with OHR in any way. Whether they are reluctant to do so for unknown reasons, or merely haven't gotten around to it, remains a mystery.

Empirical Proof of Operational Changes

Unlike the proxy measures that have been described thus far, there is a small amount of quantitative support for the notion that line managers are making use of their new-found HRM flexibility.

After a slow start, during which many agencies failed to use the powers conveyed by the Accountability Act (Hays and Whitney 1997), by 2000–2001 most agencies were selectively employing an array of salary options or other HRM reform strategies. Nearly half of the agencies that responded to an OHR survey in 2002 reported the "somewhat frequent" use of differential hiring rates, hiring new employees up to the mid-point in the salary range, and the use of skill-based pay (granting salary increases for additional skills). Performance increases were widely used in more than 60 percent of the agencies in 1999–2000, but fell slightly (to 58%) in 2000–2001 (Office of Human Resources 2002b). In all probability, this phenomenon is tied directly to the fact that the raise pool was quite limited during both those years, but especially in FY 2000–2001. Within such an environment, it's likely that some managers opt to spread the "wealth." During the years in which the raise pool was larger, 96 percent of the agencies reported the use of performance-based salary increases (Traywick 2002).

Insofar as "specifics" are concerned, the total number of flexible pay actions has risen every year since broad-banding was implemented. By way of example, performance-based increases grew from about 3,000 in FY 1996–1997 to nearly 9,500 in FY 1998–1999. In the same two-year period, the number of "additional duty increases" rose from 3,100 to 5,200, and the use of skill-based pay exploded (rising from 850 in the first year to 4,300 pay actions in FY 1998–1999). Retention increases constitute the most sparsely used pay strategy. Applied primarily in just a few very problematic job categories (e.g., information technology), only about 100 such raises are granted in the typical fiscal year.

Notably, by 2000–2001, the total number of special pay actions—a broad category that includes all raises, promotions, reclassifications, changes of duty, and other justifications for salary increases—had grown to 22,365. This means that about 31 percent of the state's workforce received some form of merit-based salary increment. While such a fact might be interpreted negatively—that is, that just about everyone is getting a slice of the pie, which implies an across-the-board strategy—the size of the raises averaged 6.79 percent when the raise pool was just 3 percent. Further, in FY 2001–2002—a year in which the General Assembly provided no raise money of any kind—14,150 workers received raises averaging 6.88 percent (Byrd 2002). Clearly, the agencies are making internal reallocations of resources in order to reward significant numbers of employees while under extreme fiscal pressures. They are able to do so by cannibalizing positions, reengineering work, and using productivity savings to enhance salaries.

These data indicate that the decentralized ability to maneuver within the HRM system is being generously utilized by line managers. Unfortunately, the data cannot tell us if managerial discretion is being used *fairly* and *wisely*. The HRM literature has long recognized that it's difficult, if not impossible, to make merit pay "work" in the public sector. Jim Perry's (2003) well-known explanations for this phenomenon include invalid performance appraisals (complicated by vague output standards), insufficient pools of merit money, and the dysfunctional competition that almost always results among groups of workers. These concerns are validated by a number of empirical studies that have placed a dark cloud over the concept of performance-based pay in government (Kellough and Selden 1997). Perhaps the most notable example—one that is especially useful in comparison to South Carolina—is the sad state of affairs in Georgia. That state's broad-based approach to merit pay ("GeorgiaGain") resembles the South Carolina program in many ways. When Georgia's workers were asked to assess GeorgiaGain after a five-year period, the results were dismal. Large majorities of employees do not believe that performance is actually being linked to pay decisions, and 68 percent alleged that "favoritism" drives salary allocations (Kellough and Nigro 2002). Flaws in the performance appraisal system, the funding mechanism, and supervisory decision making have essentially killed any credibility that GeorgiaGain may once have hoped for.

Because a comparable survey of state workers has not been conducted in South Carolina, it wouldn't be prudent to speculate about whether similar sentiments permeate the state's workforce. Suffice it to say here that, at least up until 2003, no evidence had surfaced concerning widespread angst over the revised HRM system and its method of pay administration. The unfortunate experiences with merit pay that have surfaced elsewhere, however, necessitate a cautious evaluation of the apparent "success" thus far in South Carolina.

Measures of Employee Satisfaction

As has just been noted, one would need to be very naïve to assume that every worker greeted the sweeping HRM changes with joy and celebration. Change is always threatening, especially when it affects one's livelihood. To its credit, OHR never attempted to "sell" HRM reform to agency employees. Its implementation strategy—at least insofar as broad-banding and pay flexibility were concerned— was to assume "that management would be enthusiastic, and employees would hopefully be neutral" (Byrd 2002). OHR made a concerted effort to "manage expectations," and to avoid any perception that broad-banding (etc.) would lead to a windfall for workers (Byrd 2002). During the implementation phase, emphasis was placed on explaining the perceived *administrative* advantages of salary reform (i.e., greater flexibility) without giving employees either false hopes or undue fears about its long-term impacts. Undoubtedly, some employees must have worried that their supervisors would not use the newly won discretion fairly, while it is equally plausible that high-performing workers saw opportunity for salary enhancement in a system that included both pay for performance and a tremendous range of managerial options in salary administration.

Because no systemwide employee attitude surveys have been conducted in the state, only proxy measures exist to assess worker sentiments. One very important indicator of the absence of widespread dissension is the extremely low number of complaints that have been fielded by OHR about unfair or inappropriate compensation decisions. In fact, since the reforms were introduced, the total number of employee complaints arising from salary determinations has been "less than ten" (Byrd 2002). Another notable fact is that, for a workforce of about 65,000, the number of formal grievances is very low. In a typical year, between 20 and 30 cases are adjudicated by the State Grievance Committee. Another 70 to 80 cases are successfully mediated through the new dual-track grievance process. (Assuming that the higher number occurs in a single year—resulting in 110 labor disputes—the grievance rate in South Carolina still is an incredibly low .17 percent [Wheeler and Rojot 1992]). Overall, 72 percent of labor-management disputes are resolved informally, saving both the employee and the state the considerable expense of a full-blown evidentiary hearing before the Grievance Committee.

Lessons Learned, Fears Expressed

South Carolina's foray into HRM reform appears to deserve the credit it has received for pushing the boundaries of decentralization. If judged simply on the record to date, only a true cynic could conclude that the program is failing to yield the intended results. Managers and HR directors are certainly pleased with their new powers and responsibilities, and the OHR appears to be accomplishing a great deal on a shoestring budget. The OHR's experiences with broad-banding and delegated recruitment authority will likely serve as demonstration projects for similar initiatives in numerous states during the next decade. Likewise, the consultant model, which has been crafted in South Carolina, pieces together many of the most thoughtful ideas that have bounced around for years in the academic literature. The use of personnel generalists, the forging of HR and line manager partnerships, and the cultivation of a new culture ("service") within the personnel system are all old concepts that have rarely (if ever) been combined in one public agency.

Before closing this "valentine" section of our analysis, one additional advantage of the current arrangement needs to be highlighted. As this chapter is written, the State of South Carolina is entering what will probably be the most challenging period of economic stress since the Great Depression (when the few public employees who were lucky enough to hang onto their jobs were paid in scrip that was devalued by local merchants). The problem was already severe during FY 2002–2003, leading to several mid-year budget cuts and the absence of any pay increase. Forecasts for the future indicate that the problem will get far worse before conditions improve. Whereas it might be argued that fiscal stress will blow the wheels off the reform bandwagon, the opposite seems to be true thus far. Thanks to salary flexibility and related discretionary authority, the state's managers are better equipped to cope with their current predicament than they might otherwise have been. It is not uncommon, for instance, for agencies to cannibalize positions in order to provide raises, counteroffers, or salary adjustments to employees who must necessarily assume greater responsibility. Managers are also able to alter job duties, schedules, and other conditions of employment with few restrictions. Unencumbered by wage and classification guidelines, agencies are better prepared to maneuver through the troubled financial waters. At least to date, the managerial flexibility that was gained through HRM reform has provided agencies with an effective tool to marshal their limited resources effectively.

Applicability of the South Carolina "Model"?

Having spent many pages praising the South Carolina reform experience, there is an obvious need to delineate the *caveats* that are likely occurring to any reader who is familiar with public personnel systems. The first topic, *transportability*, is clearly a limiting factor in the lessons that can be learned from this state's approach to HRM service delivery. As was discussed earlier, the absence of unions and collective bargaining made the introduction of broad-banding and other "flexibilities" much less complicated than will be the case in many other states. Anti-union sentiments run deep in the culture of the state, and the thought of organized opposition—if there had been any widespread displeasure with the reforms—would never have occurred to most of the labor force. And, if it had, their means of influencing policy decisions are very limited. With a small State Employees' Association, a few lobbyists, and a finite number of "champions" in the general assembly, state workers have few resources to resist policy initiatives.

Another "advantage" enjoyed by South Carolina was the preexisting level of decentralization that existed when the reform movement began. Somewhat ironically, the state's archaic personnel system proved to be an asset because there were few vested interests that lovingly embraced the old way of doing things. In other words, South Carolina didn't really have all that far to go to "decentralize" its HRM system. It was already decentralized in many ways, and lacked many of the institutional structures and procedural encumbrances that impede progress in other locations.

Yet, before we write South Carolina off as a complete anomaly, developments in a few other locations demonstrate that similar reforms *can* be implemented in highly unionized and bureaucratic settings. The state of Wisconsin, for example, has used interest-based bargaining to put a very impressive broad-banding arrangement into effect, and also to engineer some types of decentralization that resemble the steps taken in South Carolina (Lavigna 2003). Similar examples can be found in Maricopa County, Arizona (broad-banding in a heavily unionized setting), Hamilton County, Ohio (pay-for-performance among unionized white-collar workers), and Hennepin County, Minnesota (systemwide flexibility in a complex union environment) (Hays 2003). With effective leadership and visionary goals, reform can be achieved even in some very unlikely places.

Continuity and Standardization of HRM Services?

Decentralization of HR services to the agencies spawns another predictable concern: *inconsistency* (or even incompetence) within some agencies. In other words, the "state of the art" in HR departments in 74 separate state agencies is likely to be quite diverse. The quality of services that an agency's employees receive depends in large part on the professionalism and competence of its indigenous HR department. Meanwhile, the central OHR is not empowered to compel changes or to engineer reforms without the cooperation and participation of the agency. This means that there are undoubtedly pockets of resistance (or at least inattention) to the reform agenda and the use of expanded HR power and flexibility. OHR strives to upgrade the capacity of every agency's HR department, but wide variations probably persist nonetheless. Many of the strategies that were discussed above, notably the Partnership Index, exemplify how OHR tries to cajole and educate its entire client population. Although progress is clearly being made, no one would argue that the quality of HR services across state government is consistently high. Some agencies are simply too small to justify much of an HR function, whereas others are too large or obstinate to pay much attention to the OHR's agenda. Here, too, we encounter a trade-off dilemma that is not easily or quickly resolved.

"Politicization"?

By far the most critical *caveat* relates to the age-old problem of accountability within the civil service. The history of merit systems consists of an enduring struggle between patronage and merit (expertise versus responsiveness, or professionalism versus executive control). Merit systems evolved into bureaucratic mazes largely because politicians could not be trusted to keep their hands out of the cookie jar. Whenever public personnel systems were opened up and made more "responsive," patronage (and often incompetence) soon followed.

This is not an inconsequential concern in South Carolina. The authors of this chapter remember instances in which state jobs were actually "sold" by politicians, and agencies were ordered by members of the General Assembly to hire specific individuals (usually relatives or political supporters). Thankfully, when these situations were exposed, the perpetrators suffered severe consequences (including jail time). As a result, the prevalence of efforts to unduly influence hiring decisions seems to be very limited. While "who you know" may be a contributor to getting a public job in many settings, being qualified for that job seems to be a minimum bar that must be cleared before the appointment occurs.

The fact remains, however, that decentralization *does* expose the state to increased risks of political involvement in the civil service. Indeed, one of the first things that occurred on the introduction of cabinet government was a housecleaning at the top. Many senior public managers—the "deputy directors" of state agencies brought under the governor's authority—received letters telling them that, as of that date, they were "at-will" employees (i.e., they no longer had any claim to job security or grievance rights). The vast majority of those deputy directors—most of whom were seasoned experts and the "cream" of the state's public workforce—ended up being shifted to lesser jobs, or otherwise became casualties of reform. Inevitably, flexibility in a public personnel system means that values such as merit and professionalism can be more easily threatened. Although there is no evidence that crass political motives are driving personnel decisions at this point in time, the system in South Carolina is clearly vulnerable to such developments for the very reasons that have made reform a success.

The possibility that politicization can occur is now being heightened by an inclination on the general assembly's part to push "at-will" employment much lower in the state hierarchy. Stated differently, traditional career protections for civil servants are deeply threatened. The trend is definitely toward making the *public* workforce resemble the *private* workforce in most important ways. More and more civil servants will become at-will, job protections will gradually disappear for many, and the concept of a public sector "career" will be fundamentally altered. The state will gain flexibility in the use of its human resources, but at a cost to professionalism and expertise. These tradeoffs are ubiquitous and enduring. Striking a proper balance has always been the most difficult aspect of operating modern merit systems, but the challenges are especially pronounced today.

Another legitimate concern in this context is just how far technical fixes can go in addressing systemic budget and personnel crises.

The state appears to be near the point at which "satisficing" (HRM flexibility, for instance) represents a flimsy bandage applied to hemorraghing state agencies. Under reasonably stable circumstances, the flexibility that permeates South Carolina's civil service system is probably an asset that rarely produces blatant dysfunctional consequences (although, as noted, empirical evidence concerning the impact upon individual workers is quite scarce). Once the situation becomes worse—when fiscal demands place untenable pressures on politicians and public managers alike—the risks are compounded. Under conditions of extreme stress, the state's leaders now possess the requisite tools to take draconian actions with large segments of the public labor force. How this drama plays out will probably be the most interesting long-term facet of the South Carolina reform experience.

An implicit theme in the preceding discussion is that the South Carolina reform program is a work in progress. The system is by no means perfect, but a solid foundation has been constructed. Pitfalls undoubtedly pose a threat, and the ultimate success of this reinvented HRM system has yet to be determined.

If nothing else, though, the South Carolina certainly represents a very interesting experiment. Almost the entire reinvention agenda has been put into effect. If the long-term verdict proves to be positive, then the modern wisdom of HR—at least as articulated in the reinvention movement—will have been vindicated. If not, equally important lessons will have been learned. Whatever the ultimate verdict, it is safe to assume that the conventional wisdom of HRM practice has already been fundamentally modified, and that the character of the professional civil service is being transformed. The enduring tug-of-war between political and professional values is now leaning more and more toward the "accountability" (political) side of the ledger. Academicians and practitioners alike have a responsibility to monitor the changes and to decry any developments that tip the balance too far in either direction.

References

Argyle, Nolan (1982). "Civil Service Reform: The State and Local Response." *Public Personnel Management* 11 (1): 157–164.

Barrett, Katherine, and Richard Greene (1999). "Grading the States: A 50-State Report Card on Government Performance." *Governing* 13 (February): 17–77.

Barrett, Katherine, and Richard Greene (2001). "Grading the States 2001: A Report Card on Government Performance." *Governing* 15 (February): 20–94.

Byrd, Chris (2002). Interview. August 22.

Carter, Fred (1999). "Nomination Letter: South Carolina OHR as a Candidate for the IPMA Agency Award for Excellence for a Large Agency." Columbia, South Carolina: South Carolina Budget and Control Board, May 12.

Center for the Study of Social Policy (2002). *Human Resource Management Best Practices in Human Service Settings.* Washington, DC: Annie E. Casey Foundation.

Hays, Steven W. (2002). "Human Resource Management in South Carolina." In Charlie Tyer (Ed.) *South Carolina Government: An Introduction.* Columbia, South Carolina: University of South Carolina Institute for Public Service and Policy Research, 266–302.

Hays, Steven W. (2003). *Human Resource Management Best Practices: Success Stories in Human Services and Elsewhere.* Washington, DC: Annie E. Casey Foundation.

Hays, Steven, and Shawn B. Whitney (1997). "Reinventing the Personnel Function: Lessons Learned from a Hope-Filled Beginning in One State." *American Review of Public Administration* 27 (December): 324–342.

Kellough, J. Edward, and Sally Selden (1997). "Pay-for-Performance Systems in State Government: Perceptions of State Agency Personnel Managers." *Review of Public Personnel Administration* 17 (Spring): 5–21.

Kellough, J. Edward, and Lloyd G. Nigro (2002). "Pay for Performance in Georgia State Government: Employee Perspectives on GeorgiaGain After 5 Years." *Review of Public Personnel Administration* 22 (Summer): 146–166.

Kettl, Donald (1994). *Reinventing Government? Appraising the National Performance Review.* Washington, DC: The Brookings Institution.

Lavigna, Robert (2003). "Reforming Public Sector Human Resource Management." In Steven Hays and Richard Kearney (Eds.) *Public Personnel Administration: Problems and Prospects.* Upper Saddle River, New Jersey: Prentice Hall, 352–366.

Lowe, Harriet Rose (1973). *The History of the South Carolina Personnel Division.* Columbia, South Carolina: University of South Carolina M.A. Thesis.

Merritt, Hardy (2001). *Accountability Report: South Carolina Budget and Control Board.* Columbia, South Carolina: South Carolina Budget and Control Board (September 6).

Office of Human Resources (1995). *Civil Service Reforms in South Carolina: Trends and Experiences.* Columbia, South Carolina: South Carolina Budget and Control Board (July 11).

Office of Human Resources (1995b). *Reform of the South Carolina Classification and Compensation System*. Columbia, South Carolina: South Carolina Budget and Control Board (May).

Office of Human Resources (2002). *Return on Investment Study*. Columbia, South Carolina: South Carolina Budget and Control Board (August 5).

Office of Human Resources (2002b). *State of South Carolina Workforce Plan Addendum*. Columbia, South Carolina: South Carolina Budget and Control Board (May 1).

Perry, James (2003). "Compensation, Merit Pay, and Motivation." In Steven Hays and Richard Kearney (Eds.) *Public Personnel Administration: Problems and Prospects*. Upper Saddle River, NJ: Prentice Hall, 143–153.

Terez, Tom (2000). *22 Keys to Creating a Meaningful Workplace*. Columbus, Ohio: Workplace Solutions.

Thompson, Connie (2000). "Human Resource Initiatives in South Carolina." Presentation at the Southeastern Conference on Public Administration (SECOPA), Greensboro, NC, October 5.

Traywick, Donna (2002). Interview, May 8, 2002.

U.S. General Accounting Office (1994). *Management Reform: Implementation of the NPR Recommendations*. Washington, DC: Office of the Comptroller General.

Wheeler, Hoyt, and James Rojot (1992). *Workplace Justice*. Columbia, South Carolina: University of South Carolina Press.

CHAPTER 9

The Decentralized and Deregulated Approach to State Human Resources Management in Texas

Jerrell D. Coggburn

The state of Texas' human resource (HR) function is renowned for its decentralization and deregulation. The state is routinely cited as being the only state without a centralized HR (or, "personnel") office (Barrett and Greene 1999, 2001; Selden, Ingraham, and Jacobsen 2001). As this implies, individual state agencies are left to their own devises when it comes to designing and implementing HR. Such an approach serves to make the state a "lone star" in the public HR field, at least in the eyes of contemporary reformers advocating substantial HR deregulation and decentralization.

But, in another sense, Texas' unique approach to HR creates certain characteristics *within* Texas state government. Some state agencies might aptly be described as "lone stars" in the area of HR, that is they possess requisite HR knowledge, skills, and abilities (KSAs), they have developed modern HR programs, and they have established HR as a strategic partner to agency management. In contrast, other state agencies, lacking these same characteristics, might be better described simply as "loners." Such agencies lack HR expertise, struggle to compete with other state agencies for skilled employees, face uncertainty about the legality of their HR actions, and, as a result, generally hold more positive perceptions about the benefits of adopting a centralized approach to HR. As this suggests, there is more than meets the eye in Texas, as HR decentralization and deregulation have multiple consequences, some positive, others negative.

This chapter examines the special case of Texas HR. The chapter begins with a brief treatment of the contemporary HR reform literature and its emphasis on themes like decentralization and deregulation. Next, the chapter describes the structure of HR in

Texas, including a consideration of the agencies and officials responsible for administering the state's HR function. From that point, the
chapter moves on to examine the implications of Texas' approach on
important administrative values like equity and politically neutral
competence. The analysis is based on original survey data gathered
from HR directors in the state agencies. Finally, the concluding section of the chapter discusses the implications of the Lone Star State's
experiences for the field of public HR.

The Standing of Public HR in the Academic Literature

The academic literature on public HR is replete with references
to the rigidity, inefficiency, and ineffectiveness of traditional HR systems (e.g., Savas and Ginsburg 1973; Newland 1976; Cohen and
Eimcke 1994; DiIulio, Garvey, and Kettl 1993; Kettl, Ingraham,
Sanders, and Horner 1996; Jorgensen, Fairless, and Patton 1996;
Osborne and Gaebler 1992). Although often not supported by strong
empirical evidence, the general perception is that excessive rules and
regulations, coupled with centralized control, make the traditional
approach to public sector HR virtually unworkable: procedural
requirements increase HR costs (both pecuniary and temporal),
while arcane rules prevent public managers from hiring the most
qualified people, rewarding outstanding performers, and/or disciplining or terminating non-/under-performers. Such characteriza-
tions have gained a measure of credibility thanks, in part, to similar
findings by high-profile administrative reform commissions (Volcker
Commission 1989; Winter Commission 1993). Here, it is important
to point out that the HR reforms being proposed are not politically
neutral: To the contrary, political executives potentially gain power
relative to legislative bodies when HR is decentralized and deregulated (see Rosenbloom 1993; Moe 1994; Kellough 1998; Kearney and
Hays 1998). Thus, caution is in order when considering both the purposes of HR reform and the empirical base upon which calls for HR
reform are built.
    These caveats notwithstanding, public sector HR reform has
become the centerpiece of many contemporary administrative reform
efforts. Nowhere is this more true than at the state government level.
In fact, research suggests that the states are leading the way on
HR reform (Selden, Ingraham, and Jacobson 2001). As Selden,
Ingraham, and Jacobson (2001) report, the "penetrating changes"
occurring in state civil service systems are characterized, primarily,

by shifts from rigidity to flexibility and from centralization to decentralization. Such tendencies are reflected in recent HR reform efforts in states like Wisconsin (Lavigna 2001), South Carolina (Hays 2000), Georgia (Walters 1997; Facer 1998), and Florida (West 2002). In sum, the literature paints a compelling need for HR reform and offers numerous examples where such change has occurred or is occurring.

In contrast, research explicitly examining the outcomes of HR reform is less well developed. The evidence that does exist is mixed. For example, researchers have found empirical evidence of partisan political and equity abuses in "reformed" jurisdictions (Nigro and Kellough 2000; Condrey 2001), though not to the degree feared by many (e.g., Coggburn 2003; Kellough 1998; Peters and Savoie 1996; Kearney and Hays 1998). Others have shown that the bottom-line savings often promised by HR reform advocates are not likely to materialize (Coggburn 2000; Wechsler 1993, 1994). This evidence notwithstanding, the true effects of HR reform are uncertain. Additional research is needed, especially since HR reform seems to be accelerating even in the absence of a sound empirical knowledge base on which to build (Kellough 1999).

HR in the Lone Star State: A Brief Overview

Texas offers a perfect case study for examining the consequences of decentralized, deregulated HR. While other states have only recently adopted significant HR reform, Texas has never had a central, statewide HR office.[1] In other words, the radical model being pursued in many jurisdictions has been in place in Texas for decades. Therefore, Texas offers an opportunity to better understand the practical implications of decentralization and deregulation on widely held public HR values. But, before those questions are explored, it is important to first describe how the HR function is carried out in the Lone Star State.

State Agencies

Since the HR function in Texas state government is decentralized, with primary responsibility for HR management residing at the line agency level (Anderson, Murray, Farley 1992; Selden, Ingraham, and Jacobson 2001), it makes sense to begin this discussion with state agencies' roles in HR. Simply put, state agencies are free to develop their own policies and procedures for most every aspect of

HR, including: recruitment, selection, performance evaluation, training and development, employee discipline, and grievance. The only major caveats are: (1) state agencies must adhere to all statewide HR statutes enacted, HR provisions contained in biennial appropriation bills, and applicable federal employment laws, and (2) state agencies who are required by the federal government to develop merit systems as a condition of receiving federal aid must develop such systems.

Given this level of decentralization, it is not surprising that some agencies have developed sophisticated, comprehensive HR programs emphasizing strategic orientations, whereas others have maintained more traditional, "policing" approaches to HR (Office of the Governor 1972; Gibson and Robsinson 1993).[2] Some agencies have solid training programs, performance appraisal systems, and excellent recruitment and staffing processes, others do not (Barrett and Greene 1999; 2001). As mentioned, still other agencies have responded to federal mandates by establishing full-blown merit systems (e.g., the Texas Workforce Commission is a "merit agency"). In addition to this variation, agency-level control has also produced widely known HR problems. For example, a report on statewide HR management controls published by the State Auditor's Office (SAO 1997, 3) identified "persistent weaknesses in basic human resource controls, including performance appraisal procedures, hiring processes, staff development, and compliance with human resource regulations." Nevertheless, the point to be made here is merely that individual agencies occupy central roles in the state's HR and they operate with considerable flexibility.

State Legislature

The state legislature plays an active role in the management of the state's HR. Obviously, having the "power of the purse" means that the Texas legislature affects HR by controlling funding for state salaries, benefits, and training and development. Unlike most other states, however, the Texas legislature also plays a primary role in the promulgation of HR policies. This can come in the form of general statutory requirements or, more commonly, in provisos contained in biennial state appropriation acts (especially Article IX). For example, the legislature has passed laws placing full-time equivalent (FTE) caps on state agencies, requiring state agencies to forfeit lapsed salaries, and providing whistleblower protection to state employees. As for the biennial appropriation bills, they contain (among other things) detailed listings of all classes that can be used by state agencies in a given biennium, and set corresponding compensation schedules. Given these roles, it is easy to see why the legislature has been described as being at the top of the state's HR structure (Office of the Governor 1972).

State Auditor's Office (SAO) and the State Classification Office (SCO)

The SCO, Texas' closest approximation to a centralized HR office, is a small, professional office housed within the State Auditor's Office (SAO). Currently, the SCO is staffed by nine HR professionals, including the state classification officer.[3] Each SCO analyst holds professional HR certification through the Society of Human Resource Management (SHRM), the leading professional association for the HR field. Created by the 1961 Position Classification Act, the SCO's primary mandate is maintaining the state's classification plan and advising agencies on its application. The office also conducts periodic classification compliance audits to ensure that agencies have properly classified their positions. As this suggests, the classification function is one area of HR in Texas that remains largely centralized. State agencies can request certain classifications for new positions and reclassifications for existing positions, but the fact remains that the SCO will weigh in on these decisions. Implicitly, this serves as recognition by the state that centralization *can* serve important purposes (e.g., pay equity, efficiency) even in a otherwise decentralized setting.

The SCO's functions, however, go well beyond maintenance of the classification plan. One can gain a sense of the breadth of the SCO's activities from its mission statement:

> To be the[state of Texas'] strategic human resource management leader by providing useful information to the legislature and state agencies and institutions. The SCO's work focuses on these activities:
> - Compensation Management—To ensure the state has an appropriate and well-managed compensation system
> - Workforce Analysis—To reduce workforce risks in the state
> - HR Advisory Services—To improve human resource management in the state

The SCO fulfills it mission through a variety of HR services and activities. Among these are:

- Maintenance of the state's comprehensive HR Web site (http://www.hr.state.tx.us/), which includes an HR Question of the Month, Current Events, HR Training Opportunities, Legal Updates, and featured articles
- Development of an online *Human Resource Management Self-Assessment Guide* for state agencies
- Interpretation of state leave laws (e.g., vacation, sick, civil)
- Development and implementation of a statewide *On-line Exit Interview System*
- Maintenance of separate listservs for state HR directors and HR professionals
- Conducting wage and salary surveys and making recommendations for adjustment to the governor and legislature
- Publication of the *Texas Human Resources Management Statutes Inventory* (compiled every biennium, the inventory lists all state HR statutes and includes interpretive notes for new laws)
- Providing HR advice to state agencies through agency-specific HR consultants
- Serving on various ad hoc HR task forces
- Publishing various HR reports (e.g., *Quarterly Report on Full-Time Equivalent State Employees*; *Annual Report on Full-Time Classified Employee Turnover*)

As this admittedly incomplete list demonstrates, the SCO performs a multitude of HR roles for the state. In fact, the SCO operates very similar to the "adviser/consultant" role that reformers often advocate for central HR offices. However, it is important to note that the SCO, as a unit of the SAO, is a *legislative* entity. This is in marked contrast to every other state government and the federal government where centralized HR offices are found in the *executive* branch.

The Governor

Institutionally, Texas governors are among the weakest in the nation (Beyle 1995). Nevertheless, Texas governors impact state government HR in a number of ways. Most obvious, perhaps, is through the administrative appointment process. Given Texas' myriad of state boards and commissions, Texas' governors can anticipate making more than 4,000 appointments during a four-year term (Lamare 1998). Despite this authority, governors do not have a great deal of executive control. Appointees, for example, must be confirmed by the

Senate and must meet any statutory qualifications for positions in question. Moreover, the overlapping six-year terms of the state's multimember boards and commissions mean governors may be into their second four-year term before having appointed board majorities. Finally, beyond his/her own staff, the governor's removal power is severely constrained, perhaps "crippled" (Anderson, Murray, Farley 1992, 148), by the need to show cause for removal (Lamare 1998; Tannahill 1997).[4]

The governor does have other important HR responsibilities. First, in the area of oversight, if an SCO classification audit finds an agency has misclassified positions, the governor has the power to direct the state comptroller (discussed below) to halt paychecks for the effected positions until the problem is remedied. Second, the governor can make salary and HR policy recommendations to the legislature and can exempt positions from the state classification plan. Third, the governor's office includes divisions related to HR. The Governor's Committee on People with Disabilities (GCPD), for example, coordinates and monitors the state's compliance with the Americans with Disabilities Act (ADA)(SAO 2001). Fourth, the Governor's Center for Management Development, an executive training entity housed within the Lyndon B. Johnson School of Public Affairs at the University of Texas, provides training to state agencies in a number of management areas, including HR. Finally, the governor appoints ad hoc HR task forces commissioned to investigate various HR issues including the state's merit pay practices.

The State Attorney General (AG)

The AG is Texas' chief lawyer. As such, the AG is responsible for defending the state and its officials in lawsuits, filing lawsuits on behalf of the state, and issuing legal opinions on various matters of importance to the state. It is the last of these functions that is of the most direct concern for present purposes. Simply put, the AG, in issuing legally binding opinions on HR-related questions, is the only definitive voice on questions of HR law and policy in the state (Office of the Governor 1972). The SCO's HR Web site lists the AG's HR-related opinions, which as of June 2002 exceeded 300.[5]

Comptroller of Public Accounts

As the state's chief financial officer, the comptroller plays major roles in tax collection, revenue estimation, accounting and payroll. These responsibilities affect HR in a number of ways. By providing state revenue estimates to the state legislature, the comptroller potentially affects legislative decisions for salary increases, merit pay, and the like. More directly, the comptroller issues checks to state employees using the Uniform Statewide Payroll/Personnel System (USPS). Maintaining this system means that the comptroller is in the position of making payroll policies that are applicable to all state agencies. These policies are published in the comptroller's *Payroll Policies and Procedures Guide*. Examples include polices for dealing with payroll errors, and for awarding one-time merit increases for employees at the top of their salary group. Finally, the comptroller maintains an employee information database called the Human Resource Information System (HRIS).[6]

While these roles are important, it is the comptroller's Texas Performance Review (TPR) division that has the potential to profoundly influence state HR. The TPR, which served as a model for the Clinton administration's National Performance Review, "reviews government agencies, programs, and operations and recommends improvements to increase efficiency and effectiveness" (Comptroller 2002). Since its inception in 1991, the TPR has produced several reports, each of which has included recommendations for the state's HR function (Comptroller, various years). Many of the TPR's HR recommendations have been enacted, including the elimination of vacant state positions, requiring agencies to maintain management-to-staff ratios of 1-to-11, and a creating an HR task force to examine and publish a manual of state agencies' HR "best practices."[7]

Texas Commission on Human Rights (TCHR)

The major responsibility of the TCHR is ensuring state agencies' compliance with applicable federal and state HR laws (e.g., Title VII; Texas Commission on Human Rights Act). TCHR accomplishes its compliance mandate through regular audits, conducted on staggered six-year cycles, of state agencies' HR policies and practices. Speaking of these audits, it is worth mentioning that the TCHR Web site (http://tchr.state.tx.us/) includes several "recommended" HR polices for areas like hiring and promotions, EEO and sexual harassment, disability and reasonable accommodation (i.e., Americans with Disabilities), employee discipline, performance evaluation, and employee layoff and recall. It is impossible to say how many state agencies have adopted TCHR's recommended policies as their "own," but given that TCHR will come knocking at least once every six years surely serves as a strong incentive for agencies to do so.

In addition to its compliance role, the TCHR investigates and resolves state employee complaints of workplace discrimination. The TCHR also provides mandatory training and training materials to state agencies on compliance with employment discrimination law. Finally, the TCHR is responsible for preparing the state's two annual minority hiring practices reports: the EEO-4 report, which is filed with the federal government, and the *Minority Hiring Practices Report*, which is filed with the state legislature.

Texas Workforce Commission (TWC)

The TWC provides traditional employment services functions for the state (i.e., both public and private sectors), including administering the state's unemployment insurance program. In the area of recruitment, TWC maintains two job vacancy databases, the *Governor's Job Bank* (http://www.twc.state.tx.us/) and *Hire Texas* (http://m06hostp.twc.state.tx.us/jobmatch/jobseeker/htapp.html), which allow applicants to apply online using a standardized state application form. State law requires agencies to post position announcements with the TWC for ten days. Agencies can also request the TWC to recruit and screen applicants (Comptroller 1991), but it is not clear how many agencies actually do so. Finally, the TWC provides labor and market statistics that can be used by agencies for such things as workforce plans and minority utilization reports, and it publishes various reports on Texas workforce laws.

Employees Retirement System (ERS)

The ERS main charge is administering the state's employee retirement program. The agency also administers the state's employee benefits program, including employee group insurance, and the state's deferred compensation plans (Comptroller 1996).

Texas Workers' Compensation Commission (TWCC) and State Office of Risk Management (SORM)

The TWCC is responsible for promulgating the state's workers' compensation rules and regulations. The agency also attempts to promote safe and healthy work environments and provides information about workers' compensation rights (TWCC 2002). The SORM, on the other hand, administers the state's workers' compensation system for most employees (SAO 2001, 72). Since the state is self-insured, mitigating property, liability, and workers' compensation costs is major concern. Thus, the SORM assists state agencies with the development and implementation of risk management programs. For example, SORM maintains an online compliance manual for state agencies (see http://www.sorm.state.tx.us/volumes.htm). The manual includes a number of specific HR-related practices that agencies are encouraged to adopt.

Texas Incentive and Productivity Commission (TIPC)

The TIPC administers two state productivity plans. The State Employee Incentive Program (SEIP) recognizes and rewards individual state employees for suggestions that reduce state expenditures, increase state revenues, improve the quality of state services, or improve customer service (SAO 2001). The Productivity Bonus Program (PBB) is similar to the SEIP, but it pertains to cost savings achieved by teams, work groups, or entire agencies. In both programs, employees are afforded the opportunity to enjoy monetary awards for demonstrable cost savings.

State Agency Coordinating Committees

Although HR is decentralized in the state, it is also true that many HR issues cut horizontally across state government. Thus, the state has devised a number of multiagency structures to deal collectively with HR and other management issues. These coordinating committees are: (1) the State Agency Coordinating Council (SACC), for "large" (i.e., 800 FTEs or more) state agencies, (2) the Midsize Agency Coordinating Council (MACC), for agencies with between 101 and 799 FTEs, and (3) the Small State Agency Task Force (SSATF), for agencies with 100 or fewer FTEs.

The various agency coordinating committees consist of state agency executive personnel (typically deputy directors). The SACC and MACC utilize subcommittees, including those for HR. The SACC HR subcommittee, for example, meets monthly to discuss HR issues of mutual concern to large state agencies. The subcommittee makes recommendations to the full SACC for proposed changes to state HR policy. SACC then makes recommendations or specific HR proposals to the SCO, which, in turn, can make recommendations to the state legislature. In this way, state agencies of similar size have the potential *collectively* to effect change in the state's HR policies.

Texas Public Employees Association (TPEA) and the Texas State Employee Union (TSEU)

Texas law does not allow collective bargaining by state employees for wages, hours, or conditions of employment, nor does it allow state employees the right to strike. The law does, however, guarantee state employees the right to organize and it prevents public employers from denying employment because of someone's membership in a labor union (SAO 2001, 111). The two largest state employee organizations are the TPEA (representing some 14,000 state employees) and the TSEU (representing approximately 12,000). Both employee organizations maintain informational Web sites (http://ww.tpea.org and http://ww.cwa-tseu.org, respectively) and both seek to achieve their objectives primarily through political lobbying efforts. The TSEU's Web site, for example, lists a number of "victories" for state employees (including a 4 percent pay raise in 2001 passed by the 77th legislature) and "legislative objectives" for the upcoming legislative session.

Texas State Human Resource Association (TSHRA)

Though TSHRA is not a state entity—it is a nonprofit association of state human resources professionals—the role it plays in state HR warrants brief mention. Among the TSHRA's activities and services are: a monthly state HR newsletter, an HR web site (http://ww.tshra.org) with numerous HR links, and a variety of HR-related training and development opportunities. By providing an active, professional HR network—which no doubt spawns innumerable informal networks—TSHRA is an important piece of an otherwise fragmented state HR puzzle.

In Sum: A Complicated, Fragmented System

At the risk of stating (understating?) the obvious, Texas state government's HR function is a fragmented, complicated system. The approach confers considerable autonomy and discretion on state agencies, yet there *are* important elements of HR centralization. In a recent article that assigned "grades" for the states' management capacity, *Governing* reported that Texas' HR function suffers because there is no statewide monitoring of agencies' HR activities (see Barrett and Greene 1999). As the above discussion demonstrates, that assertion is wrong. Statewide, agencies *are* centrally monitored (e.g., SCO and TCHR post audits), just not by a single HR entity.

Despite this, it is safe to say that Texas does not come close to the levels of central control and regulation found in most other states. Thus, Texas offers a unique case for studying the practical implications of a decentralized, deregulated HR system.

The Status of HR in Texas: The HR Directors' Perspective

A number of important questions emerge from the Texas HR "model" described above. If, as in Texas, state agencies are left largely to their own devises to create HR policies and programs, then what are the consequences? For example, what are the impacts on equity, employee rights, and merit? Do some state agencies enjoy comparative advantages over others when it comes to attracting the most talented employees? More broadly, how effective are state agencies in carrying out their HR tasks? Obviously, these are important empirical questions that warrant systematic investigation.

In an attempt to answer questions such as these, a mail survey was administered to the state's HR directors. Being on the "front lines" of HR in Texas state government, HR directors have firsthand knowledge of how the HR function is administered in their respective agencies and, more generally, what the consequences (both positive and negative) of Texas' decentralized, deregulated approach are. Thus, HR directors are perfectly suited to meet the objectives of this research. It is, however, important to acknowledge up front that HR directors may be hesitant to report problems with the HR function in their own agencies since doing so might reflect poorly on their own abilities and performance. To the extent that HR directors *do* report problems, we can be confident that such problems are real.

The names and addresses of these officials were obtained by the author directly from the SCO. The SCO list included HR directors for 140 agencies, boards, and commissions. [8] Of those 140 agencies, one has been dissolved by the legislature, three have their HR functions contracted out to larger umbrella agencies, and two share the same HR director. Thus, the effective survey population was 135 state HR directors. The survey sought HR directors' perceptions of HR effectiveness in their respective agencies and in Texas state government in general. The survey also sought their opinions about the creation of a central state HR office. The survey instrument was pretested on a number of subject matter experts and was subsequently modified to eliminate duplication and any sources of confusion.

The survey was mailed at the beginning of May 2002. Following the tailored design survey method (Dillman 2000), the anonymous survey was mailed along with a detailed cover letter and a self-identifying respondent postcard. Respondents were asked to return their surveys and postcards separately, which allowed respondents and nonrespondents to be tracked without compromising their anonymity. After one week, a reminder postcard was sent. The initial mailing yielded 76 responses, or about a 56 percent response rate. A second complete mailing (i.e., a second cover letter, duplicate copies of the survey and respondent postcard) was conducted about four weeks later, during the last week of May 2002. The second mailing produced 23 additional responses, bringing the total number of returned surveys to 99, for an overall response rate of approximately 73 percent.[9]

Survey Findings

Table 9.1 displays demographic data for survey respondents. As the table shows, 70.6 percent of respondents were 45 years old or older. Approximately 60 percent of respondents were women and 40 percent were men. As for educational backgrounds, more than 70 percent reported having earned at least a four-year college degree, with a master's degree (33%) being the most frequently indicated level of educational attainment. In the area of work experience, 80 percent reported having worked in the private sector, although more than 67 percent indicated that they have worked in the public sector for ten years or longer. Finally, about 50 percent indicated that they have worked in the HR field for less than ten years.

The substantive survey findings are presented in Tables 9.2 through 9.4. Table 9.2 presents HR directors' opinions of HR as practiced within their respective agencies, Table 9.3 presents their opinions on HR as practiced generally in Texas state government, and Table 9.4 presents their opinions on the creation of a central state HR office. In each table, the first column lists the HR-related statements from the survey: respondents were asked to indicate their level of agreement or disagreement with each. Responses appear in the second, third, and fourth columns of each table: the second column lists the percentages of respondents who either "strongly agreed" or "agreed" with the listed statements; the third column presents the percentages who "neither agreed/disagreed"; and the last column lists the percentages who either "disagreed" or "strongly disagreed."

Table 9.1.
Demographic Overview of State Agency HR Directors

Age range	Percentages
24 or less	1.0
25–34	6.1
35–44	22.2
45–54	44.4
55–64	24.2
65 or over	2.0
Gender	
Female	59.6
Male	40.4
Private sector experience	
Yes	79.8
No	20.2
Years in the public sector	
Less than 5 Years	12.1
5 to 10 years	21.2
11 to 15 years	20.2
16 to 20 years	13.1
21 to 25 years	15.2
26–30 years	18.2
Over 30 Years	0.0
Years in the HR field	
Less than 5 Years	27.3
5 to 10 years	21.2
11 to 15 years	15.2
16 to 20 years	13.1
21 to 25 years	11.1
26–30 years	9.1
Over 30 Years	3.0
Highest level of academic training	
High school	7.1
Some college	12.2
2 year college degree	4.1
4 year college degree	26.5
Some graduate work	9.2
Master's degree	32.7
Ph.D.	2.0
Law degree	6.1

Source: Lone Star HR Survey of Texas state agency HR directors, conducted May–June 2002.

Note: Percentages may not sum to 100 due to rounding.

HR Directors' Opinions of HR in Their Own Agencies

Given the potential for substantial variation in HR from state agency to agency, the first part of the survey asked HR directors to offer their opinions of the practice of HR in their respective agencies. The results are presented in Table 9.2. As the table shows, there was a general sense of HR effectiveness in state agencies. For example, 74 percent of those responding agreed that their agencies have the HR expertise and staff resources needed to be effective. Given such positive views about their HR capacity, it is not surprising that 81 percent agreed that their agencies have developed effective HR programs. Importantly, an amazing 91 percent agreed that they have made good use of the HR discretion afforded by Texas decentralized, deregulated approach. This is an important finding given the uncertainty over whether HR managers would utilize newfound discretion under deregulated, decentralized HR systems (e.g., Peters 1996; Kearney and Hays 1998). Finally, strong majorities agreed that their agencies had recruitment and selection practices that allow them to quickly hire qualified candidates (86%) and to quickly deal with disciplinary problems (79%). Both of these findings stand in stark contrast to general perceptions of traditional HR systems as reported in the academic literature.

Aside from these general effectiveness issues, scholars have questioned the impact of contemporary HR reforms on employee rights and equity (Peters and Savoie 1996; Peters 1996; Kellough 1998; Coggburn 2003). Concern centers on the effects of decentralization and deregulation on the "sameness of treatment" of individuals (Peters and Savoie 1996), with at least one researcher concluding that centralized rules were needed to insure fair treatment of employees (Elliot 1985). Although many rules and regulations are viewed as irksome "red tape," most were put into place to meet important purposes: namely, to prevent corruption and political influence, ensure employee due process, and to promote fairness in HR. What, then, do the survey results suggest about these issues?

First, more than 75 percent of responding HR directors agreed that their agencies award equal pay for equal work. Similarly, almost 85 percent reported that their employees are classified properly, according to their job duties and responsibilities. Pay comparability is an obvious indicator of internal organizational equity, so these two findings offer some assurance that equity is not being compromised. Of course more egregious forms of equity abuse, such as overt discrimination, can occur. On this, however, only 2.1 percent

Table 9.2.
HR Directors' Perceptions of Agency-Level HR

In my agency. . .	Agree	Neutral	Disagree
We have the HR expertise and staff resources we need to be effective.	74.2%	7.2%	18.5%
We have used the discretion available under state law to create HR policies that meet our agency's specific needs.	90.9	7.1	2.0
We have developed an effective HR program.	80.8	14.1	5.0
Management views the HR director as a strategic partner in attaining our agency's goals and mission.	76.0	16.7	7.3
We have formulated disciplinary practices that allow problems to be dealt with quickly and effectively.	78.8	9.1	12.1
We have formulated grievance procedures that offer employees protection from unjust HR actions.	85.7	10.2	4.1
We have recruitment and selection processes that allow us to hire qualified candidates in a timely manner.	85.6	5.2	9.2
Training and development opportunities are based upon individual employee needs (assessed, for example, through "needs assessments").	68.0	19.6	12.4

(cont.) Table 9.2

We have the expertise and technical materials needed to accurately forecast our future staffing needs.	59.2	20.4	20.4
Employees are classified properly, based on their job duties and responsibilities.	84.7	11.2	4.1
Merit pay increases awarded to employees reflect actual differences in their job performance.	62.2	27.6	10.2
Employees doing essentially the same work are paid equally.	76.5	15.3	8.2
I can think of an instance(s) when someone was denied a job, promotion, or other job reward because of their race, religion, national origin, sex, age, or disability.	2.1	3.2	94.7
I can think of an instance(s) when someone's political beliefs or connections influenced a decision on hiring, promotion, or other job reward.	11.6%	7.4%	81.0%
Concern about wrongful termination lawsuits limits our use of "at-will" terminations.	22.3	21.3	56.4

Source: Lone Star HR Survey of Texas state agency HR directors, conducted May–June, 2002.

Note: Survey responses were coded as follows: 1, Strongly Agree; 2, Agree; 3, Neither Agree/Disagree; 4, Disagree; 5, Strongly Disagree; and 6, No Opinion/Don't Know. Percentages may not sum to 100 due to rounding.

Table 9.3.

HR Directors' Perceptions of HR in Texas State Government

In Texas state government...	Agree	Neutral	Disagree
Eliminating "at-will" employment would give state employees less incentive to perform.	29.0%	30.1%	40.9%
The HR advice and services provided by the State Classification Office help agencies more effectively manage their human resources.	68.0	22.7	9.3
There is wide variation in the quality of the HR function from state agency to state agency.	73.6	19.5	6.9
The HR function would improve if there was a uniform set of HR policies and procedures (e.g., a statewide "HR Policy Manual") applicable to all state agencies.	40.6	17.7	41.6
Some agencies have an advantage over others because they can offer greater salaries to attract talented employees.	89.5	8.4	2.1

Source: Lone Star HR Survey of Texas state agency HR directors, conducted May-June, 2002.

Note: Survey responses were coded as follows: 1, Strongly Agree; 2, Agree; 3, Neither Agree/Disagree; 4, Disagree; 5, Strongly Disagree; and 6, No Opinion/Don't Know. Percentages may not sum to 100 due to rounding.

Table 9.4.

HR Directors' Opinions on the Creation of State Office of HR

Creating a central state HR office would . . .	Agree	Neutral	Disagree
Decrease duplication of HR effort in state agencies.	42.4%	25.0%	32.6%
Reduce the state's liability for HR-related lawsuits.	25.6	13.3	61.1
Improve the overall effectiveness of the state's HR function.	28.3	16.3	55.4
Help protect state employees from partisan political influences.	21.8	37.9	40.2
Make it easier to address statewide HR problems and issues (e.g., employee turnover, training).	43.3	13.3	43.3
Create more equity (e.g., fair and just treatment of all employees, regardless of race, gender) in state government employment.	25.0	20.7	54.4
Take away the HR flexibility that state agencies need to be effective.	76.3	10.8	13.0

Source: Lone Star HR Survey of Texas state agency HR directors, conducted May–June, 2002.

Note: Survey responses were coded as follows: 1, Strongly Agree; 2, Agree; 3, Neither Agree/Disagree; 4, Disagree; 5, Strongly Disagree; and 6, No Opinion/Don't Know. Percentages may not sum to 100 due to rounding.

agreed that they knew of an instance of discriminatory HR behavior in their own agencies.

Employee rights are also related to the level of protection employees enjoy. Here, however, it is important to note that Texas is an "at-will" employer, meaning that both parties (i.e., state agencies or state employees) can terminate employment at any time, with or without cause. In other words, Texas state employees typically do not obtain property interests in their positions, thus they are not entitled to due process.[10] Despite this, Texas agencies must abide by anti-discrimination laws, lest they face litigation from aggrieved employees. That such a small percentage (22%) agreed that they limit at-will terminations because of fears over wrongful termination lawsuits suggests that HR directors are relatively comfortable in the propriety/fairness of their separation decisions. Moreover, almost all (86%) agreed that they have devised grievance procedures that offer employees protection from unjust HR actions.

Like equity, the potential for partisan political abuses in reformed HR settings has received considerable attention from HR researchers (e.g., Thompson 1994; Kellough 1998; Coggburn 2003; Kearney and Hays 1998). Indeed, there seems to be general consensus around Thompson's (1994) conclusion that deregulated HR systems are more vulnerable to political abuse. Given that the history of civil service reform in America has been largely a battle against such corruption (Anechiarico and Jacobs 1996), the impact of decentralization and deregulation on neutral competence and merit are fundamentally important questions.

Table 9.2 offers some information that is instructive on the politics question. Specifically, 11.6 percent of respondents agreed that they could think of an instance where someone's political beliefs or connections influenced an HR decision in their agencies (e.g., hiring, firing, promotion). Similarly, 10 percent disagreed that merit pay increases were based on actual differences in employee performance. While these findings are not enough to suggest that political abuse is endemic to Texas state government, having roughly one in ten of the state's HR directors agreeing to knowing of some HR decision being based upon something other than merit does suggest a nontrivial political influence.

In addition to the omnipresent concern over equity and politics, the HR field has increasingly stressed the need for agencies to act strategically in HR (Pynes 2003; Daley 2002; Ulrich 1997; Perry and Mesch 1997). In contrast to the reactive, control orientation of traditional HR, a strategic approach entails HR securing its place at the management table and developing HR strategies that support agency mission. For central HR offices, the goal is to shift from a traditional control or policing orientation to a consultative or advisory role.

Several survey findings speak to these broad strategic themes. First, Table 9.2 shows that 76 percent of HR directors agreed that agency management views HR as a strategic partner in meeting agencies' goals and missions. So, in the broadest terms, HR directors perceived success at gaining their place at the management table. Findings for more specific aspects of strategic HR tend to support this general view. For example, 68 percent agreed that their agency's training and development opportunities are based upon identified needs. A majority (60%) also agreed that their agencies have the resources to forecast their HR staffing needs.

To sum up, HR directors were asked to offer their levels of agreement with a variety of statements concerning the practice of HR in their own agencies. Respondents had generally positive views of their HR capacity, strategic role, and overall HR effectiveness. Their responses also suggested that equity abuses are held in check, but also that political concerns may enter HR decision making in some instances.

HR Directors' Opinions of HR in Texas State Government

Since HR directors likely have different perceptions of their own agencies' HR practices relative to those of other agencies, the second part of the survey asked respondents to provide their opinions on HR as practiced generally in Texas state government. Table 9.3 presents these findings. Looking at the table, the figure that leaps out is the 89.5 percent who agreed that the ability to offer higher salaries gives some state agencies advantages over others when it comes to attracting talented employees. Presumably, the work performed by, say, an information technology specialist would not vary appreciably from agency to agency, but this finding suggests that the level of compensation such an employee receives could. Obviously, this poses a challenge to notions of external equity (i.e., equal pay for equal work from agency to agency) within state government.

The second illuminating finding reported in Table 9.3 is the 74 percent who agreed that there is wide variation in the quality of the HR function from state agency to state agency. This is a startlingly different picture than what was painted by HR directors' perceptions of HR effectiveness within their own agencies (see Table 9.2). It seems that respondents have a generally high opinion of HR in their own agencies, but a much less sanguine view of HR as practiced in other state agencies. It is also interesting that roughly equal numbers agreed (40.6%) and disagreed (41.6%) on the ability of a statewide HR policies and procedures manual to improve HR in the state.

The survey also asked respondents their opinions of the SCO. As discussed above, the SCO is the closest approximation to a central HR office in Texas and its activities closely resemble those that are called for in reformed, strategic HR models. As Table 9.3 shows, 68 percent agreed and only 9 percent disagreed that the SCO's advice and services help agencies more effectively manage HR. This suggests general agreement that SCO fills an important role in the state's HR function.

Finally, Table 9.3 reports on general perceptions of the state's status as an at-will employer. Rhetoric surrounding calls for HR reform often touts the notion that civil service protections provide public employees too much protection, thus giving them less incentive to perform. Here, HR directors' opinions give reason to question this logic: a plurality (41%) *disagreed* that eliminating at-will employment would give employees less incentive to perform. This suggests that respondents do not view at-will employment as being instrumental to motivating state workers—a finding that differs sharply with the "conventional wisdom" espoused by would be reformers.

Findings from the second section of the survey differ in important ways from those of the first. Specifically, when asked about HR in Texas state government in general, respondents held less positive views: they agreed that some agencies hold advantages over others and that HR quality varies across state government.

HR Directors' Opinions of a Central HR Office

Finally, HR directors were asked to offer their opinions on the usefulness of a central HR office for the state. This section was designed to get at the crux of the classic centralization-decentralization debate. On one hand, a decentralized approach gives agencies greater flexibility over HR, thus potentially improving HR effectiveness. On the other hand, a centralized approach diminishes costs associated with duplication and offers greater HR consistency (see Selden, Ingraham, and Jacobson 2001; Ingraham and Rosenbloom 1992). Looking to Table 9.4, respondents generally did not see the benefits of a central HR agency. While pluralities agreed that such an office would decrease HR duplication (42%) and make it easier to address statewide HR problems (43%), only 28 percent agreed that a central HR office would improve HR effectiveness and only 26 percent agreed that it would reduce the state's liability for HR-related lawsuits.[11] The figure that really stands out, however, is the 76 percent who agreed that creating a central state HR office would take away the flexibility state agencies need to be effective. This suggests that state agencies are loath to give up the HR autonomy they currently enjoy: flexibility and autonomy won over consistency and economy, at least in these respondents' eyes.

Findings reported in Table 9.4 also speak to issues of equity and politics. First, 22 percent agreed that creating a central HR office would help protect state employees from partisan political influences. This, too, is an interesting finding. While only 11.6 percent agreed to knowing of overt political abuses in their agencies (see Table 9.2), roughly double that amount agreed that creating a central office would offer state employees greater protection. Similarly, one in four (25%) respondents agreed that creating a central state HR office would create more equity in state government employment. Here, again, the results stand in contrast to HR directors' generally positive opinions on workplace equity as reported in Table 9.2.

In summary, the HR centralization-decentralization debate is ongoing. Each approach entails costs and benefits. Survey respondents generally did not agree to seeing the potential benefits of a central office of HR for the state; rather, they tended to agree that the flexibility of a decentralized approach was necessary for HR effectiveness.

Taking Another Look: HR Expertise and Opinions on Texas HR

As stated previously, observers have suggested that HR varies considerably from agency to agency in Texas. Survey findings reported above tend to support those general assessments. The question that arises then is how to account for such variation. In an effort to see if agencies' levels of HR expertise affect HR directors' perceptions, survey respondents were divided into two groups: those who "strongly agreed" or "agreed" that they *possessed the HR expertise and staff resources needed to be effective* and those who "disagreed" or "strongly disagreed" with that statement. The "HR expertise" group contains 72 respondents, and the "no HR expertise" group contains 18 respondents. Mean (average) responses were then calculated for both groups for each survey from Tables 9.2 through 9.4. The mean responses for the two groups are compared in Table 9.5.

Not surprisingly, respondents in the "no HR expertise" group evaluated the overall effectiveness of their HR programs at significantly lower levels than those agencies possessing HR expertise.

Table 9.5.
Differences of Means on HR Issues by Perceived HR Expertise

In my agency...	HR Expertise	No HR Expertise	t	Sig.
We have used the discretion available under state law to create HR policies that meet our agency's specific needs.	1.67	2.06	-2.30	.029
We have developed an effective HR program.	1.72	3.00	-7.37	.000
Management views the HR director as a strategic partner in attaining our agency's goals and mission.	1.86	2.83	-4.97	.000
We have formulated disciplinary practices that allow problems to be dealt with quickly and effectively.	1.92	2.89	-4.42	.000
We have formulated grievance procedures that offer employees protection from unjust HR actions.	1.80	2.39	-2.57	.018
We have recruitment and selection processes that allow us to hire qualified candidates in a timely manner.	1.87	2.33	-1.57	.133
Training and development opportunities are based upon individual employee needs (assessed, for example, through "needs assessments").	2.24	2.76	-1.87	.076
We have the expertise and technical materials needed to accurately forecast our future staffing needs.	2.23	3.22	-4.11	.000
Employees are classified properly, based on their job duties and responsibilities.	1.79	2.44	-2.34	.030
Merit pay increases awarded to employees reflect actual differences in their job performance.	2.17	3.06	-4.39	.000
Employees doing essentially the same work are paid equally.	2.01	2.50	-1.95	.064
I can think of an instance(s) when someone was denied a job, promotion, or other job reward because of their race, religion, national origin, sex, age, or disability.	4.70	4.78	-.454	.651
I can think of an instance(s) when someone's political beliefs or connections influenced a decision on hiring, promotion, or other job reward.	4.29	4.61	-1.49	.144
Concern about wrongful termination lawsuits limits our use of "at-will" terminations.	3.60	3.56	-.159	.874

(cont.) Table 9.5

In Texas state government...

Eliminating "at-will" employment would give state employees less incentive to perform.	3.03	3.00	.093	.926
The HR advice and services provided by the State Classification Office help agencies more effectively manage their human resources.	2.20	2.78	-2.45	.016
There is wide variation in the quality of the HR function from state agency to state agency.	2.19	2.00	.883	.380
The HR function would improve if there was a uniform set of HR policies and procedures (e.g., a statewide "HR Policy Manual") applicable to all state agencies.	3.07	2.89	.529	.598
Some agencies have an advantage over others because they can offer greater salaries to attract talented employees.	1.86	1.65	1.16	.251

Creating a central state HR office would . . .

Decrease duplication of HR effort in state agencies.	2.96	2.87	.273	.786
Reduce the state's liability for HR-related lawsuits.	3.60	3.00	1.82	.073
Improve the overall effectiveness of the state's HR function.	3.54	2.67	2.08	.052
Help protect state employees from partisan political influences.	3.43	2.73	2.33	.022
Make it easier to address statewide HR problems and issues (e.g., employee turnover, training).	3.19	2.53	1.86	.066
Create more equity (e.g., fair and just treatment of all employees, regardless of race, gender) in state government employment.	3.52	2.87	1.77	.095
Take away the HR flexibility that state agencies need to be effective.	1.91	2.31	-1.44	.154

Source: Lone Star HR Survey of Texas state agency HR directors, conducted May-June, 2002.

Note: Survey responses were coded as follows: 1, Strongly Agree; 2, Agree; 3, Neither Agree/Disagree; 4, Disagree; 5, Strongly Disagree; and 6, No Opinion/Don't Know (the means reported do not include "No Opinion/Don't Know" responses). For the difference of means tests, respondents who "Strongly Agreed" or "Agreed" with the statement, *"We have the HR expertise and staff resources we need to be effective,"* are categorized as having "HR Expertise" (n = 72); those who "Disagreed," or "Strongly Disagreed" with the statement are categorized as "No HR Expertise" (n = 18). (There were also seven "neutral" responses and two missing responses.) The reported *t* values and significance levels (two-tailed) assume equal variances, except in those cases where Levene's test for homogeneity suggested otherwise (in which case separate variance *t* tests were used).

Although both groups expressed general agreement on their use of available HR discretion, formulation of effective disciplinary practices, and formulation of effective recruitment and selection practices, the group lacking HR expertise agreed at significantly lower (i.e., less strong) levels.

The most notable results in Table 9.5, however, are those related to the creation of a central state HR office. For five of the seven items listed, statistically significant differences are found between the two groups. Agencies lacking HR expertise and resources were more likely to view the creation of a central state HR office positively: they agreed at higher levels that such an office would help reduce the state's liability for HR lawsuits, improve the overall effectiveness of HR in the state, offer protection to state employees from patronage abuses, make it easier to address statewide HR problems, and create more equity in state government employment. While the findings reported in Table 9.4 suggested that state HR directors generally are averse to HR centralization, these findings show that significant differences of opinion exist among respondents, depending upon their perceived HR expertise.

Significant differences between the two groups can also be seen on items related to equity and politics. For example, the group lacking in HR expertise agreed at significantly lower levels that their employees received equal pay for equal work, were classified properly, and received protection from unjust HR actions through grievance procedures. In the area of political influence, the group lacking in HR expertise agreed at significantly lower levels that merit pay was awarded based upon actual differences in employee performance. The obvious conclusion is that HR expertise is necessary in order to protect equity and merit.

Finally, significant differences are also apparent in items related to strategic HR. Most broadly, there is general agreement that agency management considers HR to be a strategic partner, but the mean value for agencies lacking HR expertise is significantly lower than that of expert agencies. This same pattern is reflected in the more specific aspects of strategic HR. For example, respondents from nonexpert agencies agreed at significantly lower levels that they based training and development opportunities on identified employee needs, and had the expertise and materials to accurately forecast staffing needs. As for opinions regarding the advice and services provided by the SCO, agencies lacking needed HR expertise evaluated the SCO *lower* than agencies more expert agencies. So, those agencies who potentially stand to gain the most from the SCO tended to value the office less.

In summary, dividing respondents into expert and nonexpert groups revealed interesting differences. That almost 20 percent of respondents would disagree to having requisite HR expertise and resources is an important finding in and of itself. Furthermore, the nonexpert group expressed significantly different levels of agreement on 16 of 25 survey items presented. These findings obviously paint a more complex picture of HR in Texas than was suggested when all respondents were aggregated.

Implications and Conclusion

In recent years, themes like flexibility, decentralization, and deregulation have captured the imaginations of HR reformers. Since Texas has historically utilized the approach now being advocated, it stands as a perfect case study for understanding the consequences— both positive and negative—of the HR reform model. Survey findings reported above offer a number important lessons to the public HR field.

HR Directors Enjoy Their Autonomy and Will Use Their Discretion

The most basic finding from this analysis is that Texas' HR directors highly value the discretion they receive as a product of the state's decentralized approach. In fact, there was widespread agreement— even among those respondents lacking in HR expertise—that HR flexibility was key to state agencies' effectiveness. Moreover, the Texas case suggests that HR directors will in fact make use of their HR discretion, something that has heretofore been questioned in the academic literature. And, by and large, most respondents agreed that they have used their discretion to develop effective HR programs within their respective agencies. Of course, it is important for reformers to remember that HR directors in Texas have *always* operated in a decentralized, deregulated environment. It may well be the case that HR professionals in other jurisdictions will have to warm to the idea, but Texas shows that over time they will.

The Texas HR Model Is Not a Panacea

The second lesson to be drawn from this analysis is that Texas' approach to HR is not a panacea. The virtues and vices of both a centralized, regulated approach and of a decentralized, deregulated approach are well-known. Since the former approach has tended to be dominant in the U.S., attention has naturally focused on its shortcomings and on the benefits of the latter approach. But, as the Texas case demonstrates, the HR field may be encountering a case of Miles' Law: To those looking from the outside, Texas' approach appears to offer an enviable level of flexibility and agency-level control; to those Texas agencies lacking HR expertise who are looking (and operating) from the inside, Texas' approach appears to create inequity, political influence, and ineffectiveness, making a centralized approach somewhat more appealing. Thus, HR reformers would be wise to consider the effects of decentralization and deregulation on those agencies— especially small agencies (see Selden, Ingraham, and Jacobson 2001; SAO 2000; Comptroller 1996)—that lack sufficient HR expertise and resources: to do otherwise is to invite trouble.

Equity and Political Abuse Are Not Synonymous with Decentralization and Deregulation, But Cause for Concern Remains

The third lesson, which tends to corroborate earlier state-level research (Nigro and Kellough 2000), is that HR decentralization and deregulation have not resulted in rampant inequity and political abuse in Texas state government. Survey results showed that the most egregious forms of equity abuse (i.e., overt discrimination) and political abuse (i.e., overt patronage) were not widely perceived by the state's HR directors. This implies that deregulation and decentralization can potentially operate in HR systems without compromising long-held administrative values.

This does not suggest, however, that there is no reason for concern. To the contrary, HR directors strongly agreed that salary inequities existed across state government, one-fourth agreed that a centralized approach to state HR would make the state employment more equitable, and a sizable percentage (22%) agreed that a centralized approach would help protect employees from partisan political influences. So, while in a general sense inequity and political abuse appeared to be held in check in Texas, there was also considerable agreement that the state could do more to protect state employees. This point was only magnified in the opinions of respondents who were categorized as not having needed HR expertise.

Considering Context Is Essential

Texas tourism officials promote the state by saying, "Texas: It's like a whole other country." HR reformers would be wise to remember this motto when contemplating the adoption of Texas-style HR reforms. In other words, the fourth lesson to be drawn from the Texas experience is that context matters. Among other things, reformers need to consider the form of government and the political culture of their jurisdictions before adopting wholesale HR reform.

As described above, Texas operates with a weak executive, which is a product of the state's historically strong suspicion of centralized, active government (e.g., Tannahill 1997; Gibson and Robison 1993; Comptroller 1996). For present purposes, these political realities are important because they set the frame for HR in Texas. Once appointed, administrative officials of Texas' boards and commissions enjoy considerable autonomy. This, in turn, serves to create a layer of protection between elected officials and state employees (Office of the Governor 1973; Hill and Mladenka 1996). Thus, state employees have a built-in measure of protection from political influence.

In contrast, governors in most other states operate in the cabinet style of government, which provides more direct executive control over state agencies. So, in effect, the layer of protection from politics enjoyed by Texas employees does not exist in many other states, thus raising the specter of political abuse if and when centralized regulation and control are lifted. The practical implication is that extra diligence will be needed to ensure employees are protected from unwanted political influence.

Plugging the Holes: The Importance of Formal and Informal Networks

In the descriptive portion of this chapter, the TSHRA was identified as being an important professional network for the state's HR professionals. According to conversations with several state agency HR directors and with the state classification officer, one key to HR viability in Texas state government appears to be the emergence of network-type HR structures. The state agency coordinating committees (and their HR subcommittees), TSHRA, informal networks, and the "virtual" HR organization represented by the SCO's online HR resources all play important roles in Texas. In fact, this may well be one of the more important lessons to be gleaned from the Texas case study: a decentralized, deregulated approach to HR leaves open the possibility that voids will appear in a jurisdiction's HR function. In order to make the HR function more seamless across government, it behooves jurisdictions to facilitate the formation and maintenance of both formal and informal HR networks. In the absence of a strong, centralized HR office and a comprehensive set of HR policies and procedures, such networks represent the glue that binds Texas' HR system together.

The Importance of Considering Multiple Perspectives

Finally, the lessons presented here are subject to an important caveat: they are drawn from the perspective of the state's HR directors. As mentioned above, this raises some potential validity concerns since respondents had self-interest in portraying HR practices positively—at least in their own agencies—as this was in part a reflection on their performance. That they did not do so uniformly, however, offers a measure of confidence to the survey findings. Still, in order to gain a truly representative picture, it is important to take into account the perspectives of managers, front-line workers, and other interested groups.

It is worth noting that some employee-level data do exit for Texas. The Survey of Organizational Excellence (SOE), which assesses employee satisfaction with state government's management and HR practices, has been conducted on a biennial basis since the late 1970s (Williams 1989; Lauderdale 1999). In a recent book based on the SOE, Lauderdale (1999) identified a number of HR-related problems, including increasing employee dissatisfaction with the state's benefits package, and the general perception that raises and promotions are not connected to work performance. In other words, the SOE's employee-level data tend to corroborate certain findings of the current research. But, again, the point is that HR managers, line managers, and rank-and-file workers each have their own interests in a jurisdiction's HR system, and bearing those interests in mind when weighing the costs and benefits of HR reform is paramount.

As we move into the 21st century, there are no indications that the high performance expectations citizens and politicians place on government agencies will subside. The "more for less" mentality seems firmly entrenched in the country's psyche. Public administrators operating in this environment continually feel pressured to find ways to improve performance. Since many of government's performance problems are "people problems" (Kettl, Ingraham, Sanders, and Horner 1996), HR has become a primary target for reform. Since it is the only state operating without a central HR office, Texas has gained considerable attention from reformers. As this chapter demonstrates, opinions from within Texas state government provide cause for both optimism and concern over HR decentralization and deregulation's ability to solve government's people problems.

Notes

1. Until 1985 Texas had a Merit System Council that operated much like a traditional civil service commission for the limited number of agencies it covered. Agencies covered by the Merit Council included the Air Control Board, Department of Health, Department of Mental Health and Retardation, Department of Public Welfare, Texas Employment Commission (now the Texas Workforce Commission), Governor's Committee on Aging, Governor's Youth Secretariat, Office of Defense and Disaster Relief, Office of Human Resources (now Human Services), Office of Comprehensive Health Planning, and Surplus Property Agency (Office of the Governor 1972). The council was allowed to expire in 1985, and individual state agencies required by the federal government to maintain merit systems assumed that responsibility at the agency-level.

2. It is important to note that this research does not address the "what do individual state agencies do" aspect of HR; rather, the focus here is on the consequences of Texas decentralized, deregulated approach from the perspective of state HR directors.

3. The state classification officer is appointed by the State Auditor, subject to the approval of the state's Legislative Audit Committee.

4. It is interesting to note the degree of protection afforded administrative appointees relative to rank-and-file state employees. Governors have to demonstrate cause (e.g., gross mismanagement) to have administrative "officials" removed, while the vast majority of state employees serve "at-will" and can be separated with or without cause.

5. More precisely, the SCO's page lists 330 attorneys general opinions as of June 2002. It is important to note, however, that not all of these opinions are directly related to state government: a number of the opinions deal with local (i.e., municipal and county) government. Also, the opinions have not been cross-referenced, so there is no indication if earlier opinions have been superceded by later ones. See (http://www.hr.state.tx.us/GenInfo/AGOpinions/).

6. The comptroller is currently developing a third HR payroll and reporting system known as the Standardized Payroll/Reporting System (SPRS).

7. For a list of TPR HR reforms enacted see "Summary of Texas Performance Review Recommendations" at http://www.e-texas.org/hr/tpr.html (accessed January 2002).

8. It should be noted that the survey does not include HR directors from the state's institutions of higher education.

9. Given the relatively high response rate from the first two mailings, and given temporal considerations, I decided not to administer a third round of survey mailings as prescribed by Dillman (2000).

10. This is not true for agencies who operate merit systems or for those who have, acting on their own authority, created property interests for employees and/or just cause requirements for termination.

11. The issue of state liability for HR lawsuits is not trivial. For example, between 1992 and 1996, state agencies spent $20 million on judgments and settlements stemming from employee lawsuits (SAO 1997, 8), and, in 1999, 596 employment discrimination claims were filed with the Texas Commission on Human Rights (Government Performance Project 1999, 39).

References

Anderson, James E., Murray, Richard W., and Farley, Edward L. (1992). *Texas Politics: An Introduction*, 6th ed. New York: HaperCollins.

Barrett, K., and Green, R. (1999). "Grading the States: A Management Report Card." *Governing*, Vol. 12 (February): 17–90.

———. (2001). "Grading the States: A Management Report Card." *Governing* (February). http://www.governing.com/gpp/gp1intro.htm (Accessed June 2002).

Beyle, Thad (1995). "Enhancing Executive Leadership in the States." *State and Local Government Review*, Vol. 27, No. 1: 18–35.

Coggburn, Jerrell D. (2000). "The Effects of Deregulation on State Government Personnel Administration." *Review of Public Personnel Administration* Vol. 20, No. 4 (Fall): 24–40.

———. (2003). "Deregulating the Public Personnel Function." In S.W. Hays and R.C. Kearney, eds. *Public Personnel Administration: Problems and Prospects*, 4th ed. pp. 75–90. Englewood Cliffs, NJ: Prentice Hall.

Cohen, Steven, and Eimicke, William (1994). The Overregulated Civil Service: The Case of New York City's Public Personnel System." *Review of Public Personnel Administration* Vol. 24, No. 2 (Spring): 10–27.

Comptroller of Public Accounts (Texas). (1991). *Breaking the Mold: New Ways to Govern Texas*. First Report of the Texas Performance Review. Austin: TPR.

———. (1993). *Against the Grain: High-Quality, Low-Cost Government for Texas*. Second Report of the Texas Performance Review. Austin: TPR.

———. (1994). *Gaining Ground: Progress and Reform in State Government*. Third Report of the Texas Performance Review. Austin: TPR.

———. (1996). *Disturbing the Peace: The Challenge of Change in Texas Government*. Fourth Report of the Texas Performance Review. Austin: TPR.

———. (1999). *Challenging the Status Quo: Toward Smaller, Smarter Government*. Fifth Report of the Texas Performance Review. Austin: TPR.

———. (2000). *e-Texas: Smaller, Smarter, Faster Government*. Report of the e-Texas Commission. Austin: e-Texas Commission.

———. (2002). *Texas Performance Review*. http://www.window.state.tx.us/tpr/tpr.html (Accessed June 2002.)

Condrey, Stephen (2001). "Georgia's Civil Service Reform: A Four Year Assessment." In S. Condrey and R. Maranto, eds., *Radical Reform of the Civil Service*. New York: Lexington: 179–194.

Daley, Dennis M. (2002). *Strategic Human Resource Management*. Upper Saddle River, NJ: Prentice Hall.

DiIulio, John J., Jr., Garvey, Gerald, and Kettl, Donald F. (1993). *Improving Government Performance: An Owners Manual?* Washington, DC: Brookings Institute.

Dillman, Don A. (2000). *Mail and Internet Surveys: The Tailored Design Method,* 2nd ed. New York: John Wiley and Sons.

Elliot, Robert H. (1985). "Personnel Reform and State Employee Perceptions of Merit System Procedures: What is the Level of Support?" *Review of Public Personnel Administration*, Vol. 5, no. 3 (Summer): 26–41.

Facer, Rex L., II (1998). "Reinventing Public Administration: Reform in the Georgia Civil Service." *Public Administration Quarterly* Vol. 22, No. 1 (Spring): 58–73.

Gibson, L. Tucker, Jr., and Robison, Clay (1993). *Government and Politics in the Lone Star State*. Englewood Cliffs, NJ: Prentice Hall.

Government Performance Project (GPP). (1999). *State Government Survey: Human Resource Management Section* (Texas). (Obtained from the Texas SAO) Syracuse, NY: GPP.

Hill, Kim Q., and Mladenka, Kenneth R. (1996). *Texas Politics: Politics and Economics,* 4th ed. Belmont, CA: Wadsworth.

Ingraham, Patricia W., and Rosenbloom, David H. (1992). "The State of Merit in the Federal Government." In P.W. Ingraham and D.F. Kettl, eds., *Agenda for Excellence: Public Service in America*. Chatham, NJ: Chatham House, 274–296.

Jorgensen, Lorna, Fairless, Kelli, and Patton, W. David (1996). "Underground Merit Systems and the Balance Between Service and Compliance." *Review of Public Personnel Administration*, Vol. 19, No. 2 (Spring): 5–20.

Kearney, Richard C., and Hays, Steven W. (1998). "The Reinventing Government, the New Public Management and Civil Service Systems in International Perspective." *Review of Public Personnel Administration*, Vol. 18, No. 4 (Fall): 38–54.

Kellough, J. Edward (1998). "The Reinventing Government Movement: A Review and Critique." *Public Administration Quarterly*, Vol. 22, No. 1 (Spring): 6–20.

———. (1999). "Reinventing Public Personnel Management: Ethical Implications for Managers and Public Personnel Systems." *Public Personnel Management*, Vol. 28, No. 4 (Winter): 655–671.

Kettl, Donald F., Ingraham, Patricia W., Sanders, Ronald P., and Horner, Constance (1996). *Civil Service Reform: Building a Government That Works*. Washington, DC: Brookings Institution Press.

Lamare, James W. (1998). *Texas Politics: Economics, Power, and Policy,* 6th ed. Belmont, CA: West/Wadsworth.

Lauderdale, Michael (1999). *Reinventing Texas Government.* Austin: University of Texas Press.

Moe, Ronald C. (1994). "The 'Reinventing Government' Exercise: Misinterpreting the Problem, Misdiagnosing the Consequences." *Public Administration Review,* Vol. 54, No. 2 (March/April): 111–122.

Newland, Chester (1976). "Public Personnel Administration: Legalistic Reforms vs. Effectiveness, Efficiency, and Economy." Public Administration Review, Vol. 36, No. 5 (Sept./Oct.): 529–537.

Nigro, Lloyd G., and Kellough, J. Edward (2000). "Civil Service Reform in Georgia: Going to the Edge?" *Review of Public Personnel Administration,* Vol. 30, No. 4 (Fall): 41–54.

Office of the Governor (Texas). (1972). *Quality Texas Government: People Make the Difference.* Prepared by the Texas Research League for the Office of the Governor's Division on Planning Coordination. Austin: Office of the Governor, Division on Planning Coordination.

Osborne, David, and Gaebler, Ted (1992). *Reinventing Government.* Reading, MA: Addison-Wesley.

Perry, James L., and Mesch, Debra J. (1997). "Strategic Human Resource Management." In C. Ban and N. Riccucci, eds., *Public Personnel Management: Current Concerns,* Future Challenges, 2nd ed. New York: Longman, 21–34.

Peters, B. Guy. (1996). *The Future of Governing: Four Emerging Models.* Lawrence: University of Kansas Press.

Peters, B. Guy, and Savoie, Donald J. (1996). "Managing Incoherence: The Coordination and Empowerment Conundrum." Public Administration Review, Vol. 56, No. 3 (May/June): 281–290.

Pynes, Joan E. (2003). "Strategic Human Resource Management." In S. Hays and R. Kearney, eds., *Public Personnel Administration: Problems and Prospects,* 4th ed. Upper Saddle River, NJ: Prentice Hall, 93–105.

Rosenbloom, David H. (1993). "Have an Administrative Rx? Don't Forget the Politics!" *Public Administration Review,* Vol. 53, No. 6 (November/December): 503–507.

Savas, E. S., and Ginsburg, Sigmund G. (1973). "The Civil Service: A Meritless System?" *The Public Interest,* No. 32 (Summer): 70–85.

Selden, Sally C., Ingraham, Patricia W., and Jacobson, Willow (2001). "Human Resource Practices in State Government: Findings from a National Survey." *Public Administration Review,* Vol. 61, No. 5 (Sept./Oct.): 598–607.

State Auditor's Office (SAO), Texas (2001). *Texas Human Resources Management Statutes Inventory, 2002–2003 Biennium.* SAO Report No. 01–708. Austin: SAO.

———. (2000). *2000 Small Agency Management Control Audit.* SAO Report No. 00–023. Austin: SAO.

———. (1997). *An Assessment of Human Resource Management Controls in Texas State Government.* SAO Report No. 97–058. Austin: SAO.

Tannahill, Neal. (1997). *Texas Government: Policy and Politics*. New York: Longman.

Texas Workers' Compensation Commission (TWCC). (2002). *Agency Mission, Philosophy and Responsibilities*. http://www.twcc.state.tx.us/commission/philosophy.html (Accessed August 2002).

Thompson, Frank J. (1994). "The Winter Commission Report: Is Deregulation the Answer for Public Personnel Management?" *Review of Public Personnel Administration*, Vol. 24, No. 2 (Spring): 5–9.

Ulrich, Dave. (1997). *Human Resource Champions*. Boston: Harvard Business School.

Volcker Commission (National Commission on the Public Service). (1989). *Leadership for America: Rebuilding the Public Service*. Lexington, MA: Heath.

Walters, Jonathan (1997). "Who Needs Civil Service." *Governing* Vol. 10 (August): 17–21.

Wechsler, Barton (1993). "Florida's Civil Service Reform." *Spectrum* (Winter): 45–51.

———. (1994). "Reinventing Florida's Civil Service System: The Failure of Reform." *Review of Public Personnel Administration*, Vol. 14, No. 3 (Summer): 64–76.

West, Jonathan (2002). "Georgia on the Mind of Radical Civil Service Reformers." *Review of Public Personnel Administration*, Vol. 22, No. 2 (Summer): 79–93.

Williams, Martha S., and Schwab, A. James (1989). *The Employee Attitude Survey of Texas State Personnel Practices. Agency Comparisons for 1980, 1982, 1984, 1986, 1988*. Austin: University of Texas School of Social Work.

Winter Commission (National Commission on the State and Local Public Service). (1993). *Hard Truths / Tough Choices: An Agenda for State and Local Reform*. Albany, NY: Rockefeller Institute.

CHAPTER 10

Human Resources Reform in Arizona
—A Mixed Picture

N. Joseph Cayer
Charles H. Kime

Human resources management in Arizona reflects the state's history, political culture, and social environment. Arizona became a state in 1912 when the Progressive Movement was at its height and its constitution and government organization reflected that movement's values, especially a distrust of government (Everett 1984). These values resulted in a state government with very dispersed authority and many offices were elected such as the Corporation Commission that regulates transportation and communications. Today's Arizona is characterized as embodying the spirit of the frontier as strongly individualistic, distrustful of authority and concentrated power, and favoring decentralized government (Berman 1998; Sackton, 1980). Human resources management in Arizona historically has been very decentralized. Efforts to change the structure and to consolidate human resources functions have been the hallmark of reform efforts in the state for much of the past thirty years. In recent years, reform efforts have addressed functions, policies, and processes of personnel management.

From its very beginning, Arizona exhibited distrust of government. Even in territorial days, conflicts with centralized authority were frequent (Hansen and Brown 1987). Arizona and New Mexico together operated under territorial rule from 1862 until 1912, longer than any other state to join the union. Efforts to obtain statehood began in 1872 but were thwarted by presidents and Congress until 1912. Even as statehood became imminent, it was almost derailed by a conflict with Washington. An element of Arizona's distrust of government was a direct democracy provision in its proposed constitution that allowed recall of state officials. At the time, only Oregon allowed recall of state officials; although many local

239

governments permitted recalls. President William Howard Taft insisted that the provision dealing with recall of judges be deleted before he would issue a proclamation of statehood. The provision was deleted and statehood was proclaimed on February 14, 1912. Demonstrating their independence and view of the incident, Arizona voters restored the constitutional provision on November 5, 1912, the first election after achieving statehood (Hansen and Brown 1987; Mason and Hink 1979; Taylor 1942).

The state constitution also divided executive authority through election of seven different offices (Governor, Secretary of State, Attorney General, Treasurer, Superintendent of Public Instruction, State Mine Inspector, and the Corporation Commission). The fragmentation has continued with legislative creation of more than 150 independent boards and commissions (Berman 1998; Mason and Hink 1987).

Historically, Arizona's tax system has reflected devaluation of government as well. Tax limitations abound in terms of types of taxes that can be imposed both at the state and local levels and in terms of the processes for adopting taxes. A super majority (2/3) is required for levying of any new state taxes or raising current taxes (Mason and Hink 1987; Sackton 1997). Tax cuts, on the other hand, are very popular and the state legislature and most recent governors have staked their political careers on tax cuts. In the 1980s, Arizona went from a tax effort that was "well above to well below the national average" (Rex 1997, 21). The result is a structural deficit in which expenditures grow at a faster pace than revenue (McGuire and Naimark 1991; Watson 1991). During the good economic times of the 1990s, Arizona experienced a steady diet of tax cuts (Robb 1997; Sackton 1997; Welch 1997). The exceptions were dedicated taxes (mostly on cigarettes and gasoline) adopted directly by the voters. While a Budget Stabilization Fund, also called the Rainy Day Fund, was established, it has been raided constantly to subsidize the tax cuts. With the downturn in the economy after 2001, the state faces major deficits and the Rainy Day Fund is depleted. Nonetheless, elected officials, particularly legislative leaders, continue to talk about tax and spending cuts. The governor elected in 2002, Janet Napolitano, has established a commission to study the tax and revenue structure but still insists she does not favor any tax increase.

Human resources management in Arizona takes place in this environment. Given elected officials and a general public who believe government is a major problem for taxpayers and citizens, efforts at innovative changes face many challenges.

Background

All State of Arizona employees were appointed by elected officials until 1942. In compliance with federal government requirements to use merit as the basis for personnel systems in some programs funded by the federal government, Arizona adopted a merit system in 1942 covering affected employee groups. The merit system applied primarily to the selection process. Except for complying with mandates for federally funded programs, individual state agencies conducted their personnel functions as they wished. As a result, uniformity in hiring, classification, pay, benefits, and discipline did not exist. Protections of employee rights, to the extent that they existed, were at the pleasure of the appointing authority (Governor's Commission on Merit System Reform 1980).

By 1968 concerns arose about the inconsistencies in personnel policies across agencies. As employees formed an employee association and issues of equity began to arise, managers and employees alike led efforts to modernize the system. These concerns led the state legislature to create a statewide merit system and to establish a State Personnel Commission to administer it. The new merit system covered all state employees except for those of the three universities, the Department of Public Safety, the Governor's Office, the legislature, the courts, and the School for the Deaf and the Blind. The commission established the position of Personnel Director to which it delegated day-to-day administrative functions. The commission's functions were to adopt rules and regulations and to approve agency plans for their implementation. It also developed benefits plans and served as the appeals board for employees. Responding to inequities in classification and compensation, the commission also established a statewide classification plan and salary schedule.

In 1972 the legislature established the Department of Administration (DOA) and created the Arizona State Personnel Division as a unit within it (A.R.S. 41–701). This legislation also changed the Arizona State Personnel Commission into the Arizona State Personnel Board (A.R.S. 41–781). The personnel director became the assistant director of the Department of Administration for Personnel Administration (now the Human Resources Division). The board develops personnel rules and regulations and the Human Resources Director oversees their implementation by state agencies (A.R.S. 41–782). Each agency, however, still maintained a personnel professional position until 1977 when the state legislature abolished those positions and placed 47 new positions in the personnel division.

These efforts at centralizing the personnel function were slow to take hold and many turf battles between agency heads and the personnel division ensued.

As the national government reformed its civil service in 1978, Arizona began to do the same. In 1979 Governor Bruce Babbitt appointed the Governor's Commission on Merit System Reform to do a thorough assessment of personnel functions in Arizona government. The commission made wide-ranging recommendations mirroring much of what happened at the national level (Governor's Commission on Merit Reform 1980). While the recommendations were not fully accepted by the legislature, many became bases for change over the next several years and have had significant impact on human resources management.

Again, in 1991, the state conducted an extensive review of its human resources management. Governor Fife Symington established the State Long-Term Improved Management Project (Project SLIM) that was reminiscent of the Reagan administration's Grace Commission. As the acronym SLIM suggests, the project had as a main goal reducing government size and spending. Thus, the review by the steering committee appointed by the governor focused on cost savings and reduction in force. It also made numerous recommendations for streamlining and modernizing state government human resources management including:

- Developing a human resources management policy based on employee empowerment and employee and supervisory accountability
- Adopting a better performance evaluation system based on Total Quality Management (TQM)
- Improving the hiring process
- Improving training
- Proactive workforce planning
- Improving career path opportunities
- Providing alternative processes for employee appeals
- Reducing overall employment
- Upgrading the classification, pay, and benefits systems (State Long-Term Improved Management Project 1992).

Project SLIM resulted in some legislative action and administrative changes, but the political and legal troubles leading to Governor Symington's resignation from office interfered with his being able to carry through on all of the recommendations. Still, many became a basis for change in state government human resources management. Nonetheless, performance audits by the auditor general's office in 1993 and 1999 note problems in recruitment and hiring, performance evaluation, compensation, and benefits (State of Arizona Office of the Auditor General 1993, 1999).

The human resources system in Arizona continues to undergo scrutiny and change. Recently, the focus has been on compensation, benefits, training, and the human resources information solutions system. The rest of this chapter examines these and other human resources initiatives in Arizona. We begin with a provision of the 1972 statute establishing the personnel system dealing with delegated authority (A.R.S. 41-763).

Delegated Authority

The legislation establishing the current personnel system includes a provision that the director of the Department of Administration (DOA) may delegate the authority for conduct of particular personnel functions to operating state agencies. Individual agencies have the flexibility to design practices that fit their particular situations. Agencies must request authorization from DOA and spell out how they are going to use it. DOA then has the responsibility for monitoring the agency's implementation of the delegated authority.

The Arizona Department of Game and Fish has made good use of the delegated authority provision. In 1997–1998, Game and Fish was granted the authority to develop its own staffing system. It was taking too long to develop hiring lists once applications closed. The Game and Fish Department developed its own process and reduced the time needed to develop hiring lists from three months to three days. During times of full employment, the reduced time is very important because qualified applicants are hired by other employers and eligible lists become outdated very quickly. A quick turnaround often places the agency in a good competitive position for the best applicants.

While the delegated authority is an important element of flexibility in Arizona government, state agencies generally do not make good use of it. Agencies have been so starved for resources that they often find it difficult to initiate new practices even though they may save money in the long run. They seldom have the slack resources needed to cover start-up costs on innovative projects.

Still, within a largely centralized personnel system, the delegated authority provision offers much potential for human resources innovation by state agencies.

Compensation

Compensation of state employees has been a recurring issue from the time the state was created in 1912. The political culture of the state devalues public employees. Public employees are viewed by the public as being less competent than those in the private sector. State employee compensation consistently lags behind that of other workers. While their benefits often are better than in private sector situations, pay is relatively low. Special commissions appointed by the governor and legislative committees regularly study the compensation system and recommend steps needed to correct this situation. However, the governor and state legislature normally do not place very high priority on public employee pay. It usually is one of the last items on the legislative agenda and therefore becomes hostage to other pressing needs.

In 2000, a governor more supportive of public employees than most of her predecessors, Jane Hull, made state employee compensation one of her two top priorities. Education was the other. She convinced the legislative leadership to follow her lead on this issue. The outcome was a 5 percent state employee pay raise for the 2002 fiscal year. Another 5 percent was planned for the next fiscal year. As is common practice for the Arizona legislature, the 5 percent increase for fiscal year 2002 would not go into effect until the last quarter beginning April 2002. By the start of the legislative session in January 2002, the state was in deficit for the year and revenue prospects for the future were bleak. The legislature promptly canceled the pay increase that was to go into effect in April 2002 and also went back to a single-year budget cycle thus eliminating the promised pay increase for 2003 as well. Instead, legislators adopted a flat $1,450 pay increase for all eligible employees to begin with the start of fiscal 2003. This outcome eroded morale among state employees who had expected that they would finally be recognized for their work through a pay increase that would improve their lot, even if it still left them making less than the private sector and other public employees. Additionally, a flat across-the-board pay increase created compression problems in the pay plan, which in turn promises to undermine efforts to manage a rational classification system. Thus, the promised 10 percent increase over a two-year period disappeared with the predictable results for employee confidence in the system. Of course, the governor and legislature promised that when state revenues recovered, employees would be remembered.

Arizona adopted a Performance Incentive Pay Plan (PIPP) program providing awards for innovation and enhancement in services by agencies. The program is administered by the individual agencies. It allows one-time awards to individual employees for contributions to improved performance and performance-enhancing innovations. These awards do not increase the employees' base pay. As with many pay-for-performance programs at all levels of government, PIPP suffers from chronic lack of funding. General appropriations to agencies have been low; during difficult budget years, these discretionary funds tend to be cut. Pay incentives for performance under PIPP must be funded by the agency within its appropriated budget; therefore, agencies that are financed in part through fees for services (licenses, permits, etc.) usually are in a better position to fund the PIPP. Elsewhere in the state, it has not been a great success (Department of Administration 2003b).

Benefits

Arizona's benefits programs have been well run and in many respects are among the most innovative in the nation. Of particular interest is the system for enrolling and changing benefits selections. Arizona's employees can access the "Saguaro Program" on the Web at http://benefits.hr-services.org/ where the services are completely automated. Before the start of each fiscal year, all employees and retirees have the opportunity to enroll in particular benefits or to change current benefits selections. To enroll or change benefits, individuals may do it online or by telephone. There is no longer any paper enrollment process. Eligible employees and retirees receive information in the mail about options for the coming year. Information sessions also are scheduled and one-on-one counseling is made available for employees wanting to learn more about options and to help employees make informed decisions. Each person has a password for use in enrolling. During a specified period of time, individuals must make their choices. They then receive an immediate confirmation of what choices they have made. The system has been in effect since July of 2001 and appears to be working very efficiently (The Saguaro Program 2002).

The state also embarked on self-insurance for its employee health-care coverage beginning in October 2003. Rapidly increasing health-care premiums stimulated the state to go to self-insurance in the hopes of better controlling costs. The state has very little information on utilization rates of its current health-care program. It did not include in its contract with providers any requirement to report on utilization. Thus, the state is experimenting with self-insurance under less than optimal conditions. Some point to the state's record on self-insurance of its liability insurance and worker's compensation programs. They do not seem to be very successful. Some legislators are now proposing to sell the Worker's Comp Fund. Given the state's tendency to make hasty decisions on solutions that are promised to save money and then finding that they actually cost more, there are worries about self-insurance (Arizona Health Care Cost Containment System 2001).

Retirement

The centralization/decentralization issue is not unrelated to employee retirement systems in Arizona. Prior to 1968, retirement systems for public safety employees were decentralized and fragmented. They varied considerably in benefits and required contributions while nonpublic safety employees relied on social security. Over the years, reform efforts focused on improving retirement plans for all state employees.

Reform efforts have resulted in the creation of four basic retirement systems in the state: a system for public safety employees (including local government public safety employees) called the Arizona Public Safety Retirement System (APSRS), a retirement system for the Arizona Department of Corrections[1], a retirement system for elected officials, and a system for all other state employees called the Arizona State Retirement System (ASRS). Each of these systems provides flexibility for eligible members to retire after becoming vested in the system with a range of benefits that provide 75 to 80 percent of the highest gross salary earned and some form of cost-of-living allowance (COLA). Some employees, particularly university employees, may participate in customized retirement investment programs with approved financial investment advisors.

The Arizona State Retirement System provides pensions for all covered employees (A.R.S. 38–711). Employees are vested after ten years of service and can retire at any age. However, the fund is set so that an employee must be age 62 and have 30 years of service to receive maximum benefits with a cap of $90,000 per year. Actuarial adjustments are calculated for pensions taken before age 62. The early retirement option with just ten years of service is attractive to some employees who retire and pursue a second career.

The Arizona State Retirement System is considered to be one of the most financially sound systems in the country. It is conservative in its investment strategies and in its level of benefits. While it is not one of the better systems in terms of level of benefits, it has some innovative features.

State employees who have reached normal retirement age may participate in the Deferred Retirement Option Plan (DROP) at the discretion of the employer (Information on the Deferred Retirement Option Program 2002). Employees may work up to an additional three years but credits to the defined benefit retirement system are not made. Instead, employees and employers make contributions to a supplemental defined contribution plan. At the end of the three years (or other agreed upon period of time), employees may take the contributions to the supplemental plan in a single lump sum, two or three annual lump sums, or may purchase time in the retirement system equal to the period of time worked beyond normal retirement age.

The state also allows individuals who have been retired from state service for at least one year to return to work and receive benefits. During this employment, they do not make contributions to the retirement system, but they continue to receive retirement benefits as well as the state salary. Given the state's lack of competitiveness in the labor market, this option helps attract good employees back to the state workforce.

Firefighters in Arizona have developed into a substantial political force that has been successful in achieving reforms in human resource practices and improved benefits for all public safety personnel in the state. Prior to July 1, 1968, retirement pensions for public safety personnel were a responsibility of the local jurisdictions and those state agencies employing public safety personnel. In 1968 a new system called the Arizona Public Safety Retirement System (APSRS) brought together these disparate systems by aggregating their funds into a single system (A.R.S. 38–848). Eligible members now include all Arizona certified peace officers and career public firefighters. In 1972 legislation allowing any public safety officer, primarily police and fire, to retire at any age with a cap of 60 percent of their average salary was enacted. The APSRS has since been modified to improve benefits for its members. By 1987 firefighters and police could retire at any age with 20 or more years of service with a maximum pension of 80 percent after 32 years.

A relatively new twist for public safety retirement systems in Arizona is the concept of retiring from the public safety department without actually leaving the department until some time in the future. This option allows the member to remain in the job with a commitment to leave at some future date. The Deferred Retirement Option Plan (DROP) for public safety employees became effective July 1, 2002, in Arizona. It provides an option for APSRS eligible members to defer retirement from their department for up to 60 months. To be eligible for this option, members must retire from the APSRS program and commit to a future retirement date that is prior to or at completion of an additional 60 months of employment.

The advantages of DROP are many. Members are able to build a financial nest egg that can be withdrawn over a period of time or withdrawn upon leaving the department. Members continue employment with the department, receive the same gross salary, and retain all other personnel benefits. Those members in DROP are entitled to any and all compensation, raises, or merit increases that apply to regular employees. In addition, members discontinue contributions to APSRS and in some cases do not pay into Social Security. The net result is a pay increase of almost 8 percent. The employers also benefit because they no longer pay into the APSRS fund or Social Security, thereby lowering their indirect costs per DROP employee by almost 8 percent. The pension fund also benefits because the members actually retire at a rate less than they would have received had they remained in the system longer.

DROP does present some interesting organizational challenges to the human resource management system. The initial implementation of the system will create a period of uncertainty with regard to the number of employees who can be expected to retire in any given year. Many of those who would have retired about the time that DROP was implemented might consider delaying their retirement to take advantage of DROP, while some may choose to sign up for DROP contemplating an earlier retirement than they might otherwise have planned. This creates the potential for larger numbers of retirees than might otherwise be anticipated during the first several years.

Although departments attempt to forecast the possible effects of DROP on their human resource systems, the range of possible circumstances is extremely great and the probabilities of any particular event occurring is very much a mystery. These challenges place unusual burdens on employers to recruit, test, hire, and train large numbers of new employees but they also create what one might call a "bubble" in the personnel system. As these groups progress through the promotional systems they create ongoing problems of larger than normal numbers of eligible employees for promotions, additional continuing education requirements that are out-of-balance with the norm, and potentially a larger number of retirees at one time in the future as these employees become eligible to retire. The best data available on the consequences of these new options are anecdotal at best. However, many of the chief officers in these systems seem to believe that most members who choose this type of retirement plan, exercise their options, on average, in about two and one half years after they drop from their retirement plan. Since there are not any hard data available to support these claims at the moment, departments seem stuck with the old planning adage of "plan for the worst and hope for the best."

Human Resources Information System Reform

Since 1989 Arizona has used the Human Resources Management System (HRMS) for basic human resources and payroll information and actions. The system was outdated at the time it was installed and it did not meet the needs of state agencies for accurate and timely information. Most agencies ended up developing duplicate systems. In 1999 the State Information Management System Project was established to examine the human resources management system. It recommended replacing the HRMS with an integrated financial, purchasing, human resources, and payroll system. The most critical needs identified were in human resources and payroll. The result was development of the Human Resources Information Solution (HRIS) project.

HRIS was approved and funded in 2001 and it began the process of involving state employees in development of the system. After review of needs and examination of alternatives available, a contract was awarded in 2002 to replace the current human resources and payroll and benefits system. The contract was awarded to IBM, which uses Lawson software for the system (www.hris.strate.az.us, accessed June 21, 2002). The Lawson software includes applications for human resources, payroll, and benefits. It will allow HRIS to use a single system to administer its payroll, human resources, and employee benefits programs. The system was launched on December

29, 2003. Originally, it was expected that it would be in operation by January 1, 2003, but the date was set back to ensure greater success. It was discovered that many state agencies would not be able to assimilate the changes by the original implementation date ('Go Live' Date Revised 2002).

The launch of the HRIS system required a thorough needs analysis of state government human resources. Once the needs analysis was completed, the project began designing a system that would work for all state agencies. The system automates human resources management and payroll and benefits processes. Training of agency personnel to use the system was a very important part of HRIS.

The state expects to net a savings of more than $40 million during the twelve-year life of the project. Savings are projected to occur through increased productivity and cost savings from elimination of the outdated systems. Productivity is expected to increase as a result of employee and employer self-service features of the system and through reduced turnover as the system will be able to respond more quickly to employee needs and external job offers. No estimates on how much agencies will save on their own systems have been made. It is expected that agencies will eliminate duplicative systems once the HRIS is in place and functional.

Training

Identifying and meeting employee training and development needs are problems Arizona has wrestled with continually. As early as 1971 the state recognized its responsibility to train employees in its supervisor's manual (Arizona State Personnel Division 1971). Published by the Arizona State Personnel Division, the manual emphasizes the supervisor's responsibility for training and states: "the State Personnel Division is responsible for the development and operation of programs to improve the work effectiveness and morale of all employees in the state service including development of in-service training programs" (Arizona State Personnel Division 1971, 52). Eventually, the Department of Administration developed numerous training courses and opportunities agencies were expected to use. In an effort to address its training responsibilities, the DOA set in place a menu of required courses that all state employees must complete as well as a set of recommended courses for employees at various levels.

Until 1977 each agency did its own training and there was much unevenness in what training did occur. Some of the large agencies such as the Department of Economic Security and the Department of Corrections developed very strong specialized training programs covering everything from technical to supervisory and managerial training. The Department of Public Safety and others with law enforcement responsibilities also had extensive training programs. Still, many agencies had little training activity. In 1977 the legislature included training responsibilities as part of the Personnel Division in the Department of Administration. Those departments with well-established training programs retained their programs, but the Department of Administration began trying to centralize some activities, especially supervisory training.

DOA mandates specific courses for supervisors and managers. These courses cover leadership, performance management, and coaching and discipline. There is an effort to train supervisors and managers how to properly use the disciplinary process for personnel morale reasons and also for obvious legal reasons. All state employees who have supervisory or managerial responsibilities are required to complete a personnel management training program that covers specific topics in supervisory skills, discipline, ethics, performance measurement, and setting employee objectives.

Finding many of the DOA programs not particularly pertinent to their specific needs, many agencies began developing their own programs. The Department of Public Safety and the Department of Corrections receive peace officer training through a statewide training program specifically designed for training peace officers. This statewide training function is conducted by the Arizona Peace Officer Standards and Training Board (POST) created in 1974 (A.R.S. 41-1829). In 1984 the Arizona legislature added responsibilities to the board to include the development of a curriculum for correctional officers who work for the Arizona Department of Corrections thus establishing minimum training standards for state correctional officers. POST certifies more than 20,000 peace officers in 16 academies throughout the state.

Some departments choose to offer their own courses, with the approval of DOA, in lieu of the mandated courses for new employees; that is, orientation, ethics, and sexual harassment as well as courses that are more specific to their missions. Departments that are large enough to have their own training resources consider their culture to be somewhat unique and choose to provide as much of the training in-house as they possibly can. For example, the Arizona Game and Fish

Department and the Department of Public Safety both offer their own leadership development programs as they consider the DOA programs to be inadequate to fully meet their needs. The Department of Corrections also provides much of its training in-house.

DOA not only is responsible for training all managers and supervisors, but is responsible for maintaining a comprehensive database for the state. Agencies that have training capability in-house may choose to continue with their own supervisory and management training programs as long as they comply with DOA rules and regulations and state law. Yet, DOA only recommends that an agency's programs include the core learning objectives and core competencies rather than requiring compliance. Training specialists within DOA are available to assist agencies if they need help filling a particular gap in their program.

In 2000 Arizona Government University (AzGU) was established. It is an example of applying innovation to affect reform in government. Taking advantage of the expertise and offerings from existing educational institutions, Arizona has positioned itself to deliver a menu of courses, degree programs, certificates, and continuing education credits to cover more than 42,000 state employees in a state that has a very diverse geographic and demographic make-up. Partnering with the Western Governors University (WGU), it brings a virtual university into Arizona state government and makes its training electronically accessible to all state employees through the AzGU Web site (Arizona Government University 2003).

WGU offers distance learning from a variety of colleges, universities, and corporations throughout the United States (Western Governors University 2003). Courses offered range from high-tech Internet-based courses to traditional correspondence courses. Students can earn associate's, bachelor's, and even master's degrees. WGU is a virtual university that offers competency-based educational programs, not based on the number of college credits a student accumulates. WGU instead focuses on the essential skills needed in a particular area relying on professionals in each field to help them identify the specific competencies and skills one should possess to be successful in the work place. Work experience, educational credits, and life skills are all evaluated and can be applied toward a degree through an assessment process. Credits cannot be transferred from other universities or colleges in the traditional sense but are evaluated by WGU for inclusion in the WGU degree.

This approach gives students, especially nontraditional students, great flexibility in planning the training and education that best fits them personally and will help them grow in their chosen career. Students also are provided a mentor who is an expert in the student's field of study and whose role is to help the student develop the plan of study needed to complete the degree. WGU also has several articulation agreements that allow students to transfer their WGU degree into another university where they can pursue the next higher degree.

AzGU's governing board is made up of representatives from state agencies and an advisory council that includes representatives from WGU, each of the three state universities in Arizona (Arizona State University, Northern Arizona University, and the University of Arizona) and the Maricopa County Community College District. This partnership is a good example of how innovation can be used to meet the needs of state agencies, state employees, and the community. With its heavy reliance on technology and the use of the Internet, AzGU maximizes the advantages of online learning in a state that includes many remote areas not easily accessible to community colleges or universities. This approach also brings courses from a variety of institutions giving the student a great deal of flexibility and choice.

At this writing, Arizona arguably is going through the worst financial crisis in its history. Cutting the state budget to overcome a projected one-half billion dollar deficit in fiscal 2002, the state faced a deficit of more than a billion dollars for fiscal year 2003. State agencies have been called upon to give back up to 10 percent of their current budgets with expectations that more cuts will be needed. For a state that has a history of putting its personnel and HR system at the bottom of the budget priorities, one is hard pressed to forecast a groundswell of human resource management reform and innovation, especially in areas that require funding. Arizona Government University is an innovative and comprehensive approach that tries to facilitate the training and education needs of the state's diverse workforce. A large investment in the hardware, software, and technical personnel to make it a reality is needed.

Telework

Arizona became a leader in telecommuting when in 1989 it began a pilot project in conjunction with AT&T in which both employers permitted employees to work from home. Four state departments participated in the pilot project. The goal was to use telework as a way of reducing traffic and the air pollution problem that was becoming critical in the Phoenix metropolitan area. The telework program also was put forward as being family-friendly and as leading to greater productivity. It worked well and it was formally established in 1993 by executive order for all state agencies. The state also helped private employers set up similar programs. State agencies were given a goal of having 15 percent of their workforces on telework assignments (the governor raised the target to 20 percent in 2002). In October 1993, Arizona joined Oregon and Washington in a Telework Collaborative with the mission of sharing expertise and developing materials for other employers to use in telework programs. These three states were joined by California in 1996. The collaborative has helped employers in 26 states and 14 other countries establish programs.

Currently, 3,300 state employees (15.5%) of the 21,000 in Maricopa County (the Phoenix metropolitan area) telework. The state estimates that workers drive 4.3 million fewer miles and generate 117,000 fewer pounds of air pollution as a result. Employees also reduce their hours of stressful driving (Arizona Department of Administration 2003a). The state expects to benefit through less traffic congestion, reduced air pollution, savings on office space costs, and increasing organizational effectiveness. Increased effectiveness will be achieved through greater employee efficiency because there are fewer interruptions and distractions and because employees are less stressed. Turnover also is reduced as employees with family obligations are able to remain on the job and be at home.

Conclusion

Arizona's human resources management system is in constant flux; the legislature and other public officials often view state employees as problems rather than assets in which they should invest. The result is that when changes are made they often are not to improve the human resources system but to accomplish other goals, especially reducing the cost of government. Accordingly, recent efforts to reform the system have been piecemeal and the results mixed. Thus, the human resources system features some innovative elements and many that are outmoded.

Arizona offers an ideological environment that is conducive to innovation and there is a can-do attitude and receptivity to change. The economy of the state includes high-tech industries that place the state in the position of being a potential laboratory for experiments in the uses of technology in management. The state also has a relatively small workforce when compared with many states and experimentation should be easier in terms of change required. The political environment also fosters support for privatization and partnerships. As a result, the state has opportunities to engage in some innovative efforts utilizing public-private partnerships.

Having these advantages, the state has been largely unable to capitalize on them. Its leadership has a very conservative, minimalist perspective when it comes to the role of government. Policy makers resist making the investments required to develop innovative approaches to human resources management. Nonetheless, innovative ideas continue to percolate in the legislature and in the departments and agencies of state government. For example, since the state of Georgia went to an "at-will" model, Arizona legislators routinely propose doing the same. They have not gotten very far, usually because many also want to drop all civil protections for employees. Similarly, Arizona government often contracts with the private sector for many services and the idea of contracting out for some personnel services surfaces on occasion, but it remains only an idea for now.

Clearly, Arizona will continue to experiment with parts of its human resources system, but wholesale reform of the state system is unlikely. The prospects are that the mixed picture will be the Arizona norm for the foreseeable future. Yet there may be another chapter being written in Arizona regarding its vision of itself and its future that could affect, in a positive way, the human resources system. With the election of a new governor, Janet Napolitano, in 2002 there was renewed vigor and conversation about setting a new vision for Arizona; a vision that embraced partnering with business, a focus on the environment, setting high standards for quality education, delivering needed and quality health-care services, and particular attention to issues related to children's needs. The governor seems to recognize that the state's employees are a key factor in delivering these quality services and that it is imperative for the state to employ and maintain workers who can provide the quality services that she envisions are needed to achieve her agenda.

The governor's vision may provide even more opportunities to improve the current HR system, implement some of the creative solutions that have piloted but failed to gain full implementation, and more fully explore civil service reform that can meet the challenges of a vibrant 21st-century state government.

Note

1. The Department of Corrections (DOC) has its own pension plan called the Correctional Officers Retirement Plan (CORP). Correctional officers can retire after 25 or more years of service, at age 62 with at least ten years of service, or if their combination of age and years of service equals 80. Originally, the peace officers working for DOC were in the APSRS but later opted out in an attempt to improve their situation and to cover all of the corrections officers. The Elected Official Retirement Plan (EORP) provides elected officials with an opportunity to retire after they no longer hold an elective office in Arizona. Elected officials are eligible to retire if they are 65 or older with five or more years of service, age 62 with ten or more years of service, or at any age with twenty or more years of service. The maximum pension benefit cannot exceed 80 percent of the average annual salary or $75,000. This provides some financial stability for those individuals who make a career of public service by getting elected to serve in a number of offices throughout their lifetimes.

References

Arizona Department of Administration (2003a). "Partnering To Make A Difference," accessed at www.teleworkarizona.com/telework, 2-5-2003.

Arizona Department of Administration (2003b). "Performance-based Incentive Pilot Program," accessed at www.sasd.state.az.us/FinalReport.pdf, 2-22-2003.

Arizona Government University (2003). "Welcome to Arizona Government University," accessed at www.azgu.gov, 2-10-2003.

Arizona Health Care Cost Containment System (2001). "Statewide Health Care Insurance Plan Task Force: Review of Self-Insuring of Health Benefits," accessed at www.ahcccs.state.az.us/Studies/HRSAGrant/FinalSelf-Insurance_2.pdf, 2-22-2003.

Arizona State Personnel Division (1971). *Supervisors Manual*. Phoenix: State of Arizona Department of Administration.

Berman, David R. (1998). *Arizona Politics and Government*. Lincoln: University of Nebraska Press.

Everett, Ray (1984). *Arizona History and Government*. Tempe: Arizona State University Center for Public Affairs.

'Go Live' Date Revisited (June 2002). *HRIS Project News*, accessed at www.hris.state.az.us, June 21, 2002.

Governor's Commission on Merit System Reform (1980). *Maximizing Human Resources*. Phoenix: State of Arizona, Department of Administration.

Hansen, Gerald E., and Douglas A. Brown (1987). *Arizona: Its Constitution and Government,* 2nd ed. Lanham, MD: University Press of America.

"Information on the Deferred Retirement Option Program (DROP)" (2002). *Arizona Retirement System Financial Horizons* (Winter): 3–4.

Mason, Bruce B., and Heinz R. Hink (1979). *Constitutional Government in Arizona*, 6th ed. Tempe: Cleber.

McGuire, Therese J., and Dana Wolfe Naimark (1991). "Introduction and Overview." In T.J. McGuire and D.W. Naimark, eds. *State and Local Finance for the 1990s: A Case Study of Arizona.* Tempe: Arizona State University School of Public Affairs, 1–8.

Rex, Tom (1997). "The Facts of the Matter: Arizona's Tax Cuts." In J.S. Hall and N.J. Cayer, eds. *Arizona Policy Choices—Balancing Acts: Tax Cuts and Public Policy in Arizona.* Tempe: Morrison Institute for Public Policy, School of Public Affairs, Arizona State University, 17–34.

Robb, Robert (1997). "A Sober Case for Tax Cut Policies." In J.S. Hall and N.J. Cayer, eds. *Arizona Policy Choices—Balancing Acts: Tax Cuts and Public Policy in Arizona.* Tempe: Morrison Institute for Public Policy, School of Public Affairs, Arizona State University, 49–61.

Sackton, Frank J. (1997). "A Study of the Arizona State Tax Reduction Program." In J.S. Hall and N.J. Cayer, eds. *Arizona Policy Choices—Balancing Acts: Tax Cuts and Public Policy in Arizona.* Tempe: Morrison Institute for Public Policy, School of Public Affairs, Arizona State University, 91–96.

Sackton, Frank J. (1980). *Arizona Government in the National Context.* Tempe: Arizona State University Center for Public Affairs.

The Saguaro Program. 2002, accessed at www.hr.state.az.us/benefits, 9-1-2002.

Taylor, Clyde W. (1942). *Public Administration in Arizona.* New York: Charles Scribner's Sons.

State Long Term Improved Management Project (1992). *Project SLIM Final Report.* Phoenix: State of Arizona, Office of the Governor.

State Office of the Auditor General (1993). *Performance Audit, Department of Administration Human Resources Division.* Phoenix: State of Arizona, Office of the Auditor General.

State Office of the Auditor General (1999). *Performance Audit, Department of Administration Human Resources Division.* Phoenix: State of Arizona, Office of the Auditor General.

Watson, Mark W. (1991). *General Fund Projections: Quantifying the Structural Deficit.* In T.J. McGuire and D.W. Naimark, eds. *State and Local Finance for the 1990s: A Case Study of Arizona.* Tempe: Arizona State University School of Public Affairs, 465–483.

Welch, Nancy (1997). "Taxes: The Eternal Debate." In J.S. Hall and N.J. Cayer, eds. *Arizona Policy Choices—Balancing Acts: Tax Cuts and Public Policy in Arizona.* Tempe: Morrison Institute for Public Policy, School of Public Affairs, Arizona State University, 40–41.

Western Governors University (2003). "About WGU," accessed at www.wgu.edu/wgu/about/index.html, 2-24-2003.

CHAPTER 11

Prospects for Civil Service Reform in California: A Triumph of Technique Over Purpose?

Katherine C. Naff

The 1990s may well be remembered as the decade of reinventing government. Public institutions, facing declining confidence in government, fiscal crises, and citizens' simultaneous demands for higher quality services and lower taxes, began searching for ways to become leaner, more decentralized, flexible and innovative (see, for example, Osborne and Gaebler 1992, National Performance Review 1993). Unfortunately, human resource functions within organizations are often seen as standing in the way of progress (Hays 1996). As Wallace Sayre wrote in 1948, in its efforts to preserve standardization and uniformity as overriding values, personnel administration has "tended to become characterized more by procedure, rule and technique than by purpose or results" (Sayre 1948). Authors of the best-selling *Reinventing Government* put it this way: "The only thing more destructive than a line item budget is a personnel system built around civil service." (Osborne and Gaebler 1992, 124).

Efforts to alter outmoded systems have met with mixed results. At one end of the spectrum are Georgia and Florida, which have virtually eliminated their merit systems. At the other extreme is the state of California where, despite a cacophony of voices calling for reform, change has not been forthcoming. This chapter examines the reasons for the failure of reform in California. It begins with brief discussion of the political environment in which efforts to transform the civil service find themselves, and which plays a major role in determining the success or failure of those efforts.

259

Civil Service Reform and the Political Environment

Jerrell D. Coggburn has suggested that the success of civil service reform efforts in the states depends on a number of variables including the partisan affiliation of the governor and legislature, the characteristics of the state's administrative workforce and the state's general economic condition (Coggburn 2001). Successful civil service reform also requires the endorsement of key constituencies and a chief executive who is committed to substantial reform.

This is as much the case in the federal government as in state governments. Witness Jimmy Carter's success in securing the passage of the Civil Service Reform Act (CSRA) of 1978. It succeeded, in no small part with the support of key constituencies whose interests were carefully attended to and balanced. For example, veterans groups lobbied (successfully) to strengthen veterans preference rather than limiting it as the administration had originally planned. Unions were triumphant (ultimately) in gaining statutory ground for the federal labor management relations program (Newland 1992). Other groups, including the public administration community, lent their support to the Act focusing their recommendations on technical aspects of the bill (Schuh 2000).

This was not the case when the Clinton administration took its recommendations for reform to Capitol Hill. One reason, offered by Kettl et al., is that, "most observers of government view government management in general, and civil service in particular, as an issue that is dull as dishwater" (1996, 2). In other words, key constituents were not sufficiently concerned about reform, let alone mobilized to promote it. Instead, a letter from the heads of the four major federal unions to Clinton's senior policy advisor bluntly stated that, "we would be forced to publicly oppose this bill in the strongest possible terms should it be sent to Congress for action" (Sturdivant et al. 1995). Similarly, proposed reforms to the CSRA-created Senior Executive Service met with opposition from the Senior Executive Association (Shafritz et al. 2001).

In state government, two models of reform have been evident. One is the "modernization" effort called for by the Commission on the State and Local Public Service (also known as the Winter Commission). In its 1993 report, the Commission called for a revitalization of the public service and offered a number of recommendations for civil service reform. These reforms included decentralizing merit systems, replacing complicated grade and step systems with broad-banding, and turning more authority for staffing decisions to agencies and departments (Report of the National Commission on the State and Local Public Service 1993). Reform undertaken by the state of New York exemplifies the modernization approach (see Riccucci, chapter 13 in this volume).

The importance of the political environment and the constellation of supporters and opponents of reform is clear in this circumstance. Initial attempts to enact statutory reform were consistently defeated, in part due to strong union opposition and divided government (Ban and Riccucci 1994). Civil Service Commissioner George C. Sinnott was successful in accomplishing an "extraordinary turnaround" in part because of his personal expertise and commitment and because the task force he assembled sought input from state employee unions, other government agencies and private sector organizations (Hutchins 2001).

The other model of civil service reform in the states has been more radical. The states of Georgia and Florida dealt with their frustrations with the system by dismantling them (see chapters 6 and 7 by Nigro and Kellough and Gertz, Bowman, and West, respectively, in this volume). This fundamental rout of the civil service system was certainly enabled by its prohibition against collective bargaining by state workers as well as Georgia Governor Miller's personal dedication to the cause. Other factors contributing to the legislation's success were editorial support from the state's largest newspapers as well as from state agency leaders (Condrey 2002).

Unlike Georgia, organized labor was initially able to block the initiative Florida Governor Jeb Bush proposed for similar legislation. But despite mobilization of state workers and other unions to lobby against the legislation, it was ultimately passed by significant margins in both houses (West 2002).

If these are the two models of civil service reform in the states, then where does California find itself? As will become clear, it is off the chart. While for many years the need for reform has been apparent, and recommendations for modernization have been forthcoming, the system remains inert. Here, too, the explanation is a political one, resting to a significant degree on the strength of the unions and the nature of the state's elected leadership.

Prospects for Reform: The Case of California

California, with a population of 35 million and a trillion dollar plus economy has more than a million employees on its governments'

Figure 11.1. California State Employment 1993, 1999

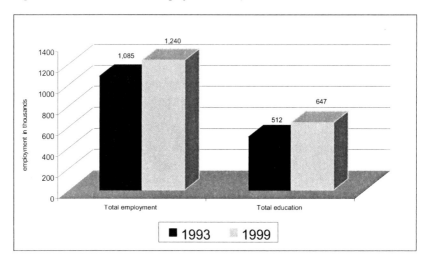

Source: http://www.census.gov/govs/apes

payroll, half of which are in education (see Figure 11.1). Of the remainder about 200,000 are within the states civil service system (State Personnel Board 2000). They fall into 4,462 classifications and are represented by 21 different bargaining units (Little Hoover Commission 1995). Despite California's reputation as a "trendsetter"; that is, the place where the tax revolt, environmental movement, and immigration debate began (Chavez 1998), the state's civil service system has changed little since the introduction of the merit system in the early 1900s.

A Brief History

In California, progressive era reforms and union potency have deep roots. After enduring "cesspools of corruption," (Newland 1999) the state established a merit system with the passage of a Civil Service Act in 1913. Following an economic depression in which state workers faced pay cuts and layoffs, the newly formed California State Employees Association (CSEA) sponsored an initiative that placed the civil service within the state constitution. The measure, passed by an overwhelming majority of voters also created the State Personnel Board (SPB). Initially, the SPB, a five-member board appointed by the governor for ten-year terms, administered a fairly straightforward system of selecting, promoting, and retaining the best qualified individuals, judged to be so by objective standards insulated from the pressures of political patronage.

However, with the Civil Rights era challenging traditional definitions of merit and unions pressing for a greater voice, the system began to show signs of stress. As a result, the State Employer-Employee Relations Act (SEERA, also called the Dills Act) was passed and signed into law in 1977. Most terms and conditions of employment became negotiable for the majority of the state's civil servants. The Act further created the Public Employment Relations Board to oversee administration of the Act.

In 1979 Governor Jerry Brown asked the Commission on California State Government Organization and Economy (later known as the Little Hoover Commission [1]) to undertake a comprehensive review of the state's personnel system. The Commission concluded that SEERA, along with affirmative action guarantees mandated by the legislature in 1977, "put strains on the State's current civil service organization structure which cannot be corrected by patchwork" (Commission on California State Government 1979, iii). Among its recommendations was the establishment of a cabinet-level Department of Personnel Administration to oversee all personnel management functions. The Commission further suggested that a constitutional amendment be passed to replace the SPB with a State Employment Equity Board to ensure the application of merit principles and serve as the neutral third party in the administration of employer-employee organization relationships. It also advocated the establishment of a streamlined personnel management system that would delegate to departments the authority to hire, promote, and reward employees; require strict performance standards for jobs and the release those not meeting those standards; and hold managers accountable for effective performance of their mission (Commission on California State Government 1979).

The governor did establish a Department of Personnel Administration (DPA), reporting directly to him, but no constitutional amendment dissolving the SPB was forthcoming. Rather, its role in day-to-day management was reduced as the DPA and unions assumed responsibility for negotiating conditions of employment, including compensation, as well as administering training programs and layoff and grievance procedures.

While the division of responsibilities between SPB and DPA may sound straightforward, it is anything but clear cut. A table of functions performed by both shows that while the DPA handles appeals of AWOL and voluntary resignation, the SPB is responsible for appeals of rejection during probation and classification appeals. DPA is responsible for drug testing of current employees, while the SPB handles drug testing of new hires. SPB is responsible for part-time employment, while DPA is responsible for the part-time, seasonal, and temporary retirement plan. Both have responsibilities with respect to position classification (e.g., creating a new classification or amending an existing one requires concurrence of both agencies), upward mobility, and employment of the disabled. Moreover, nine other state departments *also* have some responsibilities with respect to the state personnel system (see Table 11.1) (Little Hoover Commission 1995)

In the mid-1980s, California accomplished what is often recommended as part of reform proposals—the decentralization of testing and hiring to individual departments. Unfortunately, the impetus was not providing agencies with more flexibility, but a significant reduction in the SPB's budget. As a result SPB was unable to provide the training required to ensure agencies would adhere to merit principles, and some did not. In 2002, SPB published the results of a comprehensive review of the decentralized testing program. The review identified deficiencies including "insufficiently trained examination staff and poor testing practices that do not result in job-related, merit-based examination processes" (SPB 2002a, 3). Agencies were criticized for developing testing processes that were not based on the job's analytic requirements set forth in the Federal Uniform Guidelines on Employee Section Procedures, which in turn has resulted in adverse impact against candidate groups as well as for deficiencies in the examination interview process (SPB 2002a). In a hearing discussing the report, state departments complained of a lack of resources to perform job analyses in the manner prescribed by SPB as well as a lack of updated manuals and policy direction from SPB staff (Bouler 2002). Some agencies felt betrayed because they had been encouraged by the previous (Wilson) administration to be creative in their examination processes, and they were now getting beaten up for it.

Pressure for Reform

By the mid-1990s, the intricacies presented by two agencies sharing major responsibility for the civil service, and other constraints of the system as it evolved were becoming more visible. The Little Hoover Commission (LHC) and the Legislative Analysts Office (LAO) undertook studies to shed light on potential deficiencies and make recommendations for reform.

The LHC assembled an advisory committee of more than 90 people including representatives of labor, management, the public, the legislature, and academics. Its report issued in 1995 and entitled

Table 11.1
The Personnel Management Bureaucracy
(State departments with some personnel responsibilities)

Agency	Responsibility
State Personnel Board	The five-member board, gubernatorially appointed, revises classification plans, develops exam techniques, and hears employee appeals of discipline actions.
Department of Personnel Administration	Negotiates salaries, benefits, and other employment terms with unions. Administers compensation, evaluation and training programs, and layoff and grievance procedures.
Public Employment Relations Board	Protects the rights of workers to unionize and hears appeals of unfair labor practices.
Department of Fair Employment and Housing	Investigates complaints of discrimination in housing, employment, and public accommodations.
Office of Administrative Law	Reviews and approves regulations proposed by state agencies, including most personnel management rules.
Department of General Services	Reviews contracts for personnel services from private firms for legal adequacy.
Department of Finance	Analyzes department budget proposals, including the expansion and reduction of staffs.
State Compensation Insurance Fund	Offers insurance protection to employers against on-the-job injury claims, and administers benefit claims.
Public Employees' Retirement System	Contracts and approves health benefit plans for state workers; hears employee appeals on coverage disputes.
State Board of Control	Settles employee claims over "out-of-class" work assignments and unpaid benefits.
State Controller	Administers the state payroll and oversees the Personnel Management Information System.

Source: LHC 1995

"Too Many Agencies, Too Many Rules" focused on the following findings and recommendations:

- The bifurcated management structure is "hamstrung by procedures that intentionally discourage change." The Commission recommended that the SPB be abolished, unifying authority in the DPA.
- Departments lack flexibility to test, hire, and assign tasks to the most qualified people and are forced to deal with a costly and dysfunctional discipline process. The Commission suggested that departments be given more latitude over examination and classification procedures, management be given greater training, and that permanent tenure and pay raises be abolished.
- The state is "restricted from tapping the talents and efficiencies of the marketplace." The report recommended that the State Constitution be amended to "eliminate the presumption that civil servants must perform government tasks." Commissioners further recommended that labor-management advisory committees be established to resolve problems and promote innovation. (Little Hoover Commission 1995)

These and other Commission recommendations found their way into bills drafted by members of the legislature (see Table 11.2). However, only two of the more minor recommendations were passed into law.[2]

If the legislature were to enact such reforms, the 1995–1996 session would have been a prime time to do so. Previous research has found that states with greater Republican control over government are more likely to enact deregulatory measures (Coggburn 2001). In addition to having a Republican governor, the 1994 election left the State Assembly in Republican hands for the first time in 25 years, and diminished the margin of Democrats in the Senate. Moreover, the State's Legislative Analysts Office (LAO) voiced its support for reform. In a report accompanying the 1995–1996 budget, the LAO registered several objections to the current system, as it had evolved, including:

- A "merit" pay process where salary adjustments are actually automatic
- Seniority-driven layoffs, which involves a complex process where neither talent nor job performance are considered
- Awarding extra points to veterans and incumbent state

employees in the examination process, restricting managers' ability to consider the best qualified

- A "rule of three" that similarly narrows consideration of qualified candidates
- A long and expensive adverse action appeal process
- An interpretation of the Administrative Procedures Act, which has evolved to apply to the state's own internal regulations and policies, resulting in a very elaborate and time-consuming process each time the DPA or SPB intends to issue guidelines or clarifying instructions[3]
- A classification process with "minute distinctions between classifications that often borders on the ridiculous."

The LAO concluded its report by suggesting that the legislature begin a fundamental rethinking of the state civil service system. The following year, the LAO again supplemented its analysis to the 1996–1997 budget with a more specific analysis of recruitment and hiring in the state civil service. From the analysis arose the following recommendations:

- Replace the "rule of three names" with the "rule of three ranks" in examination scoring, to broaden job candidate pools that managers can consider.
- Eliminate extra examination points for nonmerit and non-job-related reasons (e.g., to veterans and current state employees).
- Eliminate the precedence given to hiring lists comprised of state employees over lists of nonstate employees.
- Increase the maximum probation period that the State Personnel Board may establish for a job class from one year to two years.
- Exempt the state's internal personnel practices from the burdensome requirements of the Administrative Procedure Act.

Some of these recommendations are problematic, however. First, it is unclear why the LAO recommended instituting a "rule of three ranks" as such a system has been in place for quite some time.[4] Moreover, there is no way the unions would agree to increasing the maximum probation period, or to eliminating the extra points that current state employees receive in the examination process. The union's power is significant. Following the legislative session, the

Table 11.2
Little Hoover Commission's Legislative Proposals on the Civil Service 1995–96 Legislative Session

Bill, Author	Summary	Status
AB 1553 Kaloogian	Creates the Quality Demonstration Project Act to allow DPA to test alternative ideas and concepts in the state's classification and compensation programs	Died in Senate Committee
AB 2503 Ackerman	Opens the examination process for Career Executive Assignment (CEA) positions to non–civil service applicants	Dropped by author
AB 2519 Kaloogian	Allows the State Personnel Board to redefine "class" to encompass a "broad-band" classification concept	Assembly Floor Failed Passage
AB 2570 Margett	Limits the Administrative Procedure Act as it applies to internal civil service personnel rules	Died in Senate Committee
AB 2709 Brulte	Eliminates automatic salary increases. Revises salary statutes so that all salary increases will be based on job performance	Assembly Inactive File
AB 2747 Ackerman	Shortens and modifies the state's layoff process to eliminate overlapping jurisdiction and responsibility between the Department of Personnel Administration and the State Personnel Board	Assembly Inactive File
AB 2772 Cortese	Limits the application of the Administrative Procedure Act as it applies to State Personnel Board internal personnel rules	Chapter 935, 1996

(cont.) Table 11.2

AB 2775 Miller	Reforms the civil service examination process	Chapter 772, 1996
AB 3282 Cunneen	Streamlines the civil service discipline process	Died in Senate Committee
AB 3427 Baugh	Reforms the civil service selection and certification process	Assembly Floor Failed Passage
ACA 11 Morrow	Eliminates the constitutional provision against contracting out	Dropped by author
ACA 22 Speier	Abolishes the State Personnel Board	Dropped by author
ACA 35 Kaloogian	Eliminates the Constitutional prohibition against contracting out. Allows the state to contract with private entities to perform state functions and services	Died in Committee
ACA 42 Poochigian	Eliminates the Constitutional prohibition against contracting out. Allows the state to contract with private entities to perform state functions and services	Assembly Floor Failed Passage
SCA 20 Monteith	Eliminates the Constitutional prohibition against contracting out. Allows the State to contract with private entities to perform state functions and services	Died in Committee

Source: LHC 1999

largest union representing California state employees, the California State Employees Association (CSEA) took credit for defeating two-dozen bills that contained what they considered to be anti-union or anti-state employee provisions ("Despite Legislative Chaos" 1996).

Additional problems in the system identified by personnel officials and others interviewed for this paper include outdated classification standards and an inordinately slow hiring process. Outdated class standards present agencies with severe difficulties because they provide the basis for qualification standards, and therefore job announcements. (The "unit supervisor" standard, for example, had not been updated since 1972). Forced to advertise a position with outdated or incomplete standards means that agencies will be presented with a long list of eligibles who do not have the required qualifications. One reason the standards are outdated is that they are within the scope of bargaining and it is assumed that unions won't go along with revising them without also demanding higher salaries for those positions. For its part, CSEA claims it has asked DPA for duty statements and has been stonewalled. Updating the standards also presents a workload issue. Revision requires the participation of all departments that use a particular classification along with DPA and the unions.

A related concern is the examination and hiring process. Examinations are offered every one to four years. This means that included on the list of eligibles from which departments are required to select are people who may no longer be interested in the job. Moreover, it takes on average six months from the time an exam is given to the time a supervisor receives a list of eligibles. This is particularly problematic because of a measure instituted as part of the 2000 budget agreement. That measure, known as the "six-month rule" requires the state controller to eliminate positions that are vacant for six consecutive months (Californian Budget Project 2002).

Why, then, has this otherwise progressive state been so slow to implement the reforms called for in the literature (e.g., Osborne and Gaebler), undertaken in some states (e.g., Georgia) and called for by its own oversight bodies (LAO and LHC)?

Whither Civil Service Reform?

The answer turns largely on the broad scope of bargaining enjoyed by state employee unions, their resistance to change, and their relationship with the governor. Another factor impeding reform is the existence of two agencies (SPB and DPA) at the helm of civil service. Far from providing unified leadership in favor of change, the two agencies sometimes find themselves at loggerheads with each other. A third reason is the lack of consensus that the system is in need of reform or any other source of leadership (à la New York's George C. Sinnott) to lead a major reform effort.

Depending on whom you ask, Pete Wilson, who served as governor from 1991 to 1998, was either the devil incarnate out to maim state civil servants, or a champion of increased efficiency through reinventing government-like reforms. If privatization constitutes a "radical" reform akin to the civil service dismantlement undertaken by Georgia and Florida, then Wilson was an insurgent. He made privatization of state services a centerpiece of his agenda and sought to overturn a provision in the State Constitution that limits the contracting out of state work. Wilson also tried to implement less momentous changes, including the implementation of a wide-ranging pay-for-performance system. His position was that every dime public employees earn—including cost-of-living increases—should be based on performance. The Wilson administration also sought changes in the layoff system and succeeded in negotiating an expedited disciplinary process for some bargaining units.

Wilson met with limited success, however, because of union opposition to his proposals. In fact, Wilson supporters and opponents agree that relationships with unions during his administration were exceptionally hostile, to the point where no matter what one proposed, the other would object. In a letter addressed to Governor Davis and legislative leaders in January 1999, LHC chairman Richard Terzian said that its 1995 recommendations "like many other 'civil service' reform initiatives, were consumed by the most serious discord between management and labor in the modern history of the state" (see Kearney's chapter 4 in this volume for more on the organized labor position on reform). In fact, while negotiation sessions took place, there were no agreements with labor for four years. DPA found itself in the unenviable position of having to reject union proposals based on philosophy rather than because they could point to a concrete management concern with the proposal.

Calling Wilson "a serial privatizer who apparently can't help himself," CSEA launched a virulent crusade against his privatization venture in which the union ultimately prevailed through successful lawsuits and the defeat of legislative proposals (CSEA 1996). CSEA also blocked the governor's efforts to impose pay-for-performance (which they called "pucker pay") on rank-and-file employees, although nonunion supervisors and managers were brought into this scheme. Only two unions, representing health-care professionals, were willing to go along with changes to the layoff system.

When the much more pro-labor Grey Davis assumed office in 1999, the climate changed dramatically. Pay-for-performance was dropped as were the changes in the layoff system, and Davis took steps to return contracted work to state employees. But with the improved climate also came the administration's reluctance to confront the unions with reforms they have long opposed. Of course, the more cynical observers might note the governor's dependence on union support for his election. Since 1997, nine of his top ten campaign contributors have been unions, including nearly $2 million in contributions from the Service Employees International Union and nearly $1 million from American Federation of State, County, and Municipal Employees (AFSCME) (Williams and Marinucci 2002). Nor are unions necessarily willing to let down their guard despite a more pro-union environment. As one union official put it, employees are no longer as fearful of losing their jobs as they were during the Wilson administration. But every four years there is a new governor. Why put reforms in place that the next governor may take advantage of at the expense of labor?

Another participant trudging in the civil service morass is the Association of California State Supervisors (ACSS). ACSS is technically an affiliate of CSEA and while they claim that does not stop them from taking positions in opposition to the union, in practice they seldom do. Supervisors are exempt from collective bargaining and therefore are in some ways the forgotten stepchild in a civil service system that revolves around labor negotiations. DPA has the authority to set supervisors' pay, but seldom gets around to it until they have completed their negotiations with unions representing rank-and-file employees. Moreover, exempt employees don't receive some of the benefits rank-and-file employees do, such as recruitment and retention bonuses. As a result, some supervisors earn less than their own subordinates. In 2002 legislation was passed with the support of the ACSS to create a salary-setting commission to recommend pay levels for excluded employees, introducing yet another body into California's peculiar human resource management milieu.

Another impediment to reform is the existence of two agencies with central roles in the civil service system and its day-to-day operations, SPB and DPA. Since the passage of the Dills Act in 1977 making most terms and conditions of employment negotiable, and the subsequent establishment of DPA to represent the governor in those negotiations, SPB has seen its authority and scope of responsibility diminish. As a result, even when unions agree to reforms in the context of labor negotiations, SPB sometimes steps in and objects.

For example, in 1997 DPA negotiated a streamlined procedure for resolving minor disciplinary appeals with the California Department of Forestry and Fire Protection. Disputes requiring an independent mediator were to be reviewed by a labor-management committee in an expedited process. From DPA's perspective, this procedure worked very well as it was considerably less time-consuming and rule-bound than the "normal" appellate process. However, SPB, asserting that the agreement encroached on its jurisdiction over the disciplinary process, successfully filed suit against DPA to block its implementation.

More recently, SPB challenged the "post-and-bid" provisions of the state's contract with three bargaining units. Post-and-bid refers to a system where a supervisor is required to hire and promote employees in certain occupations solely on the basis of seniority. SPB objected that this violated the merit system because no other performance-related or merit-based factors would be considered. This would ultimately result, SPB contended, in a less-qualified workforce, and have an adverse impact on women and minorities (SPB 2002b). DPA did not view it this way. Rather, from DPA's perspective the requirement that the selection be made from the list of eligibles ensured qualifications had already been evaluated. So why not select the candidate with the most experience? In July 2002, SPB won a restraining order in Superior Court.

Partly in response to the post-and-bid controversy, SPB recently held a hearing on a new rule that would explicitly define merit and hold that the SPB's authority over the selection process encompasses all activities from recruitment and advertising to the end of the civil service probation period (SPB 2002c). SPB had expected unions to support the rule as it states explicitly that selections must be based solely on qualifications, restricting possible subjectivity on the part of the selecting official. Instead, the unions objected to the new rule, claiming it would discriminate against women and people of color. DPA also stated its opposition to the rule.

So the broad scope of bargaining enjoyed by the unions means that reform almost has to come through the negotiation process. But these examples suggest that when such changes are agreed to, SPB may well object.

Another possible inroad to reform could be through demonstration projects, which SPB has had the authority to conduct and evaluate since 1980. The purpose of these projects is to test new personnel management practices for a period of five years, with a view to making them permanent if they appear to be successful, and all parties agree. To date, however, the only legislative change resulting from these projects was AB 1399, passed in 1999, which requires that agencies obtain written agreements from supervisors before implementing demonstrations that would affect them (they are already required to seek union concurrence for demos that affect rank-and-file employees). This legislation represented a compromise with the unions who sought to abolish demonstration projects.

Another obstacle to reform is an apparent lack of interest on the part of the State Assembly or Senate. These elected representatives and their staff take their cues from organized constituencies and the only one in the civil service arena is the union. Neither the union nor anyone else is rallying for civil service reform. Moreover, the civil service system is very complex, and the expertise to tackle it does not exist in the legislature, particularly now that term limits are in place.

In 1999 the LHC issued a second report with the purpose of recommending a "process though which top leaders and rank-and-file workers can cooperatively determine the precise changes that are needed and how those changes will be made" (LHC 1999, iv). The report urged the state's top leaders to work cooperatively with managers and employees to create a shared understanding of how the personnel system should operate in the public interest. This laudable recommendation would, at a minimum, require a leader to step in and create a vision that legislators, the governor, and all the agencies with roles in the civil service system would accept. It would also require that damaged relationships between management and labor, and between DPA and SPB be rebuilt. Such leadership does not appear to be forthcoming.

Conclusion

It is clear that any major reform in California's civil service system will not be within reach in the near future. One reason is the fundamental tension between centralized merit system and collective bargaining process, as personified in the two agencies representing these two interests. Of these two, the SPB, protector of the merit system, can better withstand pressure for reform (or dissolution) because it is "enshrined" in the State Constitution. But the majority of the civil service system is subject to bargaining, and SPB has objected to reforms agreed to by management and labor. The history of agency abuse of the merit system when hiring was decentralized, along with the low regard in which some unions hold some agencies, reinforces the importance of SPB's role in state human resource management. While the DPA attempts to maintain an equilibrium between management and labor, an anti-labor governor like Pete Wilson can undermine that effort by forcefully challenging the presumptive rights of employees to organize and indeed, to keep their jobs. Ironically, a pro-labor governor like Gray Davis can undermine reform as well by refusing to engage the unions in debate on the subject.

The call for reform has only been heard from outside evaluators and disgruntled personnel officials, without the constituency or momentum to translate their recommendations into legislative change. Having withstood a poor economy (in the early 1990s), the reinventing government movement in its zenith, and calls for change on the part of two respected entities (the LHC and LAO), it is difficult to see what, if anything, could propel this state toward significant reform. Even the renewed attention to the importance of "human capital" (Walker 2000) and the need to ensure that human resource management systems are designed to maximize the contribution and development of these assets is unlikely to generate enough momentum for reform in the Golden State. As Wallace Sayer observed in 1948, "Here, too, one may conclude that the ends have been made captive by the means."

Notes

1. Created in 1962, the Commission investigates state government operations, makes recommendations and drafts legislative proposals designed to promote efficiency, economy, and improved service in state government. By statute, the Commission is a balanced bipartisan board composed of five citizen members appointed by the governor, four citizen members appointed by the Legislature, two Senators and two Assembly members.

2. Both reforms that were passed into law affected SPB. AB 2772 exempted some SPB rules from the OAL review (see note 5). AB 2775 set some limits on the number of competitors in open exams in entry-level positions. SPB has not yet implemented regulations based on these reforms.

3. California's Administrative Procedure Act (APA) was adopted in 1945 to improve the clarity and consistency of state regulations. However, in a 1978 decision, the California Supreme Court interpreted the law to apply to the state's internal personnel policies. Therefore, before DPA or SPB can promulgate a policy, it must (1) prepare detailed documentation in support of the policy, (2) provide public notice and receive comments, (3) respond to each

comment received, (4) hold a public hearing if requested by anyone, and (5) submit the regulation and documentation to the Office of Administrative Law for its approval. (Asimov 1992)

4. Under this system percentile cutoffs are established for an occupation before an exam is given. The scores above each cutoff represent a rank, and the supervisor may select anyone who is in the top three ranks. For example, the top rank may include scores above 95 percent, the second rank scores above 90 pecent, and so forth. In some cases a "rule of the list" is used where all eligibles on the list are reachable.

References

Ban, Carolyn, and Norma Riccucci (1994). "New York State: Civil Service Reform in a Complex Environment," *Review of Public Personnel Administration* 14 (2): 28–39.

Bouler, Debra (2002). "Summary of SPB Hearing on the Status of the State's Decentralized Testing Program" Memo written to colleagues (July 10).

California Budget Project (2002). "The Civil Service Vacancy Game: Abusive Practices or Underling Structural Problems?" Sacramento: California Budget Project (May). Available at www.cbp.org.

California State Employees Association (1996). "CSEA Sues Over Yet Another Improper State Contract."

Chavez, Lydia (1998). *The Color Bind*. Berkeley: University of California Press.

Coggburn, Jerrell D. (2001). "Personnel Deregulation in the States," *Journal of Public Administration Research and Theory* 11 (2) (January): 223–244.

Commission on California State Government Organization and Economy (1979). (see Little Hoover Commission).

Condrey, Stephen E. (2002). "Reinventing State Civil Service Systems: The Georgia Experience" *Review of Public Personnel Administration* 22 (2) (Summer): 114–124.

"Despite Legislative Chaos, 1995–96 Session Does Little Harm to Workers." *Pride California* 9 (4) (Fall): 32.

Hays, Steven W. (1996). "The 'State of the Discipline' in Public Personnel Administration," *Public Administration Quarterly* 20 (Fall): 285–304.

Hutchins, Jennifer (2001). "Who Says Government Doesn't Work?" *Workforce*. 80 (3) (March): 58–61.

Kettl, Donald F., Patricia Ingraham, Ronald P. Sanders, and Constance Horner (1996). *Civil Service Reform: Building a Government that Works*. Washington, DC: Brookings Institution.

Legislative Analyst Office, State of California (1995). "Reinventing the State Civil Service." Available at http:/www.lao.ca.gov/pt5-c.html (February 1).

——— (1996). "Reinventing the State Civil Service: Recruiting and Hiring for Excellence. Available at http:/www.lao.ca.gov (February 21).

Little Hoover Commission (1979). *Personnel Management in the State Service: State of California*. Sacramento: Commission on California State Government Organization and Economy (August).

———— (1995). *Too Many Agencies, Too Many Rules: Reforming California's Civil Service*. Sacramento: Little Hoover Commission (April).

———— (1999). *Of the People, By the People: Principles for Cooperative Civil Service Reform*. Sacramento: Little Hoover Commission (January).

National Performance Review (1993). *From Red Tape to Results: Creating a Government that Works Better and Costs Less*, Washington, DC: Office of the Vice President (September 7).

Newland, Chester A. (1992). "The Politics of Civil Service Reform," in Patricia W. Ingraham and David H. Rosenbloom, eds. *The Promise and Paradox of Civil Service Reform*. Pittsburgh, PA: University of Pittsburgh Press. 63–92.

———— (1999). "The Facilitative State and Human Resources Management." *Public Personnel Management* 28 (4): 637–654.

Osborne, David, and Ted Gaebler (1992). *Reinventing Government*. Reading, MA: Addison-Wesley.

"Report of the National Commission on the State and Local Public Service" (1993). Reprinted in Thompson, Frank, ed. *Revitalizing State and Local Public Service*. San Francisco: Jossey Bass.

Sayre, Wallace (1948). "The Triumph of Techniques Over Purpose." *Public Administration Review* 8 (Spring): 134–137.

Schuh, Anna Marie (2000). *Timing Successful Policy Change: Lessons from the Civil Service*. Lanham, MD: University Press of America.

Shafritz, Jay, David R. Rosenbloom, Norma Riccucci, Katherine C. Naff, and Albert C. Hyde (2001). *Personnel Management in Government,* 5th ed. New York: Marcel Dekker, Inc.

State Personnel Board (2000). "Annual Census of State Employees and Affirmative Action Report Fiscal Year 1999–2000." Sacramento: State Personnel Board (November).

———— (2002a). "The Status of the State's Decentralized Testing Program, Preliminary Findings and Recommendations" Sacramento: State Personnel Board Policy Division (June).

———— (2002b). "Superior Court Rules that Post and Bid Provisions Violate the State Constitution and Prohibits Their Implementation." Sacramento: State Personnel Board. Available at http://www.spb.ca.gov/spblaw/ruling_1.htm.

———— (2002c). "Public Hearing to Adopt New Section 250 in Title 2 of California Code of Regulations." Available at http://www.spb.ca.gov/sitemap/cascmenu.html.

Sturdivant, John N., Robert M. Tobias, Sonya Constantine, and John Layden (1995). *Letter to Elaine Kamarck, Senior Policy Advisor to the Vice President* (May 24).

Walker, David (2000). *Human Capital: Managing Capital in the 21st Century*. Testimony before the Subcommittee on Oversight of Government

Management. Restructuring, and the District of Columbia, Committee on Governmental Affairs, U.S. Senate. March 9.

West, Jonathan (2002). "Georgia on the Mind of Radical Civil Service Reformers," *Review of Public Personnel Administration* 22 (2) (Summer): 79–93.

Williams, Lance, and Carla Marinucci (2002). "Davis' Nonstop Cash Machine," *San Francisco Chronicle* (May 19): A1, A17.

Officials Interviewed

Winter 2001

Laura Aguilera, Chief of Personnel Resources and Innovations Division, California. State Personnel Board

Chris Codiroli, staff consultant with Professional Engineers in California Government.

Jim Mayer, Director, Little Hoover Commission

Carol Ong, State Personnel Board

Bob Painter, Policy Manager, Department of Personnel Administration

Summer 2002

Tim Behrens, President, Association of California State Supervisors

Debra Bouler, Executive Office, Policy Management, California Department of General Services

Pat Chappie, Human Resource Services Director, California Employment Development Department

David Felderstein, Principal Consultant, California State Senate Committee on Public Employee and Retirement

Wayne Heine, Assistant Chief of Labor Relations, California Department of Personnel Administration

Shelley Langan, Manager, Special Projects, State Personnel Board

Jim Mayer, Director, Little Hoover Commission

Dianne Navarro, Chief of Labor Relations, California Employment Development Department

Michael T. Navarro, Chief, Classification and Compensation Division, California Department of Personnel Administration

Chester Newland, Professor, University of Southern California

Carol Ong, Manager, Policy Development, State Personnel Board

Ana Sandoval, Communications Director, California State Employees Association

CHAPTER 12

Wisconsin State Government: Reforming
Human Resources Management While
Retaining Merit Principles
and Cooperative Labor Relations

Peter D. Fox
Robert J. Lavigna

Across the nation, government organizations at all levels are
under pressure to dramatically change the way they do business. The
goal is to provide more responsive, effective, and cost-efficient services. While this demand for government reform covers virtually every
aspect of public sector performance, nowhere is the need for reform
more critical than in human resources (HR) management. What does
this mean, in more concrete terms? It means that government must
develop human resource systems that attract, develop, and retain
human capital by:

- Clearly identifying and communicating the competencies
  that are critical to organizational and individual success,
  now and in the future. Strategic workforce planning is the
  tool to do this. Clearly identified competencies should be the
  basis for all human capital systems including recruiting,
  performance management, classification and compensation,
  promotions and transfers, succession planning, and training
  and development.
- Creating efficient, timely, and effective systems to recruit
  and hire talented people.
- Providing tools and feedback to help employees candidly
  evaluate their competency levels and, just as important,
  compare where they are with where they need to be.
- Providing tools and assistance to help employees eliminate
  "competency gaps" and achieve their full potential.

- Establishing clear career paths and making sure people know how they can advance. Employees must know they have a future and how they can grow professionally.
- Creating diverse organizations and managing diversity effectively, including dealing with intergenerational issues.
- Creating flexible job classification systems that will help employees contribute and develop.
- Developing compensation systems that reward accomplishment and achievement, not just tenure.
- Forging positive and cooperative relationships with organized labor.

Unfortunately, state governments often fall short of these objectives, and that's why HR reform is more a goal than a reality in many places. Too often, human capital systems remain unresponsive, slow, rule-bound, and user-unfriendly. These shortcomings have been widely chronicled by the *National Commission on the State and Local Public Service* (Winter Commission), the *National Performance Review* (later called the *National Partnership for Reinventing Government*, Gore 1993*)* and in hearings conducted by the second Volcker Commission. The U.S. General Accounting Office, a champion of a more strategic approach to human capital, characterized federal HR as ". . . largely process-oriented and focused on ensuring agency compliance with merit system rules and regulations" (GAO 2002).

Recommendations to improve human resource systems include giving operating units more decision-making authority, making it easier to hire well-qualified new employees (and fire poor ones), eliminating restrictive rules, simplifying job classification systems, and linking compensation to performance. Unfortunately, proposals like these often remain more rhetoric than operational reality.

Some states, however, are aggressively responding to this demand for change. Georgia and Florida, for example have dramatically reformed their traditional merit systems, ostensibly to eliminate red tape and improve flexibility. Others are maintaining their merit systems, but taking aggressive steps to improve flexibility and responsiveness. The state of Washington, for example, has enacted legislation to completely review and overhaul its civil service system. States that are committed to reforming merit systems must strike the often-delicate balance between flexibility and fundamental merit principles such as openness and fairness. This requires balancing the demands of the many constituencies served by government, including elected political leaders and their appointees, legislators, line managers, rank-and-file employees, labor unions, veterans, minority groups, women's groups, personnel appeals commissions and boards, courts, job applicants, the public, and so on. These stakeholders all demand to be involved in any changes, but often disagree about what and how to change. As a result, simply managing government HR systems is tough; reforming them is a far more difficult proposition. Although the goal of the *National Performance Review*—"to make government work better and cost less"—sounds perfectly reasonable, achieving it is another matter. Reformers who do not realize that success hinges on balancing a wide range of conflicting interests and influences are doomed to failure.

The Wisconsin State Government civil service (merit) system is one of the nation's most comprehensive and oldest state systems. In 1905 Wisconsin became the third state (after Massachusetts and New York) to create a civil service system that bases hiring and advancement on ability and performance, not the whims of political leaders. The Wisconsin system is grounded in two fundamental values: merit principles and collective bargaining.

Today, Wisconsin State Government has more than 68,000 public employees, about 41,000 of whom are "classified" (civil service) employees. State law requires that all classified vacancies must be filled, "through methods which apply the merit principle, with adequate civil service safeguards." Collective bargaining in Wisconsin government traces its roots to the beginnings of organized labor in the United States. In fact, the nation's largest public sector union— the American Federation of State, County and Municipal Employees (AFSCME)—was founded in Wisconsin by state government employees in 1932. Today, almost 90 percent of Wisconsin's permanent civil service employees are represented by labor unions.

The Wisconsin Department of Employment Relations (DER) is the state government's central personnel/HR agency. The department develops and manages the centralized HR policies, practices, and systems for more than 50 state agencies, the 26 University of Wisconsin campuses, and all classified state employees. The DER also provides HR services to more than 150 local Wisconsin governments. The department is responsible for HR functions including candidate recruitment and assessment, classification and compensation, labor relations, and affirmative action. The DER secretary is appointed by the governor and confirmed by the state senate. While the DER develops statewide policies and systems, and has ultimate responsibility for Wisconsin's HR system, state agencies and university campuses handle day-to-day personnel operations. In fact, all large agencies, campuses, and most small agencies have their own HR professionals who work closely with the DER.

Wisconsin State Government has established a national reputation for public policy innovation in areas such as welfare reform. Although not as widely publicized, Wisconsin is also reforming the state's civil service system. The state has crafted its reform agenda by involving stakeholders and customers including the governor, the legislature, state agencies, labor unions, and interest groups. This consensus-based approach has resulted in major reforms in recruitment and selection, classification, and compensation, labor relations and diversity (in contrast to the California experience, see Naff, chapter 11, in this volume).

Reforming Hiring Systems to Attract Talent

To provide responsive, effective, and efficient service, government must hire talented and dedicated people. This requires civil service hiring systems that work. According to the National Commission on the State and Local Public Service (1993) report, government agencies must "end civil service paralysis" by creating more responsive hiring systems. For most civil service systems, this is easier said than done largely because of the many requirements imposed by law and regulation. The Wisconsin civil service law alone, for example, is 28 pages long. Some of its provisions are:

- All civil service appointments must be made through competitive examinations which are job-related in compliance with appropriate validation standards
- These examinations must be free, open to all, and convenient to Wisconsin residents
- Recruitment must be active, continuous, and conducted as broadly as possible
- Applicants can appeal decisions made at any step in the hiring process to an independent personnel commission that has decision-making authority.

Wisconsin's new hiring programs were driven by the realization that traditional civil service hiring processes were simply not working. In the late 1980s, it became clear that Wisconsin's hiring system was not effective either for the state agencies doing the hiring or for the applicants who wished to be hired. The civil service process was so inflexible, slow, and cumbersome that job seekers interested in public service careers were reluctant to compete for positions. The system needed reform.

In 1992 the DER conducted a customer survey to assess recruitment and hiring effectiveness. With the help of Dr. Herbert G. Heneman (University of Wisconsin-Madison School of Business; Heneman, Huett, Lavigna & Ogsten 1995) and a student intern, the department distributed a 60-question survey that included questions in five key areas identified during focus group discussions: timeliness, communication, candidate quality, examination quality, and responsiveness/service orientation. The department surveyed a total of 645 personnel professionals, line managers, and supervisors across state government. The latter two groups were particularly important because, in many cases, the DER had only limited contact with them. Almost 500 responses were received (a 70 percent return rate).

As expected, the DER received both good and bad news. Customers cited several areas where the department was performing well (accessibility, professionalism, and technical expertise). On the other hand, several areas needed improvement, notably communicating policies effectively, and creating faster and more flexible processes to assess applicants. One Department of Employment Relations manager commented that the survey showed that the department was, "slowly providing poorly-qualified candidates to agencies." Clearly, however, this was no laughing matter. The department used these data to develop a series of new programs to provide more responsive, efficient, and user-friendly service. The hiring innovations form an integrated strategy with several elements:

- Giving line agencies more decision-making authority
- Modernizing civil service laws to improve flexibility and responsiveness
- Developing more creative and user-friendly ways to evaluate job candidates
- Expanding recruiting to attract more and better candidates
- Conducting on-site (immediate) job interviews
- Using technology to provide better access, efficiency, and timeliness.

Delegating Decision-Making Authority

To improve hiring speed and responsiveness, the DER has given day-to-day hiring authority to state agencies. For example, agencies develop their own approaches to evaluate and examine applicants, accept and process applications, evaluate and rank candidates, develop lists of qualified applicants, and identify and interview the best qualified. Delegation gives line agencies direct control over hiring, enabling them to apply their knowledge of their business needs to their hiring activities. Delegation also enables the DER staff to use their technical knowledge to develop new, enterprisewide approaches to staffing, and also provide advice and consulting services to agencies on issues such as selecting the best approach to recruit and evaluate job applicants.

While state law allows the DER to delegate decision-making authority, it still has the ultimate legal responsibility to ensure that agency hiring practices follow state laws, rules, and policies. The department does this through formal policies and procedures to ensure fair and open competition, a comprehensive training program on staffing and periodic "assistance visits" (audits).

Reforming State Hiring Laws

Wisconsin civil service laws are among the most comprehensive and detailed in the nation. While this reflects the state's long-standing commitment to a strong merit system, it became clear that civil service statutes needed to be changed to make state government a more competitive employer. For example, one statutory barrier was the "rule of five" that limited the number of qualified candidates hiring managers could interview for any vacancy. Managers could interview only the five candidates with the highest civil service scores. This rule was so restrictive that if the candidates who ranked numbers five and six had identical civil service scores, the department somehow had to break the tie because only one could be interviewed. In other cases, where only a few candidates applied and all were qualified, the law made the department go through a time-consuming process to numerically rank all candidates to identify the top five. This was inefficient and ineffective.

The DER leadership convinced the state legislature to amend this restrictive law incrementally. First, in 1992, the department lobbied to modify the rule of five for two hiring situations: jobs that typically require college degrees and jobs where candidates were in critically short supply. After extensive lobbying, amendments were enacted to eliminate arbitrary restrictions on the number of candidates who could be interviewed for these kinds of positions. This change enabled the creation of two successful programs, the *Entry*

Professional Program and the *Critical Recruitment Program*. Both programs use techniques to assess applicants that are more flexible, timely, and user-friendly than traditional written examinations. The goal is to identify best-qualified candidates but minimize the bureaucratic hurdles of written exams. These job-related methodologies, which still meet Wisconsin's legal definition of "examination," include skills inventories and résumé reviews. These approaches also allow the state to use more timely alternatives to rating and ranking all applicants based on their civil service scores. These alternatives include "pass/fail" ratings and sorting candidates into categories (bands) such as "best qualified, "qualified," and "unqualified." Further, if a job included in the *Critical Recruitment Program* required a state license or certification, that credential was the "exam." Any applicant who earned that credential (e.g., certified social worker, licensed professional engineer) was qualified for an interview.

These programs made the state much more competitive on college campuses, and enabled state agencies to assess applicants quickly, interview larger numbers of qualified applicants, and hire candidates faster. For example, with these programs, the DER was able to deliver lists of qualified candidates to hiring managers immediately after application deadlines. The programs also helped diversify the state government workforce, as described below.

These two successful programs set the stage for broader reform. In 1996, then Governor Tommy G. Thompson created a *Commission on the Reform of the State Human Resource System* (1996). The commission was led by a private sector executive and included the DER Secretary, union leaders, and legislators from both sides of the aisle.

The *Commission's* December 1996 report reaffirmed Wisconsin's commitment to a merit system, but made several recommendations to improve the system's performance. To improve hiring, the report recommended that the flexibility used successfully in the *Entry Professional* and *Critical Recruitment* programs be extended to all jobs. The DER willingly crafted legislation that repealed all arbitrary restrictions on the number of qualified candidates referred to hiring managers. This proposal also eliminated residency requirements and all limits on out-of-state recruiting. The department then worked with the governor's office to forge a coalition with unions, veterans' groups, special interest groups such as the Wisconsin Association of Black Public Sector Employees, and legislators from both parties. These groups worked together to pass legislation implementing the department's proposal in 1997.

Developing Creative and User-Friendly Ways to Evaluate Candidates

In the early 1990s, more than 60 percent of the jobs in Wisconsin state government were filled using written, multiple-choice exams. While this traditional civil service approach is recognized as an effective way to predict job performance, written exams also have weaknesses, particularly in highly competitive labor markets. Candidates with other job choices often won't go through a lengthy written exam process, and written exams are particularly ineffective when competing for talent with the private sector where they are rarely used.

To make Wisconsin state government more competitive, the DER developed and implemented approaches such as skills inventories, résumé reviews, achievement history questionnaires and other "take home" exams. These approaches are now filling the majority of vacancies in the state's more than 1,900 job classifications. While each assessment instrument focuses on different job-related skills, all are content valid, which meets "appropriate validation standards" state law requires (State of Wisconsin 2002).

Combined with candidate-ranking methods such as pass/fail and banding, these approaches are faster and more user-friendly. They also make state government more competitive with other employers, including those in the private sector. Recently, the department took the next step and automated the hiring process. Now, candidates apply online and hiring managers can obtain their lists of qualified candidates online. This approach is described below.

While the DER now uses alternatives to written exams, the state has not abandoned the written exam. Multiple-choice tests are still the best approach for some jobs (e.g., office support and blue-collar positions), particularly where large numbers of candidates apply. For these jobs, the department now uses *Walk-in Testing* where applicants simply show up at state-run exam centers and take their tests without having to apply in advance.

Recruiting More Aggressively

Even the best applicant screening processes won't work unless qualified candidates apply. Traditionally, public sector staffing systems have focused on "examining" applicants to identify the best qualified. The assumption has been that there will always be enough qualified candidates. However, as the age bubble group moves into retirement, competition for talent will intensify. In these tight labor markets, government must recruit aggressively to attract qualified candidates. Because many public sector organizations are unaccustomed to marketing their job opportunities, aggressive recruiting means developing new skills and approaches. In Wisconsin, both the DER and the operating agencies have dramatically stepped up recruiting activities in several new ways:

- Until 1996 the DER had only one full-time recruiter. That year the department added a full-time equal opportunity recruiter and a full-time information technology (IT) recruiter.
- These DER recruiters conduct enterprisewide recruiting for all of state government. They promote state careers, focusing on jobs that exist across state government in fields such as office support, accounting, and information technology.
- To complement the DER recruiting activities, operating agencies have hired their own recruiters who promote specific vacancies (e.g., social workers in the Department of Health and Family Services). This sharing of responsibilities allows both the DER and operating agencies to leverage their individual resources, knowledge, and contacts.
- The DER and agency recruiters now represent state government at more job fairs and campus visits than before. In 1999 and 2000, for example, department recruiters attended more than twice as many recruiting events—more than 100 each year—as in earlier years. At many of these events, state recruiters compete head-to-head with private sector recruiters. More recently, although the economic downturn has reduced recruiting activities, overall recruiting effort is still above pre-1999 levels.
- State recruiters also work closely with community organizations across the state. The DER has a database of more than 300 community-based organizations that serve minority groups, veterans, and the disabled. Department and agency recruiters use this database to target potential recruits through e-mail, direct mail, and personal contacts.
- The DER and operating agencies recruit through the state's main Web portal, state agency Web sites, and other Internet sites. As discussed below, candidates can now apply for state jobs online, and this promises to dramatically improve the effectiveness of recruiting through the Web.

On-Site Interviewing

The Department of Employment Relations conducts on-site interviews at job fairs, particularly for hard-to-fill jobs in fields such as information technology, human services, and health care. On-site interviewing allows managers to make immediate job offers to outstanding candidates. In this process, first used in 1999, recruiters use a fast applicant screening instrument to determine basic eligibility. This instrument can consist of several "yes/no" questions about a candidate's background. Candidates who answer "yes" to all questions are immediately eligible and are interviewed by hiring managers who also attend the recruiting event.

The interviewing manager usually invites and schedules the best candidates for in-office interviews. However, hiring managers can make immediate job offers or at least make tentative offers contingent on positive references and other background checks.

Using Electronic Technology

Wisconsin state government is also using e-technology to attract and hire talent. Like most hiring organizations, the state advertises vacancies on the Internet, through the Wisconsin.gov Web portal. Beyond that, the state has also expanded into online job application. This approach was first used in 1998 to fill information technology (IT) vacancies. The prototype system allows IT candidates to apply online at any time—seven days a week, twenty-four hours a day—from anywhere. Candidates complete an online state application and an online inventory of IT skills areas important to IT managers. Applicants report their education, training, and work experience in each area they are interested in, and have skills. This checklist, which takes about twenty minutes to complete, is the "exam." When the online applicant hits "send," he or she is added to the applicant database and immediately receives an e-mail receipt. On the hiring side, the hiring manager "orders" candidates online. The manager creates a hiring profile by completing the same electronic form as the applicant, except the manager lists the qualifications needed for the job. He or she then immediately receives a list of the applicants from the database who meet the job requirements. The manager can then contact the qualified applicants, conduct interviews, and make a job offer.

The success of this online system for IT positions prompted the DER to expand the system to other jobs. Because the DER did not have the expertise or money to develop a statewide system on its own, it forged a multiagency partnership. Partners included the Wisconsin Department of Administration (the state's central administrative agency), which furnished IT architects and developers as well as most of the project funding. Other partners were the Department of Transportation, which provided project management expertise, and the Department of Electronic Government. The result is a statewide online application system or WISCJOBS—a state-of-the art system designed largely by its users. Starting in 2003, the public could access a Web-based online application process that offers applicants a "job cart," résumé builder, career agent (e-mail notification when there is a relevant vacancy), and online testing for jobs that require written exams. Applicants are also be able to create and maintain their own personal history file of applications and status. On the hiring side, agency HR staff will have a user-friendly system to announce vacancies; design, administer and score applicant assessments; and manage employment lists.

The Results

Wisconsin's hiring reforms provide hiring managers with qualified candidates faster, even for hard-to-fill jobs in fields like information technology. Programs like online application and on-site interviewing give hiring managers immediate access to qualified candidates instead of waiting for weeks to receive their candidate lists. Even the written examination process has been streamlined. Before *Walk-in Testing*, candidates had to submit written applications six weeks before test dates. The department then mailed individual confirmation notices to the 100,000 candidates who applied each year. Unfortunately, about 40,000 never showed up for their exams. Handling 100,000 applications was expensive and time-consuming, particularly with a 40 percent "no show" rate. Now, with *Walk-in Testing*, the department announces testing just three weeks in advance and invites applicants to walk in to the testing centers. This approach has reduced the testing cycle by three weeks, and eliminated the work and costs of handling and mailing more than 100,000 notices each year.

Classification and Compensation: Giving Managers More Flexibility

Wisconsin's classification and compensation system is designed to maintain pay equity among employees (internal equity), and also make the state competitive to attract and retain employees (external equity). The system does this by classifying and compensating employees based on their job tasks, duties, and responsibilities, plus what these jobs are worth in the outside labor market. Perhaps as important, the classification and compensation system should give agencies and managers the flexibility they need to attract and retain talented employees. Just as the department's hiring reforms were stimulated by customer input, new classification and compensation approaches resulted, in part, from a 1995 the DER survey of more than 600 HR and line managers and supervisors. To flesh out the survey data, the DER also held focus group discussions with 29 senior-level managers. Survey respondents and focus group participants recommended three major areas for classification and compensation improvements:

- Reward performance better
- Classify and reclassify staff faster
- Give managers more flexibility to set classifications and pay.

The DER responded by working with state agencies to develop new approaches. In particular, the Department formed two advisory groups of agency managers. These were the Compensation Advisory Council and the Information Technology Advisory Board. Both customer groups provided critical help in the design, implementation, and marketing of compensation system changes by conducting employee focus groups and feedback mechanisms in shaping final designs. Individual members of both groups also served critical roles as "champions" of change within their own agencies, thus providing "local" credibility to changes that might otherwise have been seen as emanating from the central human resource agency.

Perhaps the single most important change was adopting broad-band pay systems. Broad-banding consolidates multiple, but related, job classifications into single classifications; and multiple pay ranges into fewer, but wider, pay bands. Wisconsin's broad-band systems have two key characteristics:

- Agencies now have far more flexibility to set starting salaries. For senior managers, for example, agencies can offer starting annual salaries anywhere within a $22,000 range without DER approval. With the department's approval, the range increases to $43,000.

- Agencies also have discretion to increase salaries or provide bonuses of up to 12 percent annually. Agencies can also exceed the 12 percent cap with DER approval.

The DER first used the broad-band approach for senior managers, the highest managerial level in the civil service. The existing five senior manager levels were replaced with one broad-band classification. Through broad-banding, the DER created a performance-based compensation system for senior managers, and also made it easier to assign and transfer senior managers. For example, under the previous classification system, managers were aligned within one of the five levels even though their personal skills, knowledge, and abilities almost universally extended over a wider range than their individual classification. These managers had risen in the course of their careers to be more generalist than narrowly focused technician. With few exceptions, managers were qualified to move more freely into new assignments under the new system, and were not restricted by a laborious reclassification process imposed by the old system.

Based on this initial success, the DER then negotiated broad-banding with the Wisconsin Professional Employee Council that represents IT staff. Like most unions, this one was reluctant to agree to a system that would give managers more pay flexibility and discretion. In 1997, however, after extensive negotiating, an agreement on broad-banding was reached that covered 1,200 IT employees in state agencies. Then, in 2000, professional nonunion employees and supervisors also were broad-banded. Eight pay ranges were collapsed into three broad pay bands and several separate job classifications were collapsed or consolidated into broader classifications. This action eliminated more than 700 classifications because the broad-band pay system enables managers to award raises and bonuses rather than advance the employee through the classification system.

In the late 1990s several unionized professional employee groups became interested in the more flexible broad-band system. As a result, the DER was able to negotiate broad-band systems for occupations such as engineers, medical technologists, doctors, dentists, and psychiatrists. Again, job classifications were collapsed. In the spring of 2001, nonprofessional supervisors and confidential support staff were broad-banded. The legislature approved pay plans for these employees that only increased pay where employees needed raises because pay band minimums were increased. As a result, the new system raised payroll costs only slightly.

Results—Better Recruitment and Retention

State agencies are taking advantage of the flexibility built into broad-banding, and this flexibility is paying dividends. Currently, broad-banding covers about 10,500 employees, or 99 percent of all classified nonrepresented employees; plus unionized employees including attorneys, patient treatment and science and fiscal professionals. In 1997, the first year of broad-banding, managers used starting pay flexibility 250 times and awarded 745 bonuses or raises. In fiscal year 2002, managers awarded 1,486 raises or bonuses to broad-banded employees.

Broad-banding has helped state government achieve several goals. First, the number of classifications has been reduced from more than 2,600 to fewer than 1,900. Broad-banding has also helped recruitment and retention by giving managers more flexibility to offer competitive salaries to job candidates and to give raises and bonuses to current employees who excel. For example, broad-banding was designed in part to help reduce IT staff turnover, which in 1997 was 20 percent. In 2002 IT turnover fell to less than 3 percent (compared to the overall turnover rate of 7.5 percent for all classified state employees).

The DER evaluates the broad-banding program each year to assess its value and decide if it should be expanded to other classifications. Agency managers lauded the program and praised the DER for establishing a "meaningful process to assist us in truly managing our salary lines." A 2002 survey of state agency directors showed that 96 percent agreed that broad-banding helps recruit and retain qualified employees.

Creating Change through Labor-Management Cooperation

One of the most important responsibilities of the DER is to bargain collectively with labor unions, and then administer the negotiated labor contracts in good faith. A key aspect of the department's reform agenda has been forging strong and cooperative relationships with public sector labor unions, particularly the state's largest union, the 27,000 member Wisconsin State Employees Union (WSEU), Council 24 of AFSCME and an AFL-CIO affiliate. This cooperative relationship is based on the successful use of an innovative negotiation approach, called "consensus bargaining" that also paved the way for other HR reforms. In 1991, Wisconsin became the first state to successfully use consensus bargaining with a major union, the WSEU.

The Need for a New Approach

In 1966 labor-management relations in Wisconsin state government changed dramatically when the governor signed the State Employment Labor Relations Act (SELRA), which allowed state government employees to bargain collectively. In 1971 SELRA was amended to allow bargaining on wages and benefits. Implementing the new law did not go smoothly. Biennial negotiations were often confrontational, lengthy, and unproductive, dragging on for months with little progress. Reaching agreement always required mediation services and, in July 1977, state employees went on strike for three weeks. The situation again reached crisis in 1989–1990, when bargaining between the state and the WSEU took 14 months. The high direct costs—facilities, bargainers' salaries, and related expenses— were matched by the damaging publicity the protracted negotiations generated. These confrontational negotiations also had a longer-term cost. After bitterly negotiating for months, it was impossible for the state and the union to then shift gears and work together during the two-year term of the contract.

Consensus Bargaining

In 1991, before a new bargaining cycle began, the WSEU executive director and DER secretary decided to try a new approach to avoid another round of bitter negotiations. With the strong support of then-Governor Thompson, both sides agreed to try "consensus bargaining," a method that emphasizes consensus and problem solving over confrontation. Consensus bargaining is also known as "interest-based bargaining," "win-win bargaining," "problem-solving negotiation" and "collaborative bargaining." The consensus approach contrasts sharply with adversarial and confrontational bargaining, which is based on the assumption that labor and management have fundamentally different and conflicting interests. Consensus bargaining is radically different. It is based on the belief that both parties can be winners. The approach is grounded in the proposition that labor and management have complementary, not competing, interests.

A fundamental distinction in consensus bargaining is the difference between a "position" and an "interest." A position is one side's solution to a problem. An interest, on the other hand, is the basic need or concern the solution is designed to address. Because consensus bargaining focuses on interests, and not positions, bargainers work to identify the best approaches to meet both parties' needs, avoiding predetermined, hard-and-fast positions. The consensus process has four basic steps:

1. Bargainers work together to identify all interests, and then focus on the mutual interests, to create a constructive basis for discussions. This contrasts with traditional bargaining, which often starts with each side making firm proposals to advance their specific positions.
2. Once mutual interests are identified, negotiating teams develop options to satisfy each interest.
3. After developing these position options, negotiators agree on objective standards to evaluate each option.
4. The teams then apply these standards and identify the options on which they can reach consensus. As the teams agree to options, union and management representatives jointly draft contract language.

During the actual bargaining, committees work in small groups that include negotiators from both management and the union. These committees discuss specific bargaining issues such as hours of work, transfers, leave, health and safety, grievances and arbitrations, and layoffs. In Wisconsin, this committee approach dramatically changed the role of each side's chief spokesperson. Before consensus bargaining, the WSEU executive director and the DER chief spokesperson would face each other across the table and speak for their organizations. Now, negotiations rely on the input of labor-management teams, and these teams make decisions. Team members sit together around a table, not across from each other as they do in traditional negotiations. To an outsider, it is often impossible to quickly identify who represents management and who represents the union.

The Consensus Process Is Working

Consensus bargaining in Wisconsin began in early 1991, when about 60 WSEU and state negotiators attended a two-day training seminar conducted by Wisconsin Employment Relations Commission mediators. After this training, negotiations began in May 1991. The consensus process was first used successfully in 1991 and, since then, the state and the WSEU have reached agreement on four other biennial contracts using the same approach. The department has also used consensus bargaining to reach agreement with other unions that represent health-care workers, and scientific and other professional employees.

State and union representatives agree that the consensus problem-solving approach has created more cooperative labor-management relations. For example, 83 percent of WSEU members ratified the first consensus-based agreement in 1991. Union members have ratified subsequent agreements with similar majorities. Before consensus bargaining, union rank-and-file often approved agreements by slim majorities even after lengthy negotiations. Consensus bargaining has also saved time. In 1991 the first time the consensus approach was used, the state and the WSEU reached agreement in a then-record four and one-half months. Since then, negotiations have gone even faster, as quickly as in two months.

The consensus process has been particularly useful to shape contract language on issues other than compensation. For example, one contract change now enables employees to use leave instead of being suspended without pay for attendance and/or sick leave problems. The employee continues to work but forfeits an equal amount of leave time, thus avoiding a loss of pay. This creative solution addressed management's concern (interest) about sick leave abuse and substitute worker problems, while also meeting the union's interest in eliminating unpaid suspension as the only way to deal with sick leave abuse. Other creative provisions negotiated through consensus include:

- An alternative grievance process designed to resolve problems at the lowest level. The new process requires more discussion and problem resolution before a grievance is filed
- Allowing workers who transfer to new jobs to return to their former jobs within a few days if the new position is not working out
- A computerized *Lay-off Referral Service* that gave employees at risk of layoff first consideration for vacancies in all agencies and the University of Wisconsin system. More than 200 employees found new jobs in state government during a difficult period when agency reorganizations forced layoffs
- A "catastrophic leave" program that allows employees to donate unused vacation or personal leave to co-workers who have serious problems that could lead to loss of income
- A series of new health and safety initiatives

- Joint labor-management committees formed to review issues such as union access to new computer technology.

In addition, hundreds of grievances have been resolved through informal procedures as a direct result of significantly heightened mutual trust and confidence. These grievances covered issues such as sick leave, leave during inclement weather, discipline, work schedules, and overtime. Each of these grievances would have been grievable under the existing contract, but working from the foundation of mutual trust and confidence both labor and management focused on common interests in the individual grievances instead of disparities. Where once labor might have advocated a grievance at face value, in the new environment labor withdrew grievances recognized to be capricious or without merit. Likewise, management became more open to recognize grievances with merit and sought to resolve them with minimum delay. And, in many cases during the informal process, labor and management creatively worked together to fashion a resolution acceptable to both, which provided resolution at the lowest possible level, thus avoiding costly and protracted contractual processes. Interestingly, no occasion arose wherein a "failure to represent" charge was raised against union leadership, and no situation occurred wherein any manager raised an issue about erosion of management rights. This process averted hundreds of filed grievances from going through a full process to mediation, each of which could have cost up to $10,000. Union and management both recognized the mutual benefits of preventing unnecessary expenditures of time on unjustified grievances or unreasonable defenses against meritorious grievances, as well as diversion of scarce and finite resources to unproductive activities.

While these tangible results are important, consensus bargaining has also created a more positive labor-management relationship. Management and union bargaining team members often remark on the absence of acrimony during negotiations, even when discussing tough issues. WSEU and Department of Employment Relations representatives also now meet regularly, outside of bargaining sessions, to discuss issues and potential problems before they become crises.

Recently, despite difficult economic conditions, an unexpected dividend has been a greater understanding of each side's interests. The result is a notable period of labor peace despite a statewide fiscal crisis. For example, management and unions have worked together, without acrimony, to eliminate more than 1,250 state positions because of budget problems. In the past, this would have been a tough sell for management. As one union leader stated to the authors, "Before consensus bargaining, we would have been staging guerrilla theatre on the Capitol steps to protest these cuts."

Extending the Consensus Approach to the Workplace

The DER and the unions have built on the success of consensus bargaining to expand cooperation to the work site. One example is a joint labor-management project, Working Together, funded by a grant from the U.S. Federal Mediation and Conciliation Service (FMCS). The department and the WSEU jointly applied for and administered this grant. Wisconsin was the only state to receive an FMCS labor-management cooperation grant in 1998. The project, co-chaired by the WSEU director and DER secretary, identified and expanded "best practices" in labor-management cooperation across state government. By identifying these practices, and then expanding them to other work sites, the project was designed to create more meaningful and satisfying work. The ultimate goal, of course, was to provide better and more efficient services to the citizens of Wisconsin.

The project began with six regional labor-management forums across the state. The forums brought more than 750 labor and management representatives together to discuss and identify best practices in cooperation. After the forums, project staff sent out a survey to collect more detailed information on the most promising best practices. The project also funded the Working Together Web site and a statewide training program on how to expand best practices to other sites. The training workshops were conducted in late 1999. Each session was carefully designed to include eight two-person teams, and each team included a labor and management representative from the same work site. The teams formally applied for the workshops after receiving the endorsement of their agency's management.

The workshops were jointly conducted by a faculty of labor and management leaders. By teaching together, these labor and management leaders personally demonstrated the cooperation the workshops were designed to promote. The faculty focused on skills needed to create cooperative relationships such as listening, building consensus, making decisions, resolving conflict, developing goals and objectives, and creating action plans for change. These action plans were critical. Each team developed specific steps to address a critical labor-management issue at the team's work site. These plans included new approaches such as allowing labor representatives to participate in hiring decisions, designing more positive ways to discipline employees, involving employees in more equitable work scheduling for around-the-clock operations, reducing excessive absenteeism and sick leave abuse, creating self-directed work teams, and improving labor-management communication.

The project then sponsored five follow-up sessions where the teams reported on their progress and results. In 2000 a final session was held where all 80 teams came together to report on their results. This session culminated in a "graduation" reception at the governor's mansion where the Lieutenant Governor presented each participant with a personalized certificate recognizing their accomplishments. For many of these people, who perform lower-level jobs in remote locations across the state, this was a once-in-a lifetime experience.

The Working Together program produced both financial and nonfinancial benefits. For example, in 2000, grievances filed by employees at the participating work sites declined by 46 percent, from 990 to 532. This reduction alone saved at least $304,000 in staff time that would have been spent resolving these conflicts. In addition, the number of unresolved discharge cases awaiting arbitration declined by more than 72 percent, saving another $152,000. Both trends continued into 2003.

Although the FMCS grant expired in 2000, Working Together became a permanent program, in part through a grant from AFSCME International. According to Jerry McEntee, the International President: "The Wisconsin experience and the success with the *Working Together* project should be a national model." By early 2003, the program had new supporting partners and several other state unions were interested in a structured labor-management program. The Wisconsin Employment Relations Commission provided additional staff and financial support for the program, and there are nearly 200 teams working across state government (66 in the Department of Corrections and 74 in the Department of Health and Family Services). Both agencies are tailoring the Working Together program to their own specific missions.

The Wisconsin experience in labor-management cooperation shows that fundamental principles can cut across organizations with widely different missions. For example, the Department of Corrections, a "paramilitary" organization that employs prison guards, and probation and parole agents, has used labor-management cooperation successfully. So have several campuses of the University of Wisconsin system, where the climate is anything *but* paramilitary. Similar diversity is seen in the other participating agencies, including the departments of Military Affairs, Veteran's Affairs, Natural Resources, Revenue, Agriculture and Consumer Protection, and Commerce.

Several agencies have found the program so valuable that they have expanded *Working Together* training to entire institutions. For example, rather than beginning with two-person trainee teams from several sites, the Department of Health and Family Services sponsored on-site sessions at centers for the developmentally disabled and at an institution for mentally impaired persons convicted of crimes. Likewise, the Department of Commerce and two university campuses have sponsored on-site training. This evolutionary step, institutionalizing the cooperation program, offers great promise for the future.

Although an almost infinite number of issues can be addressed through labor-management cooperation training, topics that arise frequently are discipline and alternatives to discipline, rumor control, and other communications problems, sick leave abuse, scheduling and overtime, retention and morale, orientation for new employees, employee recognition, supervisory skills, trust and cooperation, and excessive absenteeism.

Working Together has also been recognized outside Wisconsin. For example, the National Association of State Personnel Executives awarded the program its prestigious "Eugene H. Rooney Innovation Award" in 2001 for "outstanding achievement in improving efficiency and effectiveness in state government." With a return-on-investment ratio of 10-to-1, Working Together will continue to grow. The central focus of the program—identifying and replicating best practices— has shifted to identifying and then helping work sites improve labor-management cooperation and productivity. Success so far has revealed several core principles:

- Labor and management can and will cooperate in a supportive environment to resolve work place problems that achieve mutually agreed-upon results.
- Labor and management will forge a strong partnership, starting with top-level leadership, to work together to improve cooperation.
- Joint training, assistance, support, and follow-up will create cooperation, change and improved service to the public.
- Employees want to cooperate and work better together; therefore productivity, performance, and effectiveness will improve as a result of better cooperation.

Working Together was designed to replace the traditional distrust between labor and management with cooperation based on shared mutual interests. As Working Together began, labor and management leaders worked hard to overcome fears on both sides that cooperation really meant "selling out," and overcome the historical perception that the labor-management relationship always involves one side "winning" and one side "losing." Instead, Working Together proved that labor relations could result in "win-win" outcomes. The project and its results have turned the traditional confrontational relationship in Wisconsin into a cooperative partnership. Working Together has clearly demonstrated that labor and management can cooperate to improve productivity, working conditions, and service. Case studies on the best practices developed by the Working Together labor-management teams are profiled on the Working Together Web site (http://workingtogether.state.wi.us).

Prospects for the Future

Reforming the Wisconsin HR system is still very much a work in progress. The challenge is to continue to aggressively make Wisconsin's human resource systems even more efficient and effective, while striking the often-delicate balance with basic principles of merit, fairness, and openness. Just as important, the Department of Employment Relations remains committed to labor-management cooperation. The Wisconsin HR model—centralized policies and decentralized policy implementation—has served the state well. However, one problem has been the limited statewide data on workforce demographics that results from decentralized data gathering. Recognizing this shortcoming, in early 2002 the DER organized a task force to compile the first-ever "State Workforce Fact Book." This resource provides much-needed summary information in an easy-to-access format. This data will help the state legislature deliberate issues such as employee selection, mobility and separation, compensation and benefits, collective bargaining, and equal employment opportunity.

The department will continue to press for HR change using a customer-focused approach, and it will work with stakeholders to design and implement further changes such as:

- Enacting more statutory reforms to create more civil service flexibility. These reforms include giving the DER the authority to waive personnel laws and rules for up to one year to conduct pilot programs.

- Finalizing a statewide workforce strategic plan that integrates the goals and roles of the DER, agencies, and university campuses. This plan will be the basis for recruiting, developing, and retaining state employees, as well as anticipating emerging workplace needs and changes.
- Expanding online job application to all vacancies.
- Increasing recruiting to include using the Internet more aggressively, expanding student employment programs, and creating a regional and even national recruiting presence.

- Extending broad-banded compensation to more occupations.
- Replicating labor-management cooperation "best practices" in other work sites across the state.

The DER will also continue to collect empirical data to continually evaluate and adjust programs and results. Department programs to survey hiring managers on (1) the quality of the people they interview and hire, and (2) the impacts of broad-banding are just two examples of the DER's continuing efforts to collect evaluation data. Attracting and retaining the "best and brightest" is the public sector's most critical challenge. The ability of public service to help solve the critical issues facing our nation, our states and our communities depends on attracting, motivating, and retaining talented and committed public servants. If we do this effectively, we can successfully address the toughest issues.

As the *National Commission on the State and Local Public Service* report concludes, "there are no silver bullets" to improve government. However, Wisconsin has taken positive action to show that public sector organizations can develop creative ways to provide more efficient, effective, and responsive service. As one state agency manager wrote, the Department of Employment Relations's success anticipating and responding to change has resulted in, "better people, better programs, and better state government."

References

Barrett, K., and Greene, R. (2001). "Grading the States: A Report Card on Government Performance." *Governing*, February, 2001, 20–108.

Commission on the Reform of State Human Resource System (1996). *Final*

Report. Madison, WI: Commission on the Reform of State Human Resource System.

Gore, A. (1993). *Creating a Government that Works Better and Costs Less: Report of the National Performance Review.* Washington DC: U.S. Government Printing Office.

Heneman, H., Huett, D., Lavigna, R., and Ogsten, D. (1995). "Assessing Managers' Satisfaction with Staffing Services." *Personnel Psychology,* 48, 163–172.

International Personnel Management Association (1998). *Best Practices Report.* Alexandria, VA: International Personnel Management Association.

The National Commission on the State and Local Public Service (1993). *Hard Truths/Tough Choices: An Agenda for State and Local Reform.* Albany, NY: Nelson A. Rockefeller Institute of Government.

State of Wisconsin (2002). *State Employment Relations.* Statute 230.16 (4). Retrieved June 27, 2003, from Wisconsin Statutes database.

CHAPTER 13

Civil Service Reform in New York State: A Quiet Revolution

Norma M. Riccucci

Writing more than ten years ago on civil service reform in New York State, Ban and Riccucci (1994, 28) made this observation: "Human resources management in New York state takes place within an exceptionally complex environment, both structurally and politically. That environment has made the enactment of major [civil service] reform legislation impossible." For the most part, nothing has changed in the state that would make it easier to reform the civil service system through legislative mechanisms. This is not to say, however, that there have not been some changes and improvements to human resources and public personnel practices in New York. To the extent that there have been, they have been incremental and administrative, developed and implemented by the chief personnel agency in New York State, the Department of Civil Service.

This chapter begins with a brief overview of the structure of the civil service system as well as previous efforts to legislatively reform civil service in state of New York. It then looks at the most recent administrative reforms that have transformed the practice and operation of public personnel and human resources management in the state.

Background

New York State is one of largest public employers in the country with more than 170,000 workers in the executive branch alone. The state's workforce is governed or overseen by five, often conflicting or competing organizations (see Rosenbloom and Riccucci 1986): The Civil Service Commission (CSC), the Department of Civil Service (DCS), the Public Employment Relations Board (PERB), the

303

Governor's Office of Employee Relations (GOER), and the Division of the Budget (DOB).

Similar to the federal system prior to the 1978 reform, the responsibility over traditional civil service functions in New York State is split between two, overlapping agencies: the CSC and the DCS. The CSC is the quasi-legislative and quasi-judicial body that oversees the civil service or merit system. It promulgates rules and regulations, sits in judgment of those rules and regulations, and investigates matters concerning the enforcement of its rules and regulations as well as the state's civil service law. The CSC is a bipartisan, three-member body appointed by the governor on the advice and consent of the state Senate. The president of the commission is also the commissioner of the DCS.

The DCS administers the rules and regulations issued by the CSC as well as the state's civil service law. It is responsible for such functions as recruitment, testing, transfers, promotions, and determining titles, salaries, and qualifications for state jobs. It is headed by a commissioner who is appointed by the governor on the advice and consent of the state Senate. As noted, the commissioner is also the president of the CSC.

To further complicate matters, while the Classification and Compensation Division is housed within the DCS, the director of this division has statutory independence from the commissioner of the DCS.[1] While the director of class and comp is not answerable to the commissioner, the director's decisions, however, can be overturned by the Civil Service Commission.

In 1967, with passage of the Taylor Law (formally, the Public Employees' Fair Employment Act), which granted public employees in New York the right to organize and collectively bargain their terms and conditions of employment, another agency was created: the Public Employment Relations Board (PERB). This bipartisan body, comprised of three members appointed by the governor on advice and consent of the state senate, acts as a neutral agency to administer the Taylor Law, which is actually incorporated in the state's civil service law.[2] In fact, PERB is statutorily within the DCS, but it is intended to act independently of both the DCS and the CSC. PERB, just like the CSC, has quasi-legislative and quasi-judicial authority: it can issue rules as well as adjudicate disputes arising around those rules. PERB also adjudicates disputes arising around other matters, including representation rights[3] and unfair labor practices, known as improper practices in New York State.

Then, in 1969, the GOER was established as part of New York State Executive Law[4] to "promote harmonious and cooperative relationships between the State's Executive Branch and its employees, and to protect the public by assuring the orderly and uninterrupted operation of State government." It serves as the governor's representative in executive branch collective negotiations, bargaining with fourteen different negotiating units represented by nine public employee unions across the state. In recent years, GOER has also taken on a greater role around work force initiatives. For example, an expanded agency mission seeks to "support agencies in the development, coordination, and implementation of a comprehensive human resource management program, with a particular focus on the implementation of Quality Management concepts for improved performance and service to the general public."[5] In expanding its purview over the state workforce, GOER often comes into direct conflict with the roles and purported functions of the DCS.

The public employee unions operating in the state also have some control over personnel matters in that they negotiate wages and various terms and conditions of public employment. They also have considerable influence in shaping public policy around civil service issues.

Finally, the DOB, although not a civil service agency, has control over the state's workforce in that it sets personnel ceilings and has final approval[6] over job reclassifications and the classification of new positions.

In short, the structure governing civil service in New York State is very fragmented and overlapping. This is statutorily driven. For managers and human resources specialists, it engenders a good deal of frustration and tension.[7] It was this complexity that served as the major impetus for one of the major legislative reform efforts to civil service in New York State.

Early Reform Efforts

There have been several attempts to enact legislation to reform civil service in New York. However, failing to garner enough political support, no reform efforts have ever succeeded. One of the most aggressive reform efforts occurred in the mid-1980s, when the commissioner of the Department of Civil Service at the time proposed a plan to consolidate and integrate the fragmented structural environment of civil service as described earlier. Commissioner Karen Burstein proposed the merger of the GOER with the DCS into a Department or Division of Human Resources (DHR), and the creation of a separate, independent adjudicatory body, the Merit

Protection Commission (MPC), modeled after the Merit Systems Protection Board at the federal level.[8] The new DHR would be responsible for all personnel and human resources matters, including labor relations, classification, and compensation, and the MPC would protect state employees from merit abuses. In addition, Commissioner Burstein proposed reconstituting the state's Civil Service Commission (CSC) into an independent agency, whereby it would be de-linked from the new DHR, and the president of the CSC would no longer serve as the head or commissioner of the DHR.

A formal proposal was brought to the state legislature in 1990, but faced opposition, particularly in the senate, and so, it failed to pass. While this structural rearrangement has been the only major legislative civil service reform effort in recent years, administrative reforms have been much more successful in changing the civil service system in New York.

Incremental Change through Administrative Reform

In 1995 the governor of New York State, George Pataki, issued a mandate calling for changes to civil service to make it more flexible to the state's needs while ensuring responsiveness to state workers' needs. Governor Pataki established a task force to accomplish these goals. The Governor's Task Force on the New York State Civil Service System was headed by George Sinnott, President of the New York Civil Service Commission (CSC), and Commissioner of the Department of Civil Service (DCS), and comprised by members from the Governor's Office of Employee Relations (GOER), the Division of Budget and State Operations. While the task force was comprised solely of Governor Pataki's appointees (i.e., management), Commissioner Sinnott did obtain input from, among others,[9] public employee unions.

George Sinnott was appointed to head the DSC and CSC in January of 1995. Having served for many years as the director of personnel for the town of Hempstead and for Nassau County, New York, he was not considered an "outsider," but rather, a hands-on, career public personnelist, someone well-versed in personnel and human resources matters in government. In fact, through the task force, his main strategy for accomplishing civil service reform, was to rely on the existing constitutional and statutory authority of the DCS to improve the civil service system. In other words, reforming the system would be accomplished administratively, within the DCS. This proved to be an important strategy, given the difficulty of getting reforms passed through the state legislature, and given the complicated governing structure of the civil service discussed above. In this sense, Sinnott sought to "fix" the system, not "blow it up,"[10] completely reforming it, as Georgia did in 1996. In helping to reform civil service in the state, Commissioner Sinnott worked not only with various state agencies, but also with the major public employee unions in New York State.

The primary accomplishments of the task force and ultimately the DCS, under the leadership of Commissioner George Sinnott in reforming civil service in New York State are described below.

Transfer Legislation

The task force drafted legislation that would enable the state to act as a single employer, allowing the DCS to transfer employees between and among agencies. The new transfer process was intended to make it easier to reassign employees rather than lay them off. With the support of the public employee unions, most prominently the Civil Service Employees Association (CSEA) and the Public Employees Federation (PEF), transfer legislation was passed on March 29, 1996, and added as Section 78, "Transfer to Avert Layoff," to the Civil Service Law.[11]

Reducing and Consolidating State Titles

New York State has been notorious for having one of the highest number of job titles (Ban and Riccucci 1993). And, a high number of job titles creates higher personnel costs because it necessitates holding more civil service tests. The DSC, via administrative fiat, thus, regrouped multiple, specialized titles into fewer, more broadly defined titles. Here is an illustration of how titles were consolidated:

Titles in 1995	Title Today
Laboratory Caretaker	Building Services Assistant I
Elevator Operator	
Grounds Worker	
Janitor & Elevator Starter	
Window Washer	
Supply Assistant	
Cleaner	
Parking Services Attendant	
Laborer	
Maintenance Helper	
Groundskeeper	
Executive Mansion Aide I	

The result was a significant reduction in job titles. In December 1995 there were 6,220 job titles in New York State. Within five years, more than 2,000 job titles had been reduced through title consolidation.

Reduction in job titles was not wholly supported by the public employee unions. For one thing, there was a concern with the potential impact of title consolidation on retirements; would consolidation force some employees into early retirement? The unions point to evidence that some employees who would not otherwise have retired, were left no other option but to retire. Another concern expressed by public employee unions was that title consolidation would be relied upon for attrition, and reductions in total employment, even if gradual, result in reductions in union membership.[12]

Testing Provisionals

A provisional is an employee who has been appointed to a competitive position while awaiting a competitive examination. By statute, the provisional appointment is limited to nine months, although the state has typically found ways to extend these appointments when desired. Based on the task force recommendations, Commissioner Sinnott tested virtually all provisional employees, reducing, by 79 percent, the number of provisionals. By 1998 only 0.7 percent of the 140,672 competitive class state workers were in provisional status—the lowest rate in the recorded history of civil service. In addition, the testing process was made more cost-effective and efficient by standardizing and streamlining examination methodologies while still retaining the integrity of the testing process. In effect, the DSC was able to examine a large number of candidates quickly and at reasonable cost.

The public employee unions in New York State were very supportive of testing provisional employees, because once tested, these competitive class employees were now eligible for union membership status[13] and the accompanying protections.

Promotion Testing

By January of 1996, New York State had a backlog of more than 600 titles for which no promotion tests had been scheduled. State managers were unable to plan for agency program needs and state employees were unable to optimize their chances for promotion. As a result of administrative reform, the DCS, relying entirely on internal resources, developed and administered promotion test batteries to more than 30,000 candidates. It did so by moving away from developing individual promotion tests on a title-by-title basis. Instead, the DSC relies on a two-part promotion test battery, enabling it to test many thousands of candidates at once, and providing qualified state employees more frequent opportunities to take promotion exams. In effect, the DCS is able to be more responsive to state agency needs by providing more timely eligible lists. In addition, public employees have more expedient opportunities to be promoted to higher-level civil service jobs.

Timely Scoring of Examinations

In 1994 the time required to report written test results for state examinations reached an average high of more than 150 days. The Department of Civil Service, through improved efficiency, has cut the average time to report test results to less than 60 days.

Technological Improvements

A civil service Web site now posts exam announcements on the Internet. In addition, "Employee Test Profiles" enable candidates to check their performance in each subject area of the test on the Internet. Exam applicants can also register on the telephone and they will soon have the option of paying exam fees via credit card. Overall, general information about the civil service system and jobs with the New York State government is readily available to the general public on the Department's Web site.

Reinstituting a New York State Management Internship Program

In order to ensure a continuous flow of exceptional management talent into New York State service, the DCS coordinates efforts with the Rockefeller Institute of Government, a nonprofit research institute affiliated with the State University of New York, to maximize the effectiveness and minimize the cost of a management internship program, the Public Management Internship (PMI) Program.

First developed in 1947, the PMI seeks to attract recent graduates with a master's degree in public administration or a related field with exceptional skills and abilities into management training positions in New York State government. During the two-year professional internship, PMIs participate in special projects, training and rotational assignments in state agencies. The Rockefeller Institute most recently provided the training component for the first year of the program.

When Governor Pataki took office in 1994, one of the programs he cut was the PMI. The task force reinstated the program, but in 2002, it was once again cut, due to, according to a Division of Budget spokesperson, budget shortfalls as a result of the terrorist attack on the World Trade Center on September 11, 2001. As of this writing, the future of the PMI is uncertain.

In short, a number of positive changes have been brought to New York State's civil service via concerted administrative reform. The one area that the DCS has not been successful in changing has been expanding the rule of three, a requirement to hire or promote from the top three people (or top three scores) on a civil service list. To provide managers and agency leaders with greater flexibility and discretion in hiring and promotion, the DCS sought to expand the rule of three to a rule of ten. This, however, requires legislative action, and with the public employee unions strongly opposed to such a change, proposals to expand the rule of three have failed to garner legislative support. New York State is one of three states across the country that continues to rely on the rule of three. In effect, the DCS continues to "band score" state exams, as appropriate and in accordance with common law.[14]

Band scoring allows for consideration of the fact that no test can measure a candidate's true score with perfect confidence and no test can assess all the abilities relevant to a given job. Raw scores in designated ranges are assigned the same final score. For example, all scores from 90 to 95 are given a band score of 95 and are considered to be equivalent. This considerably expands the field of candidates who can be considered for appointment to state jobs while maintaining the tenets of merit and fitness. By continuing to rely on band scoring, the DCS need not propose legislation to expand the rule of three.

Employee unions in New York continue to oppose any type of band scoring because of the hiring discretion it places in the hands of public managers. The main contention by CSEA and PEF is that merit is sacrificed by the reliance on band scoring.[15]

The Performance of Civil Service in New York State

New York State's 2001 Report Card score for Human Resources, as rated by "The Government Performance Project" of *Governing* magazine was C+, up from a C in 1999. This is not necessarily inauspicious, given that the mean human resources' grade for all states is B– with scores ranging from a high of A (South Carolina) to a low of D+ (Nevada and Alabama). In fact, Jonathan Walters (1998), in a feature story for *Governing* magazine, wrote that while "New York's state personnel system has long been considered the country's most dysfunctional. . . some pretty amazing things are happening in the Empire State these days." He went on to say that, "for decades, the king of the calcified and recalcitrant beasts has been the New York state civil service system, a monster off of whose chest comprehensive reports on reform bounced like Wiffle balls—27 of them in all since the 1970s."

But, as Walters concludes, under Sinnott's leadership and a new attitude about reform, fundamental changes have been brought to civil service in New York. Moreover, the changes have captured the attention of many national audiences, in that the New York State Department of Civil Service has received numerous national awards for its improved performance. For example, in March 2001, *Workforce* magazine presented the Department with the 2001 Workforce Optimas Award, which celebrates the best in human resource management. In 1999 the Department received the EXSL Award from the National Center for Public Productivity at Rutgers University and the Eugene H. Rooney Jr. Award for the most innovative state program from the National Association of State Personnel Executives. In 1998 the Department of Civil Service received the coveted Public Service Excellence Award from the Public Employees Roundtable and the National Governors' Association.

And, the strong leadership of Commissioner Sinnott for his role in helping to guide the reforms has also been recognized. For example, in June 2000, Commissioner Sinnott became the first public sector recipient of the Award for Professional Excellence from the Society for Human Resource Management (SHRM). In 1999 Sinnott received the National Public Service Award from the American Society for Public Administration (ASPA). In 1998 *Governing* magazine selected the commissioner as one of its Public Officials of the Year, and the International Personnel Management Association (IPMA) presented him with the Warner W. Stockberger Achievement Award, which is the Association's highest personal honor.[16]

Conclusion

New York State's civil service system continues to be administered by a very fragmented structure. Efforts to reform the structure have largely been unsuccessful because of a lack of legislative support for change. However, through administrative reform, under a strong centralized civil service department and under the leadership of an effective and popular leader, Commissioner Sinnott, some changes have been made to the New York State civil service system. While some may argue that many of the reforms seem rudimentary, they have pulled New York State's civil service up to par with other state's civil service systems. As any public personnelist will concur, civil service systems will always produce complaints and rumblings, particularly by the state agencies they are required to serve. Public managers and administrators will continue to feel hamstrung and circumscribed by civil service rules and regulations. But, it is unlikely that this will change any time soon in New York State, because one of the primary purposes served by civil service systems—abating patronage—will continue to draw the support of the strong public employee unions in New York, which balk at any effort to dismantle civil service in the state.

Notes

1. See Sections 117 and 118 of the New York State Civil Service Law. For a description of the mission of Division of Classification and Compensation, and the powers delegated to the Director, see http://www.cs.state.ny.us/cc/index.html

2. The Taylor Law is Article 14 of the New York State Civil Service Law. The law became effective on September 1, 1967.

3. Representation rights refer to the legal right of a category of employees to organize and seek representation under the Taylor Law. A recent decision involved, for example, a determination as to whether employees in a particular agency were part of the rank-and-file bargaining unit or the unit designated for supervisory personnel.

4. GOER was created by Article 24 of the NYS Executive Law.

5. See http://www.goer.state.ny.us/

6. Technically, the legislature has final approval.

7. For workers, however, it creates various avenues for job protection.

8. "Report to Governor Mario M. Cuomo on Civil Service Revitalization." Karen S. Burstein, President, New York State Civil Service Commission, January, 1986.

9. Input was obtained from, for example, the New York State Personnel Council and the State Academy for Public Administration.

10. A former Commissioner of the New York State Department of Civil Service, Dr. Walter Broadnax, when once asked how to effectively reform civil service responded, "blow it up."

11. See http://www.cs.state.ny.us/pio/introsummcsl.htm

12. Based on interviews with officials from the two major public employee unions in New York State, the Civil Service Employees Association (CSEA) and the Public Employees Federation (PEF).

13. New York is an agency fee state. Once in a bargaining unit, employees pay dues to the union, even if they opt not to join the union.

14. Legal challenges to band or zone scoring have resulted in court rulings that permit New York state to band scores, providing they do not use overly broad-bands. See Ban and Riccucci (1994), *McGowan v. Burstein, et. al.,* (1987), and *Chiles v. Burstein* (1988).

15. See *McGowan* and *Chiles, supra* note 13.

16. See http://www.cs.state.ny.us/pio/sinnott.htm

References

Ban, Carolyn, and Norma M. Riccucci (1994). "Civil Service Reform in a Complex Political Environment: New York State." 14 *Review of Public Personnel Administration*, 2: 28–39.

Ban, Carolyn, and Norma M. Riccucci (1993). "Personnel Systems and Labor Relations: Steps Toward a Quiet Revitalization." In, Frank J. Thompson, ed., *Revitalizing State and Local Public Service.* San Francisco: Jossey-Bass, 71–103.

Chiles v. Burstein, 527 NYS 2d 634 (1988).

McGowan v. Burstein, et. al., 518 NYS 2d 247 (1987).

Rosenbloom, David H., and Norma M. Riccucci (1986). "A Theoretical Approach to Public Personnel Reform." In, Donald J. Calista (ed.), *Bureaucratic and Governmental Reform.* Greenwich, CT: JAI Press, 73–87.

Walters, Jonathan (1998). "Untangling Albany," December 1998, *Governing* magazine, online, http://governing.com/archive/1998/dec/civil.txt.

CHAPTER 14

The States and Civil Service Reform: Lessons Learned and Future Prospects

Lloyd G. Nigro
J. Edward Kellough

What lessons might be drawn from the state civil service reform initiatives, major and minor, described here? What is the future likely to hold for these reforms as well as those now underway or being contemplated by policy makers in other states? In this brief concluding chapter, we will offer some observations and speculations about directions state civil service reforms might take. The first of these is likely to be entirely unsurprising to those who have read the previous chapters of this book. It is, however, fundamental to understanding civil service reform in the states, so it is at the top of our list.

A Variety of Approaches

Like their civil service systems, reforms vary greatly from state to state, and so do the reasons for undertaking them (Kellough and Selden 2003, 171–172). This diversity applies to the degree to which significant systemwide reform is contemplated by state governments and is actually taking place. In California and Arizona, such reform has been minimal, but for different reasons. In Georgia and Florida, major but significantly different reforms have taken place in contrasting political settings. Variety also characterizes the dimensions or aspects of personnel or human resources administration that are affected. In some states, like Wisconsin, the focus has been mostly on reforming (reengineering or reinventing) traditional technologies such as recruitment processes, classification systems, and training and development. In some, including Florida, the reform agenda has concentrated largely on macro-issues such as "at-will employment" and "privatization" of human resources

315

functions. Georgia offers an example of major, some say radical, reform on virtually all levels of system design and operation. There are, as a result, many species of civil service reform to be found in the states, and they continue to evolve. As noted in the introduction to this book, some reforms have focused on the modernization of civil service structures and procedures while others are based on an agenda that seeks to fundamentally change or alter the public service through the use of privatization, at-will employment, or other market-based concepts.

The drivers of reform and the contexts within which it takes place also vary widely across the states, but there are at least three categories of reasons for civil service reform initiatives in the states identified here, and in many cases, the relationships among them are for all practical purposes seamless. The first of these is *ideology*, or a belief on the part of policy makers and their associates that a particular way of handling the human resources needs and functions of state government is inherently superior and will lead to better outcomes of all sorts. Often, the explanation for performance problems boils down to this: the values, structures, and processes of the civil service system are contrary to the values and concepts imbedded in a particular ideology or belief system. This diagnosis is then paired with a set of reform prescriptions that do conform. Once these are implemented, or imposed, the performance problems in question are "solved." For many, as examples, at-will employment and privatization are to be preferred over classified civil services and direct service provision because they conform to "free market" norms and will supposedly generate lower costs and more efficient resource allocations. On the front end, reforms driven largely by ideology are seldom if ever based on empirical evidence and, on the back end, they are very unlikely to be accompanied by objective evaluation of outcomes over time.

A second category of reasons for reform is *political* or more concretely, the civil service reforms are intended to build and realign the relative power of the actors and stakeholders that depend on the state bureaucracy for a wide variety of resources. Here, civil service reforms are vehicles to establish and defend political actors' capacities to influence the "authoritative allocation of values." These capacities, of course, include the ability to carry out the agendas of elected executives, legislators, and other policy makers. Governors, like Zell Miller of Georgia and Jeb Bush of Florida, aggressively pushed reforms designed to remove merit system barriers to direct and tighten policy control over state agencies and their employees. These types of initiatives are often "sold" in terms of a need to enhance executive leadership and accountability for results and, inevitably, to allow the removal of the legions of "unresponsive, incompetent, insulated, bureaucrats" who the public is easily convinced lurk in the shadows of state agencies. The reforms serve, in other words, as potent political symbols designed to convince the public that elected officials are responsive to public opinion and are taking steps to make government more efficient and effective.

In Florida, unlike Georgia where organized labor exerted very little influence, the nature and extent of reform became the centerpiece of a fierce struggle between the governor and his allies and employee unions and their supporters. Recently, the federal government offered a classic example of how personnel systems may become arenas for political conflict involving major wins and losses for the protagonists. The Bush Administration insisted that employees of the new Department of Homeland Security serve with limited civil service protections and no collective bargaining rights. The administration's ultimate victory over organized labor and its allies in the congress on this issue illustrated clearly how, in civil service reform, politics matters. Schultz (2002) noted, "the constant change in personnel systems in the United States and elsewhere is an indication that they have adapted significantly to changing political environments" (637).

The third set of reasons for civil service reform is *technical*. It encompasses a wide range of efforts to design and implement human resource system changes that public managers, personnel specialists, and state executives believe are needed to improve performance on one or more levels of state bureaucracy. These changes center on making operational changes to human resources management methods, procedures, and techniques that are intended to increase the efficiency and technical performance of state agencies. Modernizing performance evaluation systems, streamlining and decentralizing recruitment and selection processes, and broad-banding classification structures are representative of these types of reforms. These interventions, while they may serve as vehicles for the ideological and political agendas of other interests, are the "bread and butter" of human resource professionals and specialists. Typically, once reform "packages" pass legislative and executive muster, they fade into the background and become uninteresting to elected officials and powerful organized interests. It is, of course, commonplace for civil service reforms on all levels of government in the United States to be sold to policy makers, organized interests, and the public at large as steps needed to improve bureaucratic efficiency while rooting out incompetents and low-performers. Performance management systems, particularly merit pay plans, are good examples. Legislative and executive support, budgetary and otherwise, for technical-efficiency enhancements typically declines rapidly once the underlying ideological and political goals are achieved and policy makers' attention turns elsewhere.

Civil service reform in the states has been and will continue to be a context-bound process driven by different and often dynamic combinations of ideological, political, and technical motives. Any effort to generalize about what has happened or might happen in the states must take this diversity into account (Hays and Kearney 2001). With this caution in mind, we believe the following observations about the prospects for the future may be useful.

Does Radical Reform Have a Future?

Strong support for programs of comprehensive radical reform, such as that undertaken by Georgia and to a significant extent by Florida, has not materialized in the vast majority of states. In part, no tidal wave of radical reform has washed across the states because such reforms have not (or at least cannot show they have) delivered what they promised, and they promised a great deal. Georgia's comprehensive approach was sold as *the way* to get performance and accountability (Walters 1997). Credible program evaluation was not a serious consideration in Georgia and elsewhere, so it is not surprising that there is little or no hard evidence about the results achieved by those reforms available to those contemplating reform, comprehensive or otherwise, in their states.

Suffice it to say that sweeping reforms consistently have failed to keep the promises their advocates made in the process of selling them to legislators, elected executives, organized interests, public managers, and the public at large. In the process, opportunities for real and sustainable incremental improvements may have been neglected or, if implemented, have gotten little or no administrative or political support. Downs and Larkey (1986) observed almost twenty years ago that lofty promises and subsequent disappointments had generated widespread cynicism about the motives of those advocating reform and deep pessimism about the results of all efforts to reform government, including public personnel systems. The current round of civil service reforms in the states may be approaching, if it has not already reached, the "cynicism and pessimism" stage they describe. This is not, however, to assert that more limited civil service reforms of many kinds are not needed and the evidence presented here and elsewhere suggests that there is a fair amount of reform activity ongoing in the states that is being undertaken for largely technical reasons:

> Major findings . . . indicate that penetrating changes are occurring in state civil service systems. In particular, the notion of a state civil service system with a uniform system of employment, recruitment, classification, and compensation is giving way to a more flexible and varied structure. . . . The analysis [of survey findings] reveals considerable activity is taking place in several of the personnel areas examined. We found a number of states are expending energy revamping their classifications system by streamlining the process, reducing the number of titles, or adopting broad banding systems. Similarly, several states are adopting performance management systems that link agency and individual goals and subsequently reward high performance. (Selden et al. 2001, 606)

Another reason for skepticism about the prospects of comprehensive reforms is their tendency to punish state employees. In addition to the demoralizing "bureaucrat bashing" rhetoric of the ideologically and politically driven reformers, the prospect of being "de-privileged" or deprived of their traditional merit system protections, downsized, or privatized, has mobilized resistance by public employees and their allies. Suspicion and resistance is not limited to those who work for state agencies. Growing awareness among policy makers, public employees and their organizations, and human resource professionals that many of the reforms implemented during the last quarter of the 20th century have not delivered the benefits they promised may very well dampen enthusiasm for civil service reform initiatives by the states that contemplate sudden, wholesale, changes in existing arrangements. Incremental reforms to human resource structures and processes building up from the agency level and that do not jettison traditional values of human resource management may be the more typical model (and the prescription for something approaching success) during the early decades of the 21st century. Hays and Kearney observed:

> Survey results lend support to the entreaties of . . . reformers who call out for a leaner, more responsive government with

particular reference to human resource management . . . . Yet respondents indicate. . . an abiding and even growing attachment to the core values that have guided the field for more than 100 years. As the next decade unfolds, HRM is expected to hold particularly strongly to its traditional values of equity, professionalism, executive leadership, merit, and political responsiveness, while the newer value of efficiency gains further momentum. (Hays and Kearney 2002, 594)

An important adjustment to be hoped for, if not anticipated, is a far more critical scrutiny of the seemingly sacrosanct proposition that comprehensive deregulation, privatization, and depriveleging are necessary means to efficiency and responsiveness in state governments. A much broader willingness among policy makers to sponsor objective evaluations of reforms along these as well as other lines should be very helpful (Selden et al. 2001; Thompson 2002). Altogether more likely, unfortunately, is a period during which states like Georgia and Florida merely work hard to make their reforms "work" no matter what the data say.

What Is the Future of the Employment Relationship in the Reform Scenario?

This question is likely to become pivotal in the reform debate. Civil service reform on the state as well as the federal level has sought major alterations in the formal relationships between public agencies and their employees. Somewhat paradoxically, many of the elements of civil service reform seek to establish governmental personnel practices that mirror those of profit-driven firms. Productivity, management control, and administrative discretion are core values of today's reforms, and they combine to underscore the advantages of human resources strategies that concentrate on investments in *workers having essential and scarce* qualifications. On the one hand, those workers providing organizationally critical knowledge, skills, and abilities (KSAs) are to be aggressively recruited, competitively paid, and developed as "assets" or "human capital." On the other, workers who offer easily found lower-level skills and other attributes are defined as disposable, easy to replace, and best treated as "costs" to be minimized through low wages, minimal or no benefits, and contracting out tactics. The result is a tendency for civil service reforms to encourage state employers to seek the "bottom of the barrel" in terms of how they treat all but essential employees as an element of their strategies to raise productivity, control costs, and to be more "businesslike."

Contracting out and extensive use of temporary workers are typically associated with reform, and they have had serious negative effects on the standard of living enjoyed by those who provide public services. While this impact has been felt largely on the local level where growing numbers of cities and counties are enacting laws requiring contractors to pay "living wages," there is no logical or empirical reason to assume that the states and their workers will be immune from reform's drive to cut labor costs. In addition to cutting state workforces, reform encourages minimization of employee benefits of all kinds. Historically, the benefits provided to state employees have been costly, particularly health insurance and pension plans. These are now prime targets of cost-cutters. To the degree that civil service reform in the states promotes privatization, the resulting contracting out to for-profit and nonprofit agencies allows state governments to avoid providing what have been traditionally generous (or least adequate) benefits to large numbers of workers (Lawther 1999; Ravitch and Lawther 1999). As state employers seek to fully exploit the advantages of lower labor costs and greater flexibility through contracting, the policy issues they confront regarding the future of the employment relationship will become increasingly complex and politically explosive.

The outlines of what are likely to become hotly debated policy questions are already fairly clear. Should state governments and their administrative agencies follow private sector practice and concentrate on funding competitive pay, generous benefits, and good working conditions for limited numbers of "core" high-skill workers who are deemed essential? Should they greatly downsize their permanent, full-time, workforces in favor of much larger numbers of temporary, part-time, and contract employees (so-called contingent workers)? Do they have any obligation to maintain a higher standard, to be model employers, in their treatment of workers with regard to equal employment opportunity, pay equity, employee due process protections, accommodation for the disabled, and benefits? As fundamental policy choices are made about how to provide and arrange services, how important should these values be to state policy makers as they weigh them against enhancements in efficiency, cost-effectiveness, and management control and flexibility? Lois Recascino Wise, in her analysis of three drivers of reform (social equity, democratization, and humanization of the public service) competing with efficiency and market-based reforms, observed:

> Remedies rooted in economic and market-based approaches
> may address needs rooted in normative motives. Interpreting
> the meaning of a particular reform remedy is a matter of judg-
> ing the glass half-full. For example, efforts to make working
> conditions in government and the private sector more similar
> can be interpreted as equity-based reform or as efficiency-
> based reform. Similarly, measures to promote human resource
> development may be rooted in humanistic values or may be
> grounded in efficiency. Interpretation. . . may be clouded by dif-
> ferences between rhetoric and symbolic reform and actual
> implementation. (Wise 2002, 564)

In the future, state civil service reformers will be asked to address
these complicated and socially critical issues far more seriously than
they have in the past.

Workforce Planning and Human Resource Development Challenges

In terms of the numbers of employees, the states may get
smaller, but the tasks they are asked to carry out will not get easier
in a political or technical sense. State governments, even those that
have invested heavily in contracting out, will require the capacity
needed to handle severe challenges across a broad front of public
services. A steadily growing number of state jobs will demand highly
trained and experienced professionals. These needs must be anticipated and strategies implemented to meet them. Effective workforce
planning and human resource development programs are needed,
but for the most part, they have been neglected or grossly under-
resourced by traditional civil service systems and, in practice, by
reformed systems.

Selden et al. (2001) reported "the majority of states do little to no
formal workforce planning." They concluded that the diffusion of
workforce planning in state agencies lagged well behind that of
strategic planning (602). It is clear that state government professionals and highly skilled workers must be recruited, hired, and provided the support and resources needed to continuously upgrade
their skills. Workforce planning and human resource development
have been notoriously missing pieces of traditional civil service systems and, so far, of state reform efforts. Dramatically improving

capabilities and commitments in these areas will have to be a major component of efforts to extend, refine, and consolidate civil service reform in the states. Otherwise, key assumptions about capacity underpinning major elements of reform such as deregulation, decentralization, privatization, and accountability for results will not be satisfied (Brown and Potoski 2003). Even the most promising features of reform might very well founder under these conditions. In the states, serious consideration of the challenges faced in acquiring, developing, and maintaining human capital should emerge as a high-priority piece of the reform puzzle (Ingraham et al. 2000). Although their comments are directed at the federal government, in their report on the Wye River Conference, Ingraham et al. could just as easily been addressing the states:

> Viewing federal employees as a human capital investment shifts how government perceives its workers—as assets rather than just necessary costs to be controlled. The costs, of course, remain, but the investment must be clear. To maximize this investment, agencies need a full range of tools and resources to actively acquire and develop—through recruitment, training, and reward strategies—excellent talent and leadership. . . . Human capital is an investment in talent, in capacity, and in problem-solving skills. (Ingraham, Selden, and Moynihan 2000, 59)

In combination, the managerial orientation of civil service reform initiatives, an increased willingness to consider giving human resource specialists a more central role in the strategic planning processes of state agencies, and the severe challenges posed by highly competitive labor markets may move human resource planning and development higher on state agendas. Overcoming the long-standing tendency to lose interest in these "technical" requirements of successful reform will also be necessary, and this will require coupling investments in planning and development to the political and ideological engines of civil service reform. This will not be easy.

The efforts of policy makers in the 50 states to reform their civil service systems in ways that allow them to respond successfully to the challenges they confront should be carefully studied. A far better understanding of how reform is conceived, is sold politically and administratively, is implemented and managed, and is evaluated is needed. We believe that this volume is a valuable step in this direction.

References

Brown, Trevor L., and Matthew Potoski (2003). "Contract-Management Capacity In Municipal and County Governments," *Public Administration Review*, Vol. 63, No. 2 (March–April): 153–163.

Downs, George W., and Patrick D. Larkey (1986). *The Search for Government Efficiency: From Hubris to Helplessness*. New York: Random House.

Hays, Steven W., and Richard C. Kearney (2001). "Anticipated Changes in Human Resource Management: Views from the Field," *Public Administration Review*, Vol. 61, No. 5 (September–October): 585–597.

Ingraham, Patricia Wallace, Sally Coleman Selden, and Donald P. Moynihan (2000). "People and Performance: Challenges for the Future Public Service—The Report from the Wye River Conference," *Public Administration Review*, Vol. 60, No. 1 (January–February): 54–60.

Kellough, J. Edward, and Sally Coleman Selden (2003). "The Reinvention of Public Personnel Administration: An Analysis of the Diffusion of Personnel Management Reforms in the States," *Public Administration Review*, Vol. 63, No. 2 (March–April): 165–175.

Lawther, Wendell C. (1999). "The Role of Public Employees in the Privatization Process," *Review of Public Personnel Administration*, Vol. 19, No. 1 (Winter): 28–40.

Ravitch, Frank S., and Wendell C. Lawther (1999). "Privatization and Public Employee Pension Rights: Treading in Unexplored Territory," *Review of Public Personnel Administration*, Vol. 19, No. 1 (Winter): 41–58.

Schultz, David (2002). "Civil Service Reform," *Public Administration Review*, Vol. 62, No. 5 (September–October): 634–637.

Selden, Sally Coleman, Patricia Wallace Ingraham, and Willow Jacobson (2001). "Human Resource Practices in State Government: Findings from a National Survey," *Public Administration Review*, Vol. 61, No. 5 (September–October): 598–607.

Thompson, Frank J. (2002). "Reinvention in the States: Ripple or Tide?" *Public Administration Review*, Vol. 62, No. 3 (May–June): 362–367.

Walters, Jonathan (1997). "Who Needs Civil Service?" *Governing*, Vol. 10, No. 11: 17–21.

Wise, Lois Recascino (2002). "Public Management Reform: Competing Drivers of Change," *Public Administration Review*, Vol. 62, No. 5 (September–October): 555–567.

Contributors

James S. Bowman is Professor of Public Administration at the Askew School of Public Administration and Policy, Florida State University. His primary area is human resource management. Noted for his work in ethics and quality management, Dr. Bowman also has done research on environmental administration. Professor Bowman is author of nearly 100 journal articles and book chapters as well as editor of five anthologies. He is editor-in-chief of *Public Integrity*, a journal sponsored by the American Society for Public Administration, the International City/County Management Association, and the Council on State Governments. Bowman also serves on the editorial boards of three other professional journals. A past National Association of Schools of Public Affairs and Administration Fellow as well as a Kellogg Foundation Fellow, he has experience in the military, the civil service, and business.

Chris Byrd has undergraduate and master's degrees from Clemson University. Since 1982, Chris has worked with South Carolina state government, with experience both in a state agency and in central government human resources administration. As the State Compensation Manager, Chris was heavily involved in the research, design, and implementation of the reforms to South Carolina's classification and compensation system. Chris currently serves as Assistant Director of South Carolina's Office of Human Resources with responsibility for the human resources consulting and grievance and mediation program areas

N. Joseph Cayer is Professor of Public Affairs at Arizona State University. He is the author or coauthor of numerous books in public administration including *Public Personnel Administration in the United States, Managing Human Resources, Supervision for Success in Government, and Handbook of Training and Development in the Public Sector.* Cayer also has published extensively in public affairs journals. His research interests are in public personnel/human resources, public labor relations, and general public administration.

Jerrell D. Coggburn is Assistant Professor of Public Administration at the University of Texas at San Antonio. His primary research interests include public sector human resource management and administrative reform. He is a past recipient of *Public Administration Review's* Mosher Award for best article by an academician. His work has also been published in *Review of*

325

Public Personnel Administration, Journal of Public Administration Research and Theory, and *Public Administration Quarterly*.

Stephen E. Condrey is Senior Associate and Director, Human Resource Management Technical Assistance Program at the University of Georgia, Carl Vinson Institute of Government and Adjunct Professor in the School of Public and International Affairs at the University of Georgia where he teaches in the Master of Public Administration program. He has over 20 years of professional experience in human resource management and has consulted nationally and internationally with over 300 organizations concerning personnel-related issues. He presently serves as Managing Editor of the *Review of Public Personnel Administration*, is on the editorial boards of *Public Administration Review* and *Public Personnel Management*, as well as the publications board of the American Society for Public Administration. Dr. Condrey is the editor of the *Handbook of Human Resource Management in Government*, Jossey-Bass, 1998, and *Radical Reform of the Civil Service*, Lexington Books, 2001 (with Robert Maranto). He is the 1998 recipient of the University of Georgia's Walter Barnard Hill Award for Distinguished Achievement in Public Service and Outreach. Steve is the Chair-elect of the Section on Personnel Administration and Labor Relations of the American Society for Public Administration (ASPA).

Sally C. Gertz is a clinical professor at the Florida State University College of Law. Prior to joining the faculty, she presided over labor and employment cases as a Commissioner on Florida's Public Employees Relations Commission and practiced law as counsel to a statewide school employees' union.

Peter D. Fox served as secretary of the Wisconsin Department of Employment Relations, the state government human-resource agency from 1999 to 2003. Previously, he was director of public information for the University of Wisconsin System, and was a daily newspaper editor and journalist in Wisconsin and Montana. A colonel in the Army National Guard, Fox has had significant assignments in personnel and public affairs roles. Currently he is manager of corporate communications and public affairs for Kennecott Energy Co. in Gillette, Wyoming.

Steven W. Hays is Professor of Public Administration in the Department of Government and International Studies at the University of South Carolina. A specialist in Human Resource Management (HRM) and Court Administration, he has published widely in both of those fields. The primary focus of his current research program is to assess HRM "Best Practices" and to track the diffusion of personnel reforms in state and local governments. His work has appeared in virtually all of the general and specialized journals within Public Administration, including *Public Administration Review, American Review of Public Administration,*

Criminal Justice Review, Justice System Review, and many others. Professor Hays was a founding co-editor of the *Review of Public Personnel Administration,* and served as the Managing Editor until 2001. His most recent book is *Public Personnel Administration: Problems and Prospects* (Fourth Edition, 2003), co-edited with Richard C. Kearney.

Richard C. Kearney is Professor and Chair of the Department of Political Science at East Carolina University. He has published extensively in the field of human resource management and state and local politics. He was a founding co-editor of the *Review of Public Personnel Administration.* He is the author of the 3rd edition of *Labor Relations in the Public Sector* (2001).

J. Edward Kellough is Associate Professor and Director of the Masters and Doctoral Programs in Public Administration in the Department of Public Administration and Policy at the University of Georgia. His major area of academic interest is public personnel management. His research has addressed such topics as equal employment opportunity and affirmative action, representative bureaucracy, reinventing government, and civil service reform. He is has published extensively in public administration and political science journals.

Charles H. Kime is an Assistant Professor at Arizona State University East Campus. He coordinates the Fire Services Programs in the College of Technology and Applied Sciences, which include a Bachelor of Applied Science degree in Fire Service Management and a Master of Science in Technology degree in Fire Service Administration. Prior to Joining Arizona State University, Dr. Kime spent more than 32 years with the Phoenix, Arizona Fire Department, retiring in 1999 as the Executive Assistant Fire Chief. In the fire services, his experiences range from line firefighting positions to supervisory and middle management, then to executive management positions which spanned more than twenty years. During his fire services career, Dr. Kime was very active in university education. He has taught in the graduate program of the Arizona State University School of Public Affairs and the Bachelor of Interdisciplinary Studies degree program at the same institution, in addition to his teaching of myriad fire sciences and fire services administration classes. His research interests include organizational leadership, organizational behavior, and human resource management, especially within the context of the fire service. Dr. Kime holds a Bachelors Degree in Industrial Technical Education, a Master of Business Administration degree and a Ph.D. in Public Administration.

Donald E. Klingner is a professor in the Graduate School of Public Affairs at the University of Colorado. He has written 11 books and over 60 articles and book chapters on public management and HRM. With John Nalbandian, he writes *Public Personnel Management* (Prentice-

Hall/Simon & Schuster, 5ᵗʰ edition 2003). He has been a consultant to the UN and other development agencies on public management and public personnel management capacity-building, visiting professor at the National Autonomous University of Mexico (1998–2001), Fulbright senior research fellow in Central America (1994), distinguished professor in residence with the U.S. Department of Health and Human Services (1991), member of the National Academy of Public Administration's advisory panels on federal classification reform (1990–1992) and judicial salary reform (1991–1993), chair of the American Society for Public Administration's Section on Personnel and Labor Relations (1983–1984) and Section on International and Comparative Administration (2001-present).

Robert J. Lavigna is a Senior Manager for Client Services for CPS, a public agency that helps government employers develop and enhance their human resource programs. CPS is a self-supporting public agency that provides a full range of HR products and services. From 1991–2001, Bob was Administrator of Merit Recruitment and Selection for the state of Wisconsin. In this position, he directed the Wisconsin merit civil service system. From 1998 until May 2000, he also directed a statewide Labor-Management Cooperation Program funded by a federal grant. Before being appointed by the Governor in 1991, Bob served with the U.S. General Accounting Office in a variety of positions including program evaluator, human resource director of GAO's largest field office, and assistant to the Assistant Comptroller General. In Wisconsin, Bob and his staff introduced civil service innovations that received numerous awards from professional associations. He has written a number of articles and book chapters on public sector human resources management.

Stefanie A. Lindquist is Associate Professor in the Department of Political Science at Vanderbilt University. A former law clerk on the United States Court of Appeals for the Third Circuit, Professor Lindquist also served as a research associate at the Federal Judicial Center. She has published in political science and public administration journals and law reviews, including *Administration and Society, Judicature, American Journal of Political Science, Political Research Quarterly, and Law and Society Review*. She serves as an Associate Editor for Legal Notes at the *Review of Public Personnel Administration*. Her current research focuses on judicial decision making in the federal courts.

Katherine C. Naff is Associate Professor of Public Administration at San Francisco State University. Prior to joining the faculty at SFSU, she was a senior research analyst with the U.S. Merit Systems Protection Board in Washington, DC. She has authored numerous articles and book chapters on human resource management and related topics and is co-author of a leading text in the field, *Personnel Management in Government*, 5ᵗʰ Edition (Marcel Dekker, 2001).

Lloyd G. Nigro is Professor of Public Administration and Urban Studies at Georgia State University in Atlanta, Georgia. He is currently the department chair. He received his Ph.D. in Public Administration from the University of Southern California in 1972. Before joining the GSU faculty, he held tenured faculty positions at Syracuse University and the University of Southern California. He is the co-author with Felix A. Nigro of multiple editions of two widely read texts, *Modern Public Administration* and *The New Public Personnel Administration*. He has also published numerous book chapters and articles in the areas of public personnel policy, civil service reform, administrative ethics, and public administration and American political thought.

Hal G. Rainey is Alumni Foundation Distinguished Professor at the University of Georgia, School of Public and International Affairs. His research concentrates on organizations and management in government, with emphasis on performance, change, leadership, incentives, privatization, and comparisons of governmental management to management in the business and nonprofit sectors. He recently coedited *Advancing Public Management* (Georgetown University Press, 2000) with Jeffrey L. Brudney and Laurence J. O'Toole. He is preparing a third edition of his book, *Understanding and Managing Public Organizations* (Jossey-Bass, 1997).

Norma M. Riccucci is Professor and Director of the Ph.D. Program in Public Administration and Policy at the Rockefeller College of the University at Albany, State University of New York. She has published extensively in the areas of public management, employment discrimination law, affirmative action, and public-sector labor relations. Her most recent book, *Managing Diversity in Public Sector Workforces*, is forthcoming from Westview Press. Her current research focuses on the management capacity of state and local governments to implement the Welfare-to-Work provisions prescribed by federal law.

Sally Coleman Selden is Associate Professor of Management at Lynchburg College. Her major areas of research interest include human resource management, representative bureaucracy, and public management. Her recent work has appeared in *Public Administration Review, Journal of Public Administration Research and Theory, Administration and Society, American Journal of Political Science, and Review of Public Personnel Administration*.

Jonathan P. West is Professor and Chair of the Department of Political Science and Director of the Graduate Public Administration program in the School of Business Administration at the University of Miami. His research interests include human resource management, productivity, local government, and ethics. Professor West has published over 75 articles and book chapters. His most recent books are *Quality Management*

Today: What Local Government Managers Need to Know (1995) and *The Ethics Edge* (1998) published by the International City/County Management Association. He is co-author of *American Politics and the Environment* (Longman, 2002). He is the Managing Editor of Public Integrity published by Westview Press. He taught previously at the University of Houston and University of Arizona and served as a management analyst in the U. S. Surgeon General's Office, Department of the Army, Washington, D. C.

Samuel L. Wilkins is Director of the Office of Human Resources of the South Carolina Budget and Control Board. He assumed that role on January 1, 2002. He has held previous positions with that office since 1993, including Assistant Director and Legal Counsel. He formerly was, for eight years, an Assistant Attorney General in the Office of the Attorney General of South Carolina where he was Chief of the Governmental Litigation Division. Prior to that position, he was in private practice for two years. He received his B.A. degree from Furman University, Greenville, South Carolina in 1975 and his J.D. degree from the University of South Carolina School of Law, Columbia, South Carolina in December, 1982. He was admitted to practice law in South Carolina in May, 1983, and subsequently has been admitted to practice in the United States District Court of South Carolina and the Fourth Circuit Court of Appeals. He served as a member of the editorial board for the *South Carolina Lawyer*, published by the South Carolina Bar. He currently serves as a member of the Continuing Legal Education Committee of the South Carolina Bar. He has published numerous articles on employment law issues and wrote the Public Officers and Public Employees section of *South Carolina Jurisprudence*. He is active in the South Carolina chapter of the International Personnel Management Association, having recently served as its President. He is a member of the Executive Board of the National Association of State Personnel Executives (NASPE) and chairs its taskforce on the Workforce of the Future.

Index